I0783442

HAIDA GWAII

Expanded 5th Edition

HAIDA

A GUIDE TO BC'S ISLANDS OF THE PEOPLE

GWAII

DENNIS HORWOOD

Victoria | Vancouver | Calgary

Copyright © 2016 Dennis Horwood
Fifth Edition

All rights reserved. No part of this publication may be reproduced, stored in a retrieval system or transmitted in any form or by any means—electronic, mechanical, audio recording, or otherwise—without the written permission of the publisher or a licence from Access Copyright, Toronto, Canada.

Heritage House Publishing Company Ltd.
heritagehouse.ca

Published in the US by University of Washington Press

LIBRARY AND ARCHIVES CANADA
CATALOGUING IN PUBLICATION

Horwood, Dennis, 1953–, author
Haida Gwaii : a guide to BC's islands of the people / Dennis Horwood.—Expanded fifth edition.

Includes index. Issued in print and electronic formats.
ISBN 978-1-77203-122-5 (paperback).—
ISBN 978-1-77203-123-2 (epdf).— ISBN 978-1-77203-124-9 (epub)
        1. Haida Gwaii (B.C.)—Guidebooks.
I. Title.

FC3845.Q3H67 2016   917.11'12045
C2015-908105-X   C2015-908106-8

Cover design by Jacqui Thomas
Interior design by Setareh Ashrafologhalai
Cover photos: BobEdmonson/iStockphoto.
    com (front) and (highest to lowest)
    Windy Bay pole, by Travis Doane; Sea
    lions, by Dennis Horwood; Mathers
    Creek, by Dennis Horwood; ancient
    poles at K'uuna Llnagaay (Skedans),
    by Jim Thorne (back)
Interior photos by Dennis Horwood unless
    otherwise indicated
Illustrations by Tom Parkin unless other-
    wise indicated

This book was produced using FSC®-certified, acid-free paper, processed chlorine free and printed with vegetable-based inks.

We acknowledge the financial support of the Government of Canada through the Canada Book Fund and the Canada Council for the Arts, and the Province of British Columbia through the British Columbia Arts Council and the Book Publishing Tax Credit.

The Canada Council | Le Conseil des Arts
for the Arts | du Canada

BRITISH COLUMBIA
ARTS COUNCIL

Disclaimer:

Individuals undertake the activities described in this book at their own risk. Many conditions and some information may change owing to weather and numerous other factors beyond the control of the author and publisher. Individuals or groups must determine the risks, use their own judgement, and take full responsibility for their actions, and must not depend on any information found in this book for their own personal safety. The author and publisher of this book accept no responsibility for your actions or the results that occur from another's actions, choices, or judgements.

20 19 18 17 16   1 2 3 4 5

Printed in Canada

To our enthusiastic field companions, Brenda and Doug, and to Tom Parkin, whose expertise and companionship made this book possible.

NOTE ON METRIC CONVERSIONS

All measurements included in this book are in metric. For the benefit of American visitors or others who are more familiar with imperial measurements, here are the abbreviations and conversions for the metric weights and measures that appear in this book.

Weights and Measures (multiply by)

Miles to kilometres (km) 1.6

Kilometres to miles 0.6

Inches to centimetres (cm) 2.5

Centimetres to inches 0.4

Nautical miles to kilometres (km) 1.9

Kilometres to nautical miles 0.5

Fathoms to metres (m) 1.8

Metres to fathoms 0.6

Gallons to litres (l) 4.6

Litres to gallons 0.2

Feet to metres (m) 0.3

Metres to feet 3.3

Pounds to kilograms (kg) 0.5

Acres to hectares (ha) 0.4

Kilograms to pounds 2.2

Hectares to acres 2.5

Temperatures (follow formula below)

Fahrenheit to Celsius (C) subtract 32, multiply by 5/9

Celsius to Fahrenheit (F) multiply by 5/9, add 32

MAP LEGEND

This book includes several regional maps to Haida Gwaii. Below you will find a guide to some of the symbols contained on those maps.

✳	Community	☒	Viewing tower	🏛	Watchmen site	– – –	Park boundary
☆	Site of interest	⚐	Warden station	⚓	Anchorage	⋯⋯	Trail
Ⓟ	Parking	⚘	Picnic sites	⛵	Boat ramp	– – – –	First Nations reserve
⌂	Homestead	▪	Park hiking shelter	▲	Hill/mountain	⋯⋯⋯	Ecological reserve
◩	Divesite	▲	Camping	☙	Bog	⋯⋯⋯	Ferry crossing
⋀	Sand dunes	⌁	Fresh water from a pipe			– – – – –	Gravel road

CONTENTS

PART 1 WELCOME TO HAIDA GWAII 1

1.1 Islands on the Edge 2

1.2 The Haida Nation 9

1.3 European Exploration of Haida Gwaii 14

PART 2 HAIDA GWAII, REGION BY REGION 17

2.1 Southern Graham Island 22

Crossing Hecate Strait 22

Around Skidegate Inlet 27

Rennell Sound 41

2.2 Mid-Graham Island 48

Coastal Old-Growth Rainforest 48

Of Canoes and Culture 52

Nadu—Trails to Tribulation 57

2.3 Northern Graham Island 62

Langara Island Vicinity 62

Delkatla Wildlife Sanctuary 74

2.4 Naikoon Provincial Park 79

Tow Hill Area 82

Four Corners and Cape Fife Trails 91

Tow Hill Bog 93

North Beach 98

Rose Spit 105

East Beach 110

Sand Dunes, Tlell River, and Vicinity 115

2.5 North Moresby Island 122

Gray Bay 122

Louise Island Circumnavigation 126

2.6 Gwaii Haanas National Park Reserve, National Marine Conservation Area Reserve, and Haida Heritage Site 145

Juan Perez and Darwin Sounds 152

East Coast of Lyell Island— Hlk'yah GaawGa 158

Burnaby Narrows 164

Skincuttle Inlet 172

Houston Stewart Channel 179

SGang Gwaay World Heritage Site 184

PART 3 **PLANNING YOUR TRIP 193**

3.1 Overnighting on Haida Gwaii 193

3.2 Gwaii Haanas National Park Reserve— Reservations and Orientation 217

3.3 Chartering and Tours 220

3.4 Navigation and Safety 228

3.5 Climate and Clothing *231*

3.6 The Six-Day Guide *236*

PART 4   A NATURAL HISTORY
OF HAIDA GWAII 239

4.1 Birds *240*

4.2 Marine Mammals and Reptiles *252*

4.3 Land Mammals and Amphibians *261*

PART 5   THEIR PLACE TO BE 267

APPENDICES 283

A.1 Checklist of the Birds of Haida Gwaii *283*

A.2 Checklist of the Land Mammals and
Amphibians of Haida Gwaii *288*

A.3 Checklist of the Marine Mammals
and Reptiles of Haida Gwaii *289*

A.4 Hunting on Haida Gwaii *290*

ACKNOWLEDGEMENTS 293

FURTHER READING 295

INDEX 298

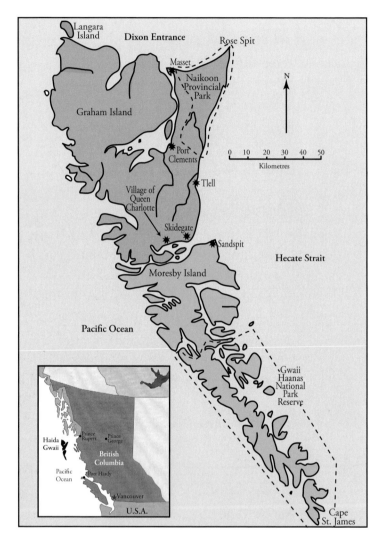

Langara
Island

Dixon Entrance

Rose Spit

Masset

Naikoon
Provincial
Park

Graham Island

Port
Clements

0 10 20 30 40 50

Kilometres

N

Tlell

Village of
Queen
Charlotte

Skidegate

Sandspit

Hecate Strait

Moresby Island

Pacific Ocean

Gwaii
Haanas
National
Park
Reserve

Haida
Gwaii

Prince
Rupert

Prince
George

**British
Columbia**

Pacific
Ocean

Port Hardy

Vancouver

U.S.A.

Cape
St. James

HAIDA GWAII

PART 1

WELCOME TO HAIDA GWAII

HAIDA GWAII (formerly known as the Queen Charlotte Islands) consists of a tight cluster of islands lying 50 to 150 kilometres off the northwestern coast of British Columbia. For millennia, it has been a remote, mysterious, and inaccessible place, but developments during the last four decades have raised the profile of this unique and beautiful region.

Haida Gwaii has always been a distinctive place, and the first people to settle here developed an exceptional cultural identity. Long before European contact, the Haida were revered and feared, from what is now Alaska south to Washington State and beyond.

As early as 1774, British and American sailors were drawn here to trade for the pelt of sea otters. When the fur trade eventually declined due to the otters' almost complete annihilation, the islands drew the attention of mining, fishing, and forest companies.

The forest industry did well: the trees on Haida Gwaii are among the finest of any temperate rainforest. But as the rate of cut increased, so too did the clear-cuts. This motivated the Haida, along with many other residents and off-island groups, to lobby for a reduction in or an end to the logging. During the 1970s a series of articles, books, and television programs began to publicize the exceptional nature of the islands' environment and the people who lived there. Suddenly, everyone seemed to be talking about Haida Gwaii.

Native land claims and the struggle to protect the natural environment during the 1980s continued to promote national and international awareness of the islands, and in 1987 the Gwaii Haanas National Park Reserve and Haida Heritage Site was created. This remarkable park, with its ancient Haida village sites, is just one of the major attractions here. The superb beaches in Naikoon Provincial Park and excellent recreational fishing also draw visitors from around the world.

Tourists who visit Haida Gwaii tend to be adventurous, active, and aware of the natural environment. They also tend to spend more time on these islands than tourists do in other, more typical, destinations. These visitors are eager to understand Haida Gwaii, and they often leave with a profound appreciation of their experience.

If that sounds appealing, this guidebook is for you.

1.1 ISLANDS ON THE EDGE

The archipelago of Haida Gwaii rises from the outer edge of the continental shelf along British Columbia's northwest coast. Although BC's coast includes thousands of islands, these are the most isolated. In fact, no other island group anywhere in Canada is so distant from the main continent. A broad inshore channel called Hecate Strait separates them from the mainland, and the heaving gap of Dixon Entrance lies between Haida Gwaii and the islands to the north that form the Alaskan panhandle.

Viewed on a map, the roughly 150 islands have a shape somewhat like a stylized Olympic torch. The largest, Graham Island, embraces the flame. Runners grasp the tapered handle of Moresby Island. The many smaller islands like Langara, Louise,

Tow Hill is the most recognized landmark in Naikoon Provincial Park. A trail leads to the summit and offers excellent views of North Beach out to Rose Spit.

Welcome to Haida Gwaii

Balance Rock is located just minutes away from Skidegate. The glacial erratic, a leftover from the ice age, is a favoured spot to pose for a playful photograph.

Lyell, Burnaby, and Kunghit might be jewels decorating the torch from top to bottom.

The total land area is approximately 9,940 square kilometres. This is considerably smaller than Vancouver Island (the largest island along the west coast of the Americas), but almost twice the size of Prince Edward Island, Canada's smallest province.

When European explorers began sailing throughout the Pacific Ocean, the existence of Haida Gwaii was completely unknown to them. Recognition of this area being separate from the mainland occurred on August 3, 1787. After a month of trading and exploring, Captain George Dixon realized he was circumnavigating a network of islands and named them after his ship and sovereign, Queen Charlotte (wife of George III of England). Her name would appear on charts and maps for the next 223 years.

Since Queen Charlotte never crossed the Atlantic, let alone visited here, her attached name has been an irritant for many associated with the islands. On June 10, 2010, after much

St. Mary's spring along Highway 16 has had a lasting effect on the many visitors who have sipped its clear, cool water.

discussion and political lobbying, the federal and provincial governments announced the official name would revert back to Haida Gwaii, meaning "Islands of the People."

The name Haida Gwaii deservedly recognizes the long history and original residents of the islands, the Haida Nation. However, the name "Queen Charlotte" remains in other geographical places such as the Queen Charlotte Mountains and Queen Charlotte Sound. Some island communities, businesses, and societies have also retained the queen's title. Books and other publications written prior to 2010 will, of course, always retain her name. Hopefully, this rightful re-naming will not be confusing to anyone new to Haida Gwaii.

TOPOGRAPHY

The islands of Haida Gwaii encompass an enormously varied landscape. In a 1968 provincial research paper, geologist A. Sutherland Brown likened them to BC in miniature, since most of the terrain found elsewhere in the province is represented here. There are broad beaches of sand, rising columns of sandstone, sea-carved caves, and cliffs of volcanic bedrock. There are glacial sediments and rock strata renowned for fossils.

This is a wild place. The Queen Charlotte Mountains form a divide along the western edge of Graham and Moresby Islands, a ridge of rugged and steep terrain incised by numerous straits and fjords. The surf-smashed west coast lies wide open to North Pacific winds, and its inaccessibility means that this beautiful area sees few visitors. Moresby Island is narrow, with steep slopes and few lakes, while Graham has rolling plateaus and muskeg lowlands on its eastern side. The heart of Graham Island is washed by the salt water of Masset Inlet, known to locals as "The Lake." Freshwater streams and rivers run everywhere.

Over all of this clambers coastal vegetation as dense as any tropical jungle. In grandeur, the giant conifers of Haida Gwaii are unsurpassed in Canada. These towering cedar, spruce, and hemlock trees are among the best examples of temperate rainforest in North America and were essential to the development of Aboriginal culture. In 1987 some of these magnificent stands were protected when part of Haida Gwaii was designated the Gwaii Haanas National Park Reserve and Haida Heritage Site.

ECONOMY

Outside the parks and reserves, the huge conifers are still the chief measure of commerce on the islands. The forest industry is the biggest single employer here. Often, and quite understandably, the conservation of lands hasn't sat well with those whose livelihood depends on the harvesting of trees. While many residents are beginning to accept the long-term importance of conservation and careful land management, change comes at a price. The loss of forest jobs means full-time employment is harder to come by in a region that otherwise offers only commercial fishing or the rare mining job. No natural resources are processed here, and government employment and tourism previously represented only minor opportunities.

Many people feel that tourism now presents the greatest potential for economic growth. In the past, sport fishing was the main draw. More recently, however, eco-tourism has become firmly established and is expected to boost the islands' economy well into the future.

COMMUNITY

Eight main communities dot the islands today, along with several villages and former townsites that have retained a few occupants. From north to south, Graham Island has active communities at Old Massett, Masset, Port Clements, Tlell, Skidegate (now called Hlgaagilda 'llnagaay), Skidegate Landing, and the Village of Queen Charlotte.

Old Massett and Masset are the most northerly communities. Commercial fishing is the economic mainstay at Masset. Port Clements ("Port" for short) combines fishing with logging. Tlell is a hamlet, but is home to a collection of artisans and B & Bs, as well as the provincial park office and a small ranch. The centrally located Village of Queen Charlotte, Skidegate, and Sandspit (on Moresby Island) have the largest hospital and airport, moorage for watercraft, and an information centre for Gwaii Haanas National Park Reserve and Haida Heritage Site.

PEOPLE

About four thousand Canadians of varied ancestry live on Haida Gwaii today. Like islanders everywhere, they enjoy their isolation and lifestyle and are often resistant to change. They're particularly interested in maintaining local control over the developments that influence their lives. They prefer a certain amount of challenge to modern convenience.

Although some islanders demonstrate the *mañana* attitude, don't be fooled into thinking these are backwater folks. Many are multi-talented; being a jack-of-all-trades comes with the territory in a place where work and supplies are often expensive or in short supply. Here, financial achievement is not the only measure of success; personal accomplishment and individuality seem equally important. As a result, you'll find a high level of confidence and personality among the locals. "Characters" tend to find plenty of nourishment in this environment. Don't be surprised when you hear monikers such as Sid the Wrench, Huckleberry, or Stickleback Tom.

A series of islander profiles in Part 5: Their Place to Be offers a glimpse into the lifestyles and passions of some of the people we've had the pleasure of meeting over the course of numerous visits to Haida Gwaii. Since every islander seems to have several pearls in the closet, these profiles cannot possibly speak to the experiences of all. Instead, they present a snapshot of a few of the folks who make these islands their home, and, perhaps most importantly, give some insight into why they have stayed. One thing is certain. Meeting the people of Haida Gwaii will provide as many memorable moments as exploring the spectacular landscape.

We would be remiss if we did not warn you about one particular feature of Haida Gwaii—the curious effect of the waters of St. Mary's Spring. The spring's location is marked by a chainsaw sculpture of a woman by the side of Yellowhead Highway (#16), just north of Lawn Hill. Legend has it that whoever partakes of the spring's cool, natural champagne will someday return to the islands. It has certainly had that effect on us.

We hope you, too, will find a reason to return to Haida Gwaii.

1.2 THE HAIDA NATION

Geography made it easy for Haida society to develop. The islands enjoy a relatively warm maritime climate with plenty of rain, which enables rich stands of spruce, hemlock, and cedar to flourish. Meanwhile, island shores are washed by nutrient-rich waters teeming with intertidal life, where fish, birds, and mammals feed in abundance. Surrounded by such generous natural resources, the Haida developed a self-sustaining hunting-and-gathering society, rich in oral language and tradition.

The western red cedar was pivotal to Haida society. The species' immense size, straight grain, soft wood, and resistance to rot made it ideal for house construction. The Haida cut the trees, selected a house site, and undertook the actual construction with great care and precision. Houses had a dual purpose. They were practical, in that they provided their occupants with shelter, and they were also ceremonial centres. Entering their oval doorways marked passage into the spiritual world, bringing occupants into close association with their cultural traditions.

An important act in house building, along with a potlatch celebration, was the raising of a frontal pole bearing the crests of the resident family. Poles carved from cedar were erected both inside and outside houses. The figures on poles depict more than just animals: some represent natural phenomena; others are supernatural beings. The crests belonged to specific families and were jealously guarded. New crests could be added during a potlatch.

Sadly, few original poles remain in their original locations. The villages of K'uuna Llnagaay (formerly Skedans) and SGang Gwaay Llnagaay (formerly Ninstints) have the most poles still on site. The Haida Heritage Centre in Skidegate displays a few more. (In 2001, six new poles were raised here.) Others can be viewed at the Royal British Columbia Museum in Victoria or the

Old Haida villages are one of the main attractions on the islands. Many have watchmen who will guide you throughout the site.

Cumshewa Village once had about 280 inhabitants. This was one of the last village sites to be abandoned in the southern islands. Circa 1890. BC ARCHIVES, C-09294

UBC Museum of Anthropology in Vancouver. In 1981 UNESCO granted SG̱ang Gwaay (formerly Anthony Island) World Heritage Site status. This ranks the Village of SG̱ang Gwaay Llnagaay with the Egyptian pyramids and the Inca estate of Machu Picchu. (See "SG̱ang Gwaay World Heritage Site," page 184.)

As impressive as their houses and poles were, the Haida were unequalled in canoe building. From massive cedars they carved graceful craft varying in length from 22 metres to the more manoeuvrable 4- and 7-metre models. The largest could easily transport forty people and 2 tonnes of supplies. With these boats, Haida men and women paddled through temperamental Dixon Entrance and crossed the treacherous shallows of Hecate Strait. On trading or raiding forays they travelled as far south as

Six contemporary Haida poles are a key feature at the Haida Heritage Centre located at Skidegate. This pole was carved by Garner Moody. (See page 274.)

present-day Victoria and Puget Sound, Washington. They were superlative seafarers, staying out of sight of land for days without navigational aids. See "Of Canoes and Culture" (page 52) for more about these historic vessels.

No discussion of Northwest Coast Indigenous culture would be complete without mention of potlatches. These ceremonial celebrations are held to mark significant cultural events. In preparation for such events, guests from other villages were invited and huge feasts were prepared.

These celebrations have historically been an extremely important part of Haida culture. They allowed marriages to be witnessed, families to intermix, a chief's successor to be named, and an individual's or family's status to be confirmed. Eating, gift giving, dancing, and storytelling were an integral part of each gathering. Since the Haida relied heavily on their oral history, much was irretrievably lost during the colonial period when their villages were ravaged by European diseases. Later, when the Canadian government outlawed potlatches, Haida culture was further diminished. During the last fifty years, however, the Haida have revived and reshaped many age-old traditions.

The resurgence of their art is one of the most appreciated aspects of this renaissance. Many Haida artisans, among them weavers and carvers of silver, gold, argillite (a soft black shale quarried on Slatechuck Mountain), and wood, have gained international reputations. An item from one of these master crafters makes a great conversation piece when you talk about your visit to Haida Gwaii. Equally memorable is viewing the cedar canoe at the Haida Heritage Centre, or visiting K'uuna Llnagaay or SGang Gwaay. Attending a potlatch will deepen your understanding of Haida heritage and may serve as a reminder that the world came close to losing this magnificent culture.

1.3 EUROPEAN EXPLORATION OF HAIDA GWAII

On July 17, 1774, a Spanish explorer, Captain Juan Perez of the ship *Santiago,* sighted a prominent headland on the archipelago's northwest tip. The next day a fleet of Haida dugout canoes paddled out to visit his ship. This historic event marked the first European contact with one of the most sophisticated Indigenous societies in North America. It didn't take long for other navigators to follow Perez, venturing into the region from New Spain (now California) in 1775 and 1779.

The great British explorer Captain James Cook bypassed these islands altogether on his trip up this coast in 1778. Upon reaching Alaska, however, he traded for sea otter pelts that eventually sold in China for an astronomical sum. So began the maritime fur trade, an enterprise so profitable it ultimately annihilated all the sea otters in the area, and very nearly extinguished the entire species.

By 1786, British ships direct from England, India, and the Far East were competing for trade with First Nations all along the Pacific Northwest coast. Captain George Dixon sailed close to Hippa Island along the west coast of Haida Gwaii that year. The following year he returned and, after further exploration, named the entire group of islands after his ship and his king's consort, Queen Charlotte.

The islands eventually became a trading territory for Americans as well. Sadly, the aggressive attitude of these efficient competitors had serious consequences for both the Haida and other traders. The intimidation and force used by one Captain Robert Gray initiated a series of violent reprisals by the First Nations. As the sea otter population declined, trade methods became more ruthless. There was murder on both sides.

Less hostile relations were re-established in 1831 when British traders of the Hudson's Bay Company (HBC) began

The old village of SGang Gwaay Llnagaay has the highest number of original poles still standing. Most of them are mortuary poles.

constructing permanent trading posts on the north coast. The company restricted the sale of firearms, ammunition, and liquor. Although this reduced HBC profits, it resulted in a good deal more stability. With the British establishing colonies on the south coast and the Russians firmly in control of the north, the Americans eventually left the territory.

For the Haida, the introduction of western civilization was devastating. Disease, illegal alcohol, firearms, and money combined to destroy what had been one of the strongest Indigenous cultures on the coast. Missionaries also arrived to Christianize the First Nations. In their fervour, some of these missionaries did more damage than good; others were trusted and respected.

The first was an Irish clergyman named William Henry Collison. His memoir, *In the Wake of the War Canoe*, offers fascinating insight into many aspects of traditional Haida life before further European influence resulted in major cultural changes.

These eyes greet visitors arriving at the Haida Heritage Centre, reminding them that these islands are Haida territory.

The early post-contact history of the islands follows a fairly typical pattern characterized by the usual parade of missionaries, resource developers, and homesteaders. The churches were persistent in their quest to spread the gospel. The lumber industry has diminished but is still profitable. Only a few homesteaders, however, found the climate and terrain hospitable.

PART 2

HAIDA GWAII,
REGION BY REGION

THIS SECTION WILL help you explore all that Haida Gwaii has to offer. We have highlighted the main recreational spots and unique locales that showcase the islands' Indigenous history, European settlement, geology, geography, and natural history.

We begin by crossing Hecate Strait, one of the most interesting waterways along BC's coastline. Next, we highlight southern Graham Island, then travel northward through Tlell, Port Clements, and on to Masset. Graham Island's undisputed "top spot" is Naikoon Provincial Park. Every first-time visitor to Haida Gwaii should spend a few days exploring the beaches and trails within the park boundaries.

Southern Haida Gwaii is equally exciting to visit. Unfortunately, access to most places south of Moresby Camp is limited to boats or aircraft. Louise Island, K'uuna Llnagaay (Skedans), and all areas to the south within Gwaii Haanas National Park Reserve and Haida Heritage Site are like nowhere else in the world. SGang Gwaay has been ranked as one of the world's most significant cultural sites. If you have time and the means, don't pass up an opportunity to visit this exceptional area.

A particularly nice aspect of Haida Gwaii is that you don't need a bulging budget to have a memorable experience. Beach and forest walks—all free—have been as wonderful as our more expensive boating and flying ventures. No doubt you, like us, will find a few spots that might have been included in this guidebook. Keep them as your secret—they should be your own special memory.

PRINCE RUPERT—THE GATEWAY TO HAIDA GWAII

For most visitors travelling to Haida Gwaii, the first leg of their journey usually follows one of two main routes: the Yellowhead Highway from Prince George or BC Ferries via Port Hardy. Some visitors travel via the Alaska state ferries to Prince Rupert or the CN passenger train that parallels the Yellowhead Highway. Regardless of your route, all of these terminate in Prince Rupert.

Departure times for the Haida Gwaii ferry from Prince Rupert can be early morning, midday, or even late into the evening. Arriving several hours before the departure time is highly recommended. Once you have located the terminal and confirmed your boarding time, you can spend any extra time exploring this historic north coast port.

If you only have a few hours, the city offers two walking tours that give a flavour of the recent and distant past. The waterfront tour guides you past a variety of restaurants, museums, and gift shops. Be sure to stop at the Pacific Mariner's Memorial Park. One of the most interesting boats along the entire coast is displayed in an outdoor pavilion. In 1987, the *Kazu Maru* was found wrecked on Haida Gwaii. Upon investigation, it was discovered that the boat's owner disappeared while fishing

Prince Rupert's waterfront boasts numerous shops, restaurants, and activities all within walking distance.

two years prior—in Owase, Japan! The capsized boat was salvaged a mere 7,000 kilometres from its homeport. It is now restored and can be viewed in a most fitting backdrop.

You won't see any boat like this on Haida Gwaii. Similarly, railroads are almost non-existent on the islands, but Prince Rupert has plenty of railroad history. In 1910, Prince Rupert was chosen as terminus for the Grand Trunk Pacific Railway (today the Canadian National Railroad, or CNR). The Kwinitsa Station, relocated to the Rotary Waterfront Park, has plenty of railroad memorabilia. It is a must-see for rail enthusiasts.

The downtown walking tour features many buildings constructed when railroad activity peaked. The hundred-year-old architecture helps make it easier to imagine what railroad boomtowns experienced. This compact area of a few city blocks can be strolled at your leisure within two hours.

When planning your trip, you might find you have enough time to spend a day or more in the Prince Rupert area. If so, there

In 1987, the *Kazu Maru* washed ashore in Skidegate Channel on Haida Gwaii. It was soon discovered the small craft had drifted across the Pacific Ocean from Owase, Japan.

are two world-class attractions worthy of your time and unlike anything you might experience on Haida Gwaii.

About a century ago, fish canneries were scattered along the Pacific Coast from Alaska to California. Almost every major inlet seemed to have a cannery anchored along the shoreline. Today, most of these fish processing plants have been decommissioned, dismantled, or simply abandoned. The North Pacific Cannery, located at Port Edward, was one plant that operated for over a hundred years. As this industry waned, attention shifted to preserving this industrial heritage. In 1989, the North Pacific Cannery was designated as a National Historic Site. The cannery now hosts thousands of visitors from May through to September. Spending a few hours here is by far the best way to gain an appreciation of this once-thriving coastal industry.

Allow twenty-five minutes when driving to the cannery from Prince Rupert. Public transit serves Port Edward and its immediate surrounding area on a routine schedule.

Visiting the North Pacific Cannery gives visitors a chance to envision how the fishing industry operated along the BC coast. JIM THORNE

During your time on Haida Gwaii, it is possible you may see black bears along the beaches or on an estuary meadow. If you want to see grizzly bears, however, you will have to plan this adventure before heading over to the islands. Prince Rupert has one of the premier grizzly-viewing locations anywhere in North America. The 44,000-hectare Khutzeymateen Grizzly Bear Sanctuary can only be reached by boat or aircraft. You are almost guaranteed to see the bears in their natural environment if you visit in spring or early summer. Depending on the season, you can safely observe them munching on tidal grasses, catching fish, courting, or watching over their cubs. If grizzly bears are on your must-see list, this excursion will not disappoint.

Scheduled day or extended trips to the Khutzeymateen leave from Prince Rupert Harbour.

Whether you spend a few hours, a day, or longer in this historic coastal community, your time here will be special.

VISITOR SERVICES AND INFO CENTRE

Located in the Museum of Northern BC

100 First Avenue West

PO Box 669, Prince Rupert, BC

V8J 3S1 Canada

Toll Free: 1-800-667-1994

Phone: 250-624-5637

Fax: 250-627-8009

Email: prinfo@citytel.net

Website: visitprincerupert.com

2.1 SOUTHERN GRAHAM ISLAND

CROSSING HECATE STRAIT

Upon arriving at Prince Rupert, put your problems in your pocket and make way for thrills and adventure. A six- to eight-hour ocean cruise to the famous Misty Isles lies ahead. The ferry ride across Hecate Strait is one of the longest and most interesting ferry rides across open water in Canada. Once aboard, claim a couch near the large windows or find a seat on the semi-enclosed rear deck. Keep your binoculars handy and settle in for the crossing.

In summer, Hecate Strait is usually calm. But even when the swells grow, the clouds move in, and spray sweeps the decks, you can still appreciate the rougher side of its personality. For the first hour you travel through the busy waters of Chatham Sound. This sheltered waterway is part of the Inside Passage, a marine route between Alaska and Vancouver Island. Watch for other passenger liners, freighters, tugs, yachts, fishboats, and pleasure craft travelling in all directions.

The canoe pictured here was carved on Haida Gwaii prior to 1883. It is 19.5 metres long and is on display at the American Museum of Natural History in New York City. GORDON MILLER

After the ferry reaches Edye Pass, the Hecate crossing begins. You might expect this broad expanse of water to be deep. In fact, for most of its 200-kilometre length, Hecate Strait averages only 17 fathoms. At the northern end, depths are as shallow as 7 fathoms. The strait links Dixon Entrance, to the north, with Queen Charlotte Sound, to the south.

To understand why the basin is so shallow, you have to look to geological time. On several occasions over the last million years, sheets of ice covered both Haida Gwaii and the mainland. The ice, carrying large quantities of rock and sediment, moved slowly from the mountains to the sea, where it either floated away as icebergs or melted. Debris carried by the ice accumulated in Hecate Strait. Exploratory offshore drilling by oil companies has revealed more than 3 kilometres of sediment on the seabed.

The MV *Northern Adventure* serves Haida Gwaii during the summer season. Reservations are highly recommended, particularly for over-length vehicles.

Shallow water like this can produce rapid changes in marine conditions. The strait amplifies tidal flows: when the winds are strong, huge waves can suddenly appear. With very little warning, calm water can erupt into a frenzy. Hecate Strait is reputed to be one of the roughest stretches of water on the Pacific Ocean. During winter gales, Hecate's fury is so great that ferries have little choice but to wait out rough weather at dockside—departures may be postponed for forty-eight hours or more. "If you want a real pounding, you need to cross in the winter," said Second Officer David Parry when he was quizzed about the rough seas.

In his book, *In the Wake of the War Canoe*, Rev. William Collison, the first missionary on Haida Gwaii, recounts crossing Hecate Strait for the first time:

As the wind increased, the sea arose and threatened to engulf our frail bark in its yawning depths. In six hours we had lost all sight of land, and even the mountain tops had disappeared. None of us were able to retain our seats on the thwarts, nor would it have been well to have done so, as they are only sewn to the sides of the canoe with thongs of cedar withes, and might easily have given way under the increased strain. In addition, she rode better with the ballast low down, consequently all save the steersman had to remain huddled up in the bottom of the canoe. An occasional wave broke over us, which kept us all on the alert, and soon all four of our young sailors were seized with that dread ailment mal de mer. I, together with my steersman and bowman, remained unaffected, for which I felt thankful, as it required all our efforts to keep our frail craft afloat...

Just as we were congratulating ourselves on our success, we sighted a dark ridge or wall of water rushing up rapidly toward us from the south. Apprehensive of being swamped or capsized, we furled sail, and, grasping our paddles, headed our canoe around to meet the approaching danger. It proved to be but the turn of the incoming tide, which rushes shoreward from the ocean at this point with great force.

After thirteen hours at sea, the exhausted crew staggered ashore at Rose Spit.

The waters of Hecate Strait are as rich in fish as they are in history. At one time Prince Rupert was known as the halibut capital of the world, but overfishing has severely reduced the region's catch. Commercial fishers still seek delicious halibut and smaller groundfish, and crab pots are also set in the tens of thousands. In summer you may notice the fluorescent orange floats marking the ends of their lines. Hecate Strait is also fished heavily by salmon trollers. These smaller boats drag lures from lines attached to poles that lean out from the hull, catching fish on individual hooks. Other salmon boats use seine or gill nets.

Besides fish, a large number and variety of seabirds spend the summer in the strait. Shearwaters are easily recognized by their habit of skimming low over the waves. Their sabre-like wings sometimes appear to shear the swells, hence their name. Shearwaters, usually seen in open water, return south before winter storms begin. Stay close to a window to observe them, or better still, stand outside on the open deck. Of four species recorded in Hecate Strait, sooty shearwaters are the most numerous. Watch for their dark bodies gliding effortlessly over the waves or sitting duck-like in groups of fifteen to twenty. Sometimes they mass in flocks of more than 100,000, and sightings of a quarter-million have been documented here.

Shearwaters are not alone in their preference for seas where squid and small oceanic fish are plentiful. The gull-like fulmar and the larger black-footed albatross also depend on this special diet. Since both these species are uncommon here, it is all the more thrilling when you do spot one. Bird enthusiasts will sometimes go to a lot of expense chartering vessels in the hope of seeing such species. With many pelagic birds spending up to five months in Hecate Strait, the ferry is still your best bet for some inexpensive birding.

Birdwatchers will notice the bird fauna change as the low-lying land of Haida Gwaii appears. The number of shearwaters tapers off as they are replaced by grebes, pigeon guillemots, and scoters. Approaching Lawn Hill along the coast of Graham Island, the ferry makes a sharp turn and follows an ocean trench visible only by depth sounder. Soon you'll pass the Haida community of Skidegate, then Torrens and Jewell Islands, before easing into the dock at Skidegate Landing. You have now entered Skidegate Inlet.

GETTING THERE

Most people cross Hecate Strait by boat. BC Ferries' *Northern Adventure* has scheduled crossings between Prince Rupert on the mainland and Skidegate Landing on Haida Gwaii. This vessel can accommodate all types of RVs, cars, bicycles, and walk-on passengers. You can even carry on your kayaks. The upper decks have several lounges, a restaurant, and overnight berths. One lounge becomes an informal sleeping area after 10:00 p.m. Scheduled flights via a smaller airline cross Hecate Strait from Prince Rupert to Masset. Scheduled flights from Vancouver serve Sandspit and Masset airports.

For more, see Part 3: Planning Your Trip.

AROUND SKIDEGATE INLET

For many visitors, Skidegate Inlet provides the first close-up view of Haida Gwaii. This marine channel separates Graham Island, to the north, and Moresby, to the south, the largest islands in the chain. More than 12 kilometres wide at its eastern mouth, Skidegate Inlet winds between islands and mountains for 30 kilometres before it becomes Skidegate Channel, which connects to the west coast. These waterways provide terrific opportunities to explore homesteads and old Haida village sites, to watch seabirds and marine mammals, to find fossils and examine intertidal life or to fish for salmon. Skidegate Inlet lends itself nicely to exploration by either boat or car, as described below. There are numerous options for accommodations in this area. (See "Part 3: Planning Your Trip.")

Haida Gwaii, Region by Region

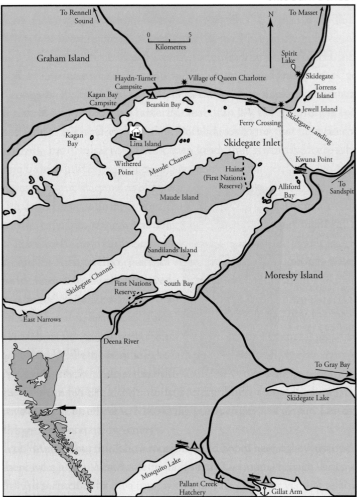

Exploring by Boat

You can begin a circle trip around the inlet at the concrete airplane ramp located between Skidegate Landing and the Village of Queen Charlotte, where there is plenty of parking and public washrooms. Unfortunately, strong westerly winds can make launching troublesome at times. In adverse conditions you may opt to take the shuttle ferry M V *Kwuna* across to Moresby Island. On the Moresby side, you can slide your boat in at Sandspit Harbour or the government dock in Sandspit. Small boats navigate easily throughout the inlet, but a chart is essential as numerous rocks and shallows make boating hazardous for those new to the area.

If you begin your trip at the airplane ramp, take a moment to examine some of the boulders along the beach. Ammonites (extinct, coiled marine shells) and clams almost pop from the rocks, their black fossils contrasting sharply with the sandstone that imprisons them. Many fossil sites have been discovered in Skidegate Inlet, imprints of creatures that lived here between 65 million and 140 million years ago. Such fossils are invaluable to scientists attempting to learn more about ancient animal and plant species.

Once underway, head toward the Village of Queen Charlotte. You'll pass exquisite sand beaches on Maple, Gooden and Roderick Islands. Modern homesteads have been built on some of these islands—please respect private property.

One of the larger islands, Lina, shows evidence of numerous previous inhabitants. The Haida dwelt in at least three places around Lina's perimeter. On the extreme east end, several tiny islets shelter a clearing that was once the site of Lina Village. Depressions in the tall grass are now the only trace of the former houses.

During pioneering days, eight non-Indigenous families homesteaded on the island. Their buildings have vanished as well, a common occurrence on Haida Gwaii. Farmers have come and gone, but their gardens remain. If you search carefully along the south shore you should find gnarled apple trees, an oversized holly tree, and several flowering shrubs. Tall stems of foxglove, an introduced flower, often mark these former cultivations, which are dotted throughout the islands.

Haida Gwaii, Region by Region

This ammonite, *Dubariceras freboldi*, from Maude Island is a very important fossil in the Jurassic period of North America. Although related to the modern nautilus, this marine mollusk lived here about 195 million years ago.

After rounding Withered Point on Lina Island, you'll find yourself in Kagan Bay. Also known as Waterfowl Bay, this shallow basin lives up to its name. In midsummer, we once recorded ten bird species jammed together on one small rock. Thousands of scoters and grebes pause here during their migration. Numerous rocks, islets, and extensive mud flats guarantee hours of good birdwatching. Kagan Bay and connecting Maude Channel are also pleasant places to canoe or kayak. Tidal currents swirl past the tips of some islands, creating eddies and small whirlpools.

Depending on the amount of time available, you have two options while in Maude Channel. A shortcut between Maude and Graham Island leads west via Skidegate Channel. Kayakers, in particular, will enjoy the east and west narrows, since the flood tide coming from Hecate Strait has a range roughly twice that coming from the Pacific side. This can create a maelstrom of eddies, currents, standing waves, and whirlpools. Since many

The small inter-island ferry *Kwuna* shuttles passengers, vehicles, and large RVs across Skidegate Inlet. JIM THORNE

boats find these channels tricky to negotiate, we recommend passage only at slack water. To reach the open Pacific you'll have to paddle or motor more than 30 kilometres.

If you turn east past Sandilands Island, you can explore the south side of Maude Island. This sausage-shaped island bears the scars of successive logging operations. Lush spruce and hemlock now cover the wounds. Boats can usually motor right next to the sheer cliffs along this side. At low tide you'll be treated to a spectacular array of intertidal life. Thousands of brown or white anemones dangle from the cliff face like dripping wax. Water normally supports their characteristic barrel shape, but their muscles stretch as the tide drops. Fossils discovered along this shoreline have made Maude Island famous within the geological community. Each layer of rock has such exquisite specimens that these fossils have become the comparative base for others of this time period throughout the world.

After visiting the numerous shops and restaurants in the Village of Queen Charlotte, a walk along the waterfront introduces you to Skidegate Inlet.

At the extreme east end of Maude Island, look for the grass-covered point and a tiny island. Haina Village, or Sunshine Town, was once located here. When west coast villages were decimated by disease in the late 1800s, survivors moved to this village site. Haida homes and totems were raised alongside a Methodist church. By 1893, however, the residents had moved on to form the larger community of Skidegate Mission. Because this is a First Nations reserve, you need permission to explore it.

With Maude Island behind you, head for the islets near Kwuna Point. Three seabird species nest on these tiny islets. Watch for pigeon guillemots with black bodies and white wing patches. As they scoot across the water or squat on a favourite rock, their brilliant red legs leave no doubt as to their identity. Often gathering near kelp beds, they dive in search of skinny, eel-like fish called blennies. They can hold several fish in their bills as they return to nests under logs or in rock crevices.

The Spirit Lake trail begins directly behind Skidegate Village. Suitable for hikers of all ages, the 3-kilometre forested trail around the perimeter of the lake takes about 1.5 to 2 hours.

Haida Gwaii, Region by Region

The gazebo at Onward Point provides welcome shelter on wet days. Whales, porpoises, and seabirds can all be watched from this prominent headland.

Glaucous-winged gulls also feed and nest here. Unlike guillemots, they build exposed nests on islets that have little or no vegetation. In June and early July the small islets appear snowy as parents incubate their speckled eggs. Once hatched, the scruffy grey chicks scamper from the nest, and by summer's end they're large enough to fend for themselves.

The other nesting seabird may be harder to find. Almost the size of gulls, black oystercatchers are the buffoons of the inlet. Like a clown with an exaggerated appendage, this absurd, red-billed shorebird balances its chunky body on elongated pink legs. A golden eye rimmed in red completes the costume. With such brilliant colouration the oystercatcher might seem an easy bird to spot. However, they prefer secluded islets where they lay their eggs just above the high-tide line. Look for the adults resting on boulders or flying together offshore. Their loud, monotonous "queep" carries halfway across the inlet.

In September, anglers easily outnumber bird species around these islets. They are attracted by the coho salmon, which seem

Foxglove was introduced to the islands. It has spread and grows profusely near settlements or in disturbed areas. JIM THORNE

to like the deep, clear waters around Maude Island and nearby Kwuna Point. For years the popular local technique was drift fishing with buzz bombs or similar lures. Fishermen now take a creative approach, spin-casting lures and spoons over ledges and near submerged rocks. Trollers prefer flashers and hoochies, guarding their colours like a best-kept secret. We trolled a flasher with a broken back and a green hoochie at thirty-minute intervals. During line checks, a few ounces of weight were added if nothing touched the lure. These fish feed primarily near the surface.

Another popular fishing method involves criss-crossing the shoals near Sandspit. Although these shallow waters are exposed to the seas of Hecate Strait, local anglers love to spend the long summer evenings out here, fantasizing about bent rods and whirling reels. During June and July, coho weighing about 2 kilograms feed in water up to 30 metres deep. We enjoyed being out in the open, but our timing was off—only a small pink salmon took our hoochie. We would have done better here in the fall. Skidegate's fishing really heats up in late September and remains

Black oystercatchers have an unmistakable robust red bill and pink legs. Their name implies oysters are their main meal, but in fact, they relish limpets, snails, chitons, and other small shellfish.

productive throughout October. Good catches at that time of the year reach 7 kilograms, but winners in the annual coho derby usually weigh in at 9 kilograms—beauties.

Whether your pleasure is fishing, boating, birding, or exploring, eventually you'll have to head in. Leave Alliford Bay, pass Maude Island, and cross Bearskin Bay. A visit to Torrens and Jewell Islands is a delightful detour in fair weather. A pebble beach on Torrens Island makes for easy landing, where you can enjoy a picnic amid the driftwood or go searching for deer in the undergrowth. Make your way back to the boat ramp by following the shoreline into Skidegate Inlet.

Exploring by Car

Begin your road trip by driving to Skidegate. Opposite the George Brown Recreation Centre is a parking lot and the trailhead for Spirit Lake. This 3-kilometre trail system is suitable for most hikers. The trails have several loops, allowing hikers to return within two hours or to stay longer, picnicking at tables near the lake. The trail passes through a second-growth forest, then enters an old-growth stand. Several large cedars have been culturally modified: the Haida obviously used this area for harvesting cedar bark and, undoubtedly, other forest plants.

If you end your Spirit Lake hike before noon, there is still plenty of time to cross Skidegate Inlet and visit Moresby Island. The shuttle ferry MV *Kwuna* transports vehicles and passengers from Skidegate Landing to Alliford Bay across the inlet. The twenty-minute ride is a must, especially if you don't have the opportunity to tour the inlet in your own craft. A small lounge provides protected viewing during rain, but on nice days, outside on deck is the place to be. We've seen storm-petrels in spring, porpoises in the summer, and hundreds of migrating birds in the fall. And keep a sharp lookout for whales.

Grey whales pass by here twice each year, migrating to and from the Arctic. These whales are primarily bottom feeders, which helps explain why they linger around the shallow areas within this inlet. Greys position their jaws sideways, very close to the sandy bottom. By folding their lips outwards and quickly retracting their tongue, they can suck in large amounts of sand and living organisms. Their baleen plate filters unwanted sand and water, retaining thousands of tiny, 2- or 3-centimetre-long amphipods and other small organisms. Between each feed they usually surface to breathe. Watch for a 2-metre, lollipop-shaped spout or a smooth, mottled grey back with a series of bumps or "knuckles" located near the tail.

After disembarking from the ferry, drive toward Sandspit. You will soon reach the Onward Point trailhead on the seaward side of the road. This looped trail, manageable for families with small children, can be strolled inside thirty minutes. A gazebo, perched on a rocky bluff, makes an excellent whale-viewing spot, particularly in wet weather.

Beach Road follows the shoreline right to bustling Sandspit Airport. Many private homes and small businesses front this 14.6-kilometre paved road. Heading south from Sandspit, Copper Bay Road will take you to Gray Bay, Skidegate Lake, Pallant Creek, and Cumshewa Inlet. Maintained logging roads allow you to travel in a circle, beginning and ending at the Alliford Bay ferry. Many people drive this loop for a day's outing. (See "Gray Bay," page 122.)

A walk out on the spit is a pleasant alternative to driving the back roads. A well-worn trail through the beach grass begins at the government dock. Extensive offshore shallows attract all kinds of birds. During migration, shorebirds rest and regroup along the beaches. Farther out, thousands of scoters may cover the water like a black sheet. Their spring arrival coincides with the spawning of Pacific herring. If a mischievous eagle or an overzealous boater puts them to flight, their wings produce a high-pitched, tremulous whistle.

Anglers enjoy the spit as much as birdwatchers do. On an incoming tide, winds and currents may combine to form large eddies within casting distance of shore. Buzz bombs or krocodiles cast into the swirling water hook many coho salmon.

We also recommend visiting Sandspit Airport. Displays in the main foyer highlight local and aerial history.

Don't forget your ferry return to Graham Island; sailing times are posted at both docks. On several occasions we missed the boat due to a long line of cars. Arrive half an hour before departure to ensure your vehicle gets on board. You can spend the waiting time beachcombing nearby.

Both grey and humpback whales frequent the waters of Skidegate Inlet. Watching the display of a humpback breaching leaves most viewers almost speechless.

GETTING THERE (SKIDEGATE INLET)

The *Northern Adventure* ferry unloads vehicles and passengers at Skidegate Landing. Also at Skidegate Landing, the MV *Kwuna* ferries vehicles and passengers back and forth across the inlet at scheduled times. The Village of Queen Charlotte has a float-plane base. Helicopters generally depart at Sandspit Airport on Moresby Island. Small boats enter Skidegate Inlet from Hecate Strait, or from the west via narrow Skidegate Channel.

CYCLING HAIDA GWAII

Cycling has to be one of the nicest ways to explore Haida Gwaii. Whether you are pedalling the highway from Skidegate Landing to Tlell or riding the sandy expanse of North Beach, you will have unique experiences. The hardest decision may be what kind of bike to bring along: the trusty tourer or the rugged mountain bike.

Cycling North beach is a leisurely way to explore the drift line. You are almost certain to find a bottle that has travelled all the way from Asia or a unique shaped shell.

BC Ferries has very low rates for cyclists and your bicycle travels free aboard MV *Kwuna*, the ferry that crosses Skidegate Inlet. The roads connecting Sandspit, the Village of Queen Charlotte, Skidegate, as well as north to Tlell, Port Clements, Masset, and Old Massett, all have asphalt surfaces. Visiting any other island location, however, means travelling on gravel roads. Newly arrived cyclists tend to spend their first evening near the Village of Queen Charlotte. B&Bs, motels, and a few camp-grounds are close by. The next day is usually spent around town or riding to Tlell, about 41 km north along Yellowhead Highway (#16). It is 21 km farther to Port Clements, and an additional 40 km to reach Masset. Some cyclists leave their bikes in Masset and catch a ride to North Beach; others choose to tackle an additional 25 km of mostly gravel road.

Cycling time between the communities varies according to the rider and the weather conditions. You can expect hard rain and strong winds, even during summer months. Make sure your bike is in excellent condition, and carry an emergency repair kit. Bicycle service is almost non-existent here, and stores carry very few parts.

RENNELL SOUND

Within an hour's drive of the Village of Queen Charlotte, you can reach Rennell Sound, the only vehicle access point to the west coast of Haida Gwaii. The sound is 15 kilometres across in places, and cuts 30 kilometres deep into Graham Island. It offers wonderful beaches, hidden coves, a diversity of wildlife, and good camping sites, as well as excellent fishing and boating—altogether an ideal combination for experiencing the power, beauty, and excitement of the open ocean.

At the base of the steep hill, you will reach a T intersection. The left turn leads to private property; turn right and within a minute you'll arrive at Rennell Sound Recreation Site. We recommend starting your exploration here.

The BC Forest Service cleared seven places large enough for tents or trailers, and small boats can be launched at this spot. A sign indicates public roads, beach trails, and picnic areas. Thirteen

42

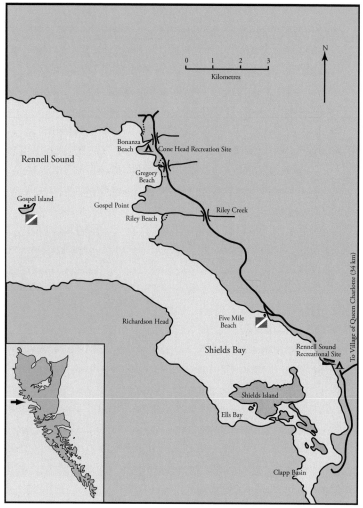

kilometres farther along, there are two more campsites at Cone Head Recreation Site (between Bonanza and Gregory Beaches). Both recreation sites have tables, fire pits, and outhouses. Allow at least a day to explore these west coast beaches.

The first trail begins near the dryland log sorting area, which can't be missed as you continue 4 kilometres past the campsite.

The road splits here. Take the left fork through the sorting area and watch for the sign indicating Five Mile Beach. From here it's a two-minute walk to the water's edge. At low tide, an isthmus connects with a tiny island. Sharp rocks splashed by Pacific swells support a healthy range of intertidal life. Look for shells of abalone and turban snails on the rocks. If you're lucky, you may discover *Dentalium*, the "money-tusk" shell, on the beach. These pencil-shaped shells were once a form of currency, their value being partly determined by length. Shells of more than 7 centimetres were so valuable that only wealthy Haida chiefs owned them.

The best beaches, Gregory and Bonanza, are farther along. To reach them, continue for another 8 kilometres to Gregory Beach or 11 kilometres to Bonanza Beach. Large, clear signs indicate vehicle pullouts and trailheads. Short, well-maintained trails suitable for small children lead directly to sand and surf. Both beaches are less than 500 metres from the road, which makes it relatively easy to pack in your tent and supplies should you want to stay overnight.

Rocky outcrops at both ends of these beaches enclose the soft sand, but heavy surf often breaks against them with tremendous force. Only creatures that can withstand the impact of tonnes of water live on such exposed places. Chalky white gooseneck barnacles and large California mussels are permanent residents of this violent world. The barnacles cement themselves to rocks via a tough, leathery neck. California mussels use fibrous strands as anchors on hard surfaces. Rough-skinned sea stars, such as *Pisaster,* move slowly over beds of mussels and barnacles. Their thousands of tube feet serve two important functions. They hold the sea stars firmly against the rocks when waves smash upon them, and they assist when the sea stars feed. The tube feet pry mussel shells apart, then the sea star inserts

When the tide recedes, the soft sand of Bonanza Beach is perfect for bare feet and sand castles. JIM THORNE

its stomach into the shell and digests its contents. What a way to go!

At low tide, the exposed headlands abound with intertidal life. But as the tide turns and the channels begin to fill, you can easily shift your attention to wave watching. The rising water soon forces a retreat to higher ground, as breaking waves race up the channels to explode in a seething froth. This titanic force is spellbinding.

Pacific swells often deposit unusual articles on shore, such as tropical plants, bits of sea life, and international garbage from ships. Interest in their mysterious origins is surpassed only by the captivating nature of waves. Rollers that have the strength and fury to smash logs into oblivion can possess, at the same time, the agility to carry delicate light bulbs and Japanese glass fishing floats and gently deposit them, intact, amid the stones.

To view these beaches from the water, return to the Rennell Sound Recreation Site. Launch your boat and consider heading

The beach camping at Rennell Sound is excellent. Driftwood will fuel your fire and rolling waves will lull you to sleep. JIM THORNE

directly across the bay. Shields Island and several islets resemble a peninsula from shore. These islands form a protected harbour that will accommodate smaller boats. Shallower water between the islands hides numerous rocks and shoals. With a chart in hand, it's safe to meander among them in a canoe or small craft.

These islands host a tremendous variety of intertidal life. Living organisms cover virtually every square centimetre of rock. Blue mussels are so numerous they sometimes envelop the rocks that support them. Within the length of your boat, you can see hundreds of sea stars. As you stare into the clear depths, rock scallops' orange lips grin back at you, and silver flashes betray schools of needlefish fleeing for cover. In suitable weather, cruise out past these islands. Bald eagles seem to escort you toward the horizon. The mountains behind you form the northern Queen Charlotte Range. On a calm day, the reflected vistas beg to be photographed. Anglers search out the 20-fathom zone to jig for cod and halibut. If

Every tide pool has something worth looking at, especially for young inquisitive minds. TRAVIS CARTER

HAIDA GWAII

you're searching for salmon, troll the shoreline. To round out the day, head for the quiet retreat of Gospel Island. A sheltered, sun-splashed beach awaits you, and you may discover sea lions and seals basking on its western edge.

The west coast of Haida Gwaii has a deserved reputation for being wild and unpredictable. Thundering waves and howling winds delight some people, while others prefer a calm sea with gentle breezes. Rennell Sound has all these attributes and much more. A day or two camping at Rennell Sound will give you a good taste of the west coast's diverse personalities.

GETTING THERE

Rennell Sound is located on the west coast of Graham Island and can be reached easily via gravel roads leading from the Village of Queen Charlotte or Port Clements. Logging trucks also travel these roads. Contact the Ministry of Forests in the Village of Queen Charlotte at 250-559-6200 for the latest road use report.

From the Village of Queen Charlotte office, drive west for 0.5 km. The road to Rennell Sound runs north for 22.5 km to the Rennell turnoff. An alternative route leads from Port Clements southward through the interior for about 51 km, until meeting the same turnoff to Rennell. Follow the marked route and watch for the sign indicating a steep hill with a 25 percent grade.

This hill may seem forbidding, but 4 × 4 camper trucks and vehicles towing small boats regularly go up and down success-fully. If you have a heavy trailer, there is an area near the top where you can leave it temporarily. You may wish to inspect the 1-km-long grade before proceeding down.

2.2 MID-GRAHAM ISLAND

COASTAL OLD-GROWTH RAINFOREST

Giant trees with their sweeping canopies, lichen-laden branches, and moss-carpeted roots dominated British Columbia's coastal areas for millennia. Species such as spruce, cedar, hemlock, and Douglas fir grew to enormous heights and often attained girths that made them the most massive single living organisms to inhabit the planet. Over the last hundred years, logging operations cut many but not all of the largest trees. Massive trees still flourish on Haida Gwaii, but viewing the finest specimens usually involves air and watercraft.

Thankfully, a fine example of an old-growth forest with very large trees has been preserved along the bank of the Yakoun River. Yaaguun Gandlaay Protected Area can be reached by car, has a wide, wheelchair-accessible trail, and is suitable for all ages. You can spend a few minutes or an hour walking slowly along the trail and will experience what it feels like to walk among botanical behemoths.

Don't be surprised if you feel humbled and perhaps even speechless when entering an old-growth rainforest. The maze of trunks creates cloisters with cathedral-like qualities. Buttressed wooden pillars taper up to a fresco of dark needles and bright sky. On a sunny day, shafts of sunlight penetrate the high canopy and illuminate the forest floor like beams through a stained-glass widow. Tapestries of lichen droop from lower limbs, while thick mosses mantle fallen limbs and logs along the trail. Gazing upward among such giants might make you feel like you have shrunk in size. Everything around you is on a grand scale.

Such forests can also be quiet, solemn spots. Along the trail, a few benches offer the opportunity to rest and be still. You will

Massive trees such as this cedar allowed the Haida to construct their houses and ocean-going canoes. The roots and inner bark of Sitka spruce (background) were used for hats and food preparation.

Haida Gwaii, Region by Region

Single Delight blooms in damp coniferous forests with an abundance of moss. The Haida used the roots in a tea for numerous ailments and for good luck.

soon notice that moss and lichens combine to muffle voices and bird song alike. Many visitors enjoy such peacefulness and tranquility. Being quiet and reflective can be as refreshing as a drink from a clear mountain stream.

Taking a few restful moments will also give you a chance to look closely at the ground beneath your feet. Amid the moss, look for flowering Single Delights. Their pale, waxy blossoms poke out shyly just above the moss carpet. Purple coral root also grows in such moist environments. Their vibrant flowers and stems lack life-sustaining chlorophyll but survive by drawing nourishment from the abundance of decaying wood and plants beneath the moss.

In numerous places along the trail and on tree trunks you will notice small interpretive plaques placed by the Haida. The trees in this grove were and still are an important part of their culture. The brief messages on each sign explain that cedar and spruce have been used extensively by First Nations. The wood has provided shelter, fuel, implements, artistry, and even clothing. Cedar is still used for making masks, paddles, bowls, and ceremonial regalia. Without cedar trees, human habitation along our coastline would have been severely limited.

This grove of virgin forest giants is small but highly representational of what once covered the entire island archipelago. Since logging companies wait a short eighty years to cut new growth, we cannot expect to see an extensive return of such large trees. So parks, ecological reserves, and enclaves such as this will be the only places to view such magnificent biological specimens. Given the rarity of such environments, why not take a few extra moments to linger and fully engage the sights, sounds, and scents of a rich, coastal rainforest?

GETTING THERE

Drive into Port Clements and continue through town along the main road. Continue 3.5 km past the Sunset RV Park and Campground. You will reach an obvious pullout with signs marking the Yaaguun Gandlaay Heritage Site. There is ample parking for cars, trucks, and motorhomes.

All tribes of the Pacific Northwest built dugout canoes. These craft set the standard for transportation, trade, hunting and fishing, and for conducting raids. Haida canoes, however, were prized up and down the coast for their craftsmanship, size, and seaworthiness. The moist climate of Haida Gwaii produced superior cedar for building the largest canoes, and the Haida's seamanship in open water gave them dominance over rival nations. Other First Nations were unwilling to attack them in their homeland because the Haida were renowned for their ferocity and were well protected by the difficult crossing. The very sight of their war canoes approaching struck terror into tribes as far south as Puget Sound. The Haida also had a deserved reputation as shrewd traders, and they carved canoes for barter as well as for their own use.

Until recently, the last big canoe carved on Haida Gwaii was commissioned in 1909, when Alfred and Robert Davidson undertook to build one 17 metres long for the Alaska–Yukon–Pacific Exposition in Seattle, Washington. That giant eventually sold to the National Museum of Canada in Ottawa and was on display in the Canadian Pavilion during Expo 86 in Vancouver.

Such a canoe could carry 4.5 tonnes of cargo. In his 1872 travelogue, Francis Poole recounts a trip from Haida Gwaii to Victoria in a canoe containing three dozen people. *Queen Charlotte Islands: A Narrative of Discovery and Adventure in the North Pacific* describes a three-week journey during which Indigenous paddlers demonstrated phenomenal stamina and skill. That story, and similar accounts by Rev. William Collison of crossing Hecate Strait in severe weather, will convince even the hardiest river canoeists that whitewater paddling is mere child's play. For the Haida, every oceanic trip posed a life-threatening risk.

At one time, the carving of canoes was an important occupation. The Haida made a variety during the winter months, then

This canoe was shaped but never made it to the water's edge. For unknown reasons, several such canoes were abandoned in the forests near Juskatla.

Haida Gwaii, Region by Region

paddled them to the mainland each spring for trade. Their success in this commerce was due in part to the size and quality of the cedars that grow in these temperate rainforests. The Haida made virtually everything from this soft, straight-grained conifer. Hilary Stewart, in her book *Cedar,* aptly calls it the "tree of life" and explains in detail how the Haida selected, cut, and shaped the trunks into canoes.

Evidence of this activity is visible all over the islands. One important location was Masset Inlet on Graham Island. Villagers from Old Massett went there in January to fell trees, as the wood contains little sap at that time of year. Old cedars frequently rot, so the Haida sounded the trunks by pounding on them to discover whether they were suited for canoe or house construction. Once a suitable candidate was selected, they would usually cut a test hole into the heartwood to confirm its soundness. If found to be solid, the tree would be felled after an appropriate ceremony. Logs destined to become canoes would be rough-shaped on site before being dragged or towed back to the village.

The introduction and use of European-designed boats soon spelled the end for such physically demanding labours. Regenerating trees and thick moss eventually concealed all evidence of canoe-building activity. In recent decades, hikers and loggers have encountered stumps, treetops, and even blanks (unfinished canoes) forgotten in the woods. Several such blanks can be seen in Masset Inlet, but the most accessible is in an old clear-cut near Port Clements. The bow of that unfinished canoe faces the stump from which it was felled, fully 3 kilometres from the nearest beach. The job of dragging the cured and hollowed hull through the forest would be done by slaves and hired men who specialized in canoe carving. The final shaping, steam-spreading, and painting would take place back at the village.

Scores of dugouts were once drawn up on the beach below Skidegate. At low tide, canoe runs are still visible on the southern edge of the beach. These are paths perpendicular to the shore where beach stones were cleared to allow canoes to land and launch without damage to the hull.

Almost a century went by before craftsmen once again took up the challenge of constructing a canoe. When the Bank of British Columbia commissioned one for exhibition at Expo 86, the designer and construction foreman was acclaimed Haida artist Bill Reid, whose hometown was Skidegate. The completion of his 18-metre craft is chronicled in a video display at the Haida Heritage Centre. Rediscovery of forgotten techniques was crucial to execute this immense project. The Haida are justifiably proud of this canoe, named *Lootaas*, which means "wave Eater." It is symbolic of their renewed tribal vigour.

On July 11, 1987, *Lootaas* arrived in Skidegate after several crews spent three weeks paddling it north from Vancouver. Two thousand people crowded the beach as *Lootaas* swept toward its ancestral home. Its bow wave sparkled in the bright sun. While a long way from shore, the flash of synchronous paddles signalled the canoe's progress. As it came on, ten bare-chested men could be seen driving pointed paddles forward and back to the beat of a tambourine drum. *Lootaas* sliced through the water with barely a ripple as the paddlers' deep "oooh-ah" chant resonated across the water. Bill Reid sat in the stern ahead of the steersman, a blue fedora shielding his proud face. His heart justifyably throbbed to that chorus!

That night, a thousand guests were invited to a Skidegate potlatch. The feasting, singing, dancing, oratory, and gift giving made that evening the event of the decade on the islands. The ceremony will be a lifelong memory for everyone who attended.

Haida Gwaii, Region by Region

That such canoes are worthy of regional and national recognition indicates the value of Haida heritage to all Canadians. We hope *Lootaas* will gnash these waters for years to come.

GETTING THERE

The two canoes described in this chapter are located a considerable distance apart. Some visitors choose to examine the blank or partially finished canoe first, then drive to the Haida Heritage Centre in Skidegate to view the famous *Lootaas* on display in the open shelter.

To view the blank canoe in the woods, drive into Port Clements. Continue along the main road through town to the Sunset RV and Camping Park. From the park, continue an additional 11 km on the gravel road toward Juskatla. A canoe sign on the left side marks a side road. Driving this narrow road is not advised. Instead, pull off close on the gravel shoulder and walk about 0.3 km to the trailhead. At the trailhead, you will see two logs that appear to have been honed. Continuing along the trail for about five minutes brings you to the best example of a traditional canoe in its infancy.

PADDLE THE *LOO PLEX*

During your visit to Haida Gwaii, consider paddling *Loo Plex*. This canoe is a replica of a cedar canoe carved by renowned Haida craftsman Bill Reid. It takes twelve to twenty people to propel this type of watercraft. The canoe leaves directly from the

The *Loo Plex* can seat twenty adults. Individuals or groups wishing to paddle a canoe of this size should sign up at the Haida Heritage Centre office. HAIDA HERITAGE CENTRE

beach at the Haida Heritage Centre, and, depending on the wind and weather, glides through the waters washing the beaches of Skidegate or the small islands nearby. For a price of $15 per person, it will be a most memorable experience. For more information, contact the Haida Heritage Centre at 250-559-7885.

NADU—TRAILS TO TRIBULATION

At the end of Nadu Road, on Masset Sound, a relatively short walk and scramble graphically illustrates the broken dreams found in so many places on these islands. Here moulder the remnants of a homestead and a failed business enterprise. After spending a couple of hours here, you will come away with a glimpse of the isolation, loneliness, and hardships experienced by early homesteaders.

The side road into Nadu was originally built during the 1920s to supply inland subsistence farmers from the water's edge. The highway did not exist then, so transportation was by steamship. The road's slope near the sound was logged in the 1970s. Today, hemlock and alder trees are growing rapidly covering this scar. Their vigorous growth conceals much of what the early homesteaders left behind.

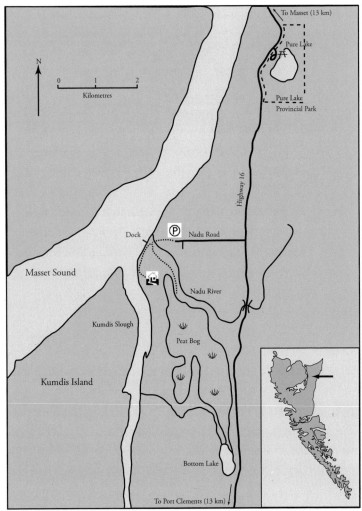

To Masset (13 km)

Pure Lake

N

0   1   2
Kilometres

Pure Lake
Provincial Park

Highway 16

Dock   P   Nadu Road

Masset Sound

Nadu River

Kumdis Slough

Peat Bog

Kumdis Island

Bottom Lake

To Port Clements (13 km)

    You'll reach a rock breakwater at the former homestead by following the shoreline south from the old dock. For easiest walking, begin your journey about two hours after high tide and return before it comes in. (Add two hours to the Masset tide tables for accurate timing.) Overhanging vegetation makes the shoreline traverse very difficult during high tide.

The unmortared breakwater, built of beach cobbles, is only 1 kilometre away. The even sides and attention to design are marks of a skilled stonemason. After seven decades only a small portion has collapsed. This was truly a labour of love and is an indication of the care put into all the construction at this site.

A narrow trail leads up the embankment behind the footings of an old boathouse. It winds through the cedars to a clearing with a "fruitless" apple orchard. In 1911 the promising new home of the Edward Evans family stood here. Three huge rhododendron bushes are evidence of Mrs. Evans's efforts to domesticate the wilderness. These transplanted southern shrubs have grown to 6 metres tall and display gorgeous blooms during the first week of July.

The smooth adze marks and even joints on the last remaining portions of the walls speak to the skills of an artist. We immediately suspected a Scandinavian influence. Later we read in Kathleen Dalzell's *The Queen Charlotte Islands, 1774–1966*, that "master axemen" Ole Anderson and Alec Johnson were hired by Evans to build this substantial house. The craftsmanship and aesthetic touches evident in this homestead only serve to enhance the sense of despair that pervades the place—so much for naught.

It must have been devastating to leave these dreams and dollars behind, a story typical of farming on Haida Gwaii. Encouraged by exaggerated agricultural claims and government land giveaways, many pioneers devoted everything they had to their farms. Today, no one on the islands earns a living solely from crops or cattle.

In 1967 another enterprise started at Nadu with the same high hopes that had inspired previous pioneers. Bering Industries of Victoria, BC, spent $1 million constructing a peat moss plant to process a nearby bog into a horticultural product. The moss was extracted by draining the bog, allowing the dry top layer of moss to be suctioned off.

The stone breakwater remains largely intact, even though the homestead has been long abandoned. The rocks were placed without the aid of mortar.

Ironically, the very qualities that render peat useless for farming are excellent attributes when the moss is added to proper soil. Its sterility, lightness, compressibility, absorbent nature, and organic composition make it easy to work and valuable for gardening and other uses.

From the dock you may wish to follow a heavily overgrown road up a gentle incline to the bog workings about 1.6 kilometres away. The walk passes through a mixed wood to a bench above Nadu River. There are no views until the trees give way at the edge of the bog. Little remains at this extraction site, but if you haven't visited a bog before, seize the opportunity to look around with an exploratory spirit.

The reason for the business failure is unclear, although the distance to markets must have been a factor. Peat-harvesting operations in the lower Fraser Valley would have presented serious competition. Evidently, only one shipment was ever made from the Nadu plant. The foundations of the buildings and a slowly rotting dock are all that remain of this venture.

Of all the efforts to earn a living attempted on these islands, only fishing and logging have met with continued success. As we learn more about the importance of careful management of our so-called renewable resources, however, even their future seems uncertain. In the midst of all this, a new economic opportunity is beginning to pay off on Haida Gwaii: tourism. With international attention focused on the richly rewarding adventure of touring these beautiful islands, there is the potential for even greater economic benefit to flow from the area's stunning natural attributes. Here, at last, is an enterprise that can maintain and enhance the independent lifestyle so cherished by islanders. We hope tourism will continue to thrive even if Nadu fades away forever.

GETTING THERE

Nadu Road is marked on the Yellowhead Highway 19 km north of Port Clements or 21 km south of Masset. From the highway, this gravel road runs straight for 1.6 km. There is plenty of room to park at the road end. A narrow, overgrown road continues a farther 0.4 km, ending at a small landslide. Farther along, a deep washout and numerous leaning alders inhibit your progress. After about 30 minutes, you will reach the remains of concrete pads and a rotting dock. An additional twenty minutes south along the beach will be required to access the breakwater and remains of a homestead. If you begin your beach walk two hours after high tide there should be plenty of time to explore and return with dry feet. Visitors will also need a pioneering spirit to straddle crisscrossing alders and follow faint pathways to reach these interesting sites.

NOTE Gumboots are highly recommended for this shoreline and bog outing.

2.3 NORTHERN GRAHAM ISLAND

LANGARA ISLAND VICINITY

Called North Island by some, Langara is a forested, low-profile rocky isle of about 25 square kilometres. Lying off the north-western tip of Graham Island, it is fully exposed to the pounding Pacific. Wind, waves, and a serrated shore give it a frightening sort of beauty. The scenery is spectacular. Every bluff, bay, and rock pillar promises something new and exciting.

This location, often too remote for spur-of-the-moment visitors, has attracted every sort of inhabitant over the years: Haida villagers, trading sailors, fishermen, environmental students, lightkeepers, and biologists. Originally the Haida lived around the island in several villages, the largest being Kiusta on nearby Graham Island. This site was abandoned in about 1850 when most of the residents migrated to the Alaskan panhandle and eastward toward Masset. Kiusta has been used only seasonally since.

First Nations use of this area is long-standing. In 1986, archaeologists uncovered campfire charcoal dating back 10,400 years. Subject to further verification, this will go down as one of the oldest known sites of human activity in British Columbia. Such ancient Aboriginal colonization lends perspective to "discovery" of Haida Gwaii by European navigators.

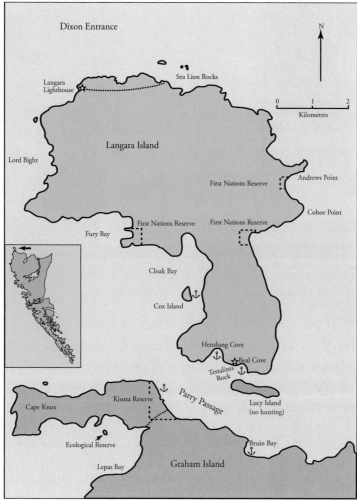

In 1787, English fur trader George Dixon was the first European to circumnavigate this archipelago. As well as naming the group of islands after Queen Charlotte, he named Langara "North Island" and "Cloak Bay" following a profitable purchase of furs: "There were 10 canoes about the ship, which contained, as nearly as

The wild northwest coast of Haida Gwaii has many rock walls and pillars formed by wave and wind erosion. TOM PARKIN

I could estimate, 120 people; many of these brought most beautiful beaver cloaks, others excellent skins, and, in short, none came empty handed, and the rapidity with which they sold them was a circumstance additionally pleasing; they fairly quarreled with each other about which should sell his cloak first . . ." These were the first days of the infamous sea otter trade. The exchange of sea otter pelts for resale in China continued until the mid-1800s. It would have continued had not the entire otter population on Haida Gwaii been completely annihilated.

In contrast to the sea otter's fate, fish still thrive around Langara Island. The commercial fleet has been enjoying superlative salmon catches in this vicinity for years. Now the lucrative sport-fishing industry has discovered the area as well.

In recent years a floating lodge was anchored in Henslung Cove to cater to fly-in clients. One patron declared the experience "the best fishing I've had in 30 years on the BC coast." Weight records at

Peregrine Falcons are commonly seen around Langara Island. Rock faces or pillars, such as those on the opposite page, provide protected ledges ideal for nesting.

Langara Lodge exceed 139 kilograms for halibut, 35 kilograms for spring salmon, and 10 kilograms for the largest coho salmon ever landed. Large ling cod and chum salmon supplement the take. The lodge has gained a worldwide reputation and capacity bookings as a result of such tremendous catches.

Several other floating resorts have since sprung up in the area. All these operations are relatively expensive and open to reserved guests only. (For more, see "Part 3: Planning Your Trip.")

Meanwhile, Haida adolescents who participate in a program called Rediscovery forgo such luxurious accommodation and live close to the land. These island teens use the rustic cabins at Lepas Bay as their base. Every summer, consecutive two-week programs provide hands-on learning in environmental awareness, outdoor skills, and respect for traditional Haida culture. Rediscovery has been so successful that the program's originators have given training workshops to instructors in the United States.

The lightkeepers at Langara are the only people who live on the island year-round. Langara lighthouse is notoriously difficult for boat landings because there's no moorage. Most people come and go by helicopter. These lightkeepers are Canada's most westerly residents. They serve us all by operating directional beacons and taking weather and seismograph (earthquake) readings. Since submarine earthquakes sometimes generate tsunamis, this lighthouse is the vanguard of the Canadian early warning system. The station was established in 1913 at the same time as its companion on the southern tip of this island chain—Cape St. James.

Like their rocky counterpart to the south, Cape Knox and Lepas Bay on Graham Island are completely exposed, and both provide plenty of rugged scenery. Cape Knox also offers the possibility of cave exploration. Out from Pillar Bay's beach, facing Dixon Entrance, towers a 29-metre column of conglomerate rock and sandstone. There are similar, though smaller, features in Cloak Bay: one called Porthole Rock has a 2-metre hole through it.

Another geological oddity is Plum Pudding Rock, or Testatlints, in Parry Passage. This enormous boulder, accessible at low tide, is topped by a thicket of trees and sits on the shore of Langara Island. Recognized by geologists as an erratic feature, it was deposited by glaciers during the ice age. A shaman whose grave lies on its summit gave the stone its Haida name.

Walking about on land is the best way to really appreciate these locations. Just within the trees at Kiusta, a row of depressions outlines what were once houses in the former village. Only a few corner posts remain upright to mark their perimeter. Roof beams covered in moss lie across the pits, and the rainforest crowds close—a scene typical of abandoned Haida villages. Unusual here is the three-pole mortuary, which once supported the remains of a Haida chief. Called the Edenshaw pole, this triple

Salmon or halibut fishing around Langara Island attracts fishers from around the world. The lodges in this area are fly-in and upscale in comfort and convenience.
LANGARA LODGE

totem is the only one of its kind in existence. At the far end of the beach behind it, faces stare from rocks at the tide line. Although ground out by the Haida, the meaning and function of such petroglyphs remain a mystery.

A trail leads across the wooded peninsula from Kiusta to the famous crescent beach at Lepas Bay. A spectacular 55-kilometre coastal hike begins here. The route south takes you to caves and misty rainforest, beachcombing treasures, and freshwater fishing. Sea-run cutthroat trout can attain sporting size in the deeper coastal creeks.

A visit to Langara Island would not be complete without seeing its peregrine falcons. These streamlined hunters are admired the world over for their speed and finesse in flight. At one time the population here was phenomenally dense: up to twenty pairs nested on the cliffs. Since 1968, only five to seven nests have been

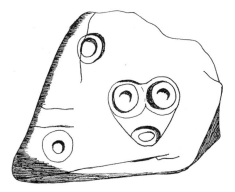

Petroglyphs on a beach boulder near Kiusta. The age and purpose of these rock carvings remain a mystery.

active. Some scientists believe their decline is due to the falling numbers of ancient murrelets, a major food source.

Murrelets once numbered more than twenty thousand pairs, making Langara Island the site of the world's largest ancient murrelet colony (along with other burrow-nesting seabirds). Unfortunately, Norway rats were introduced to the island and wreaked havoc with the vulnerable nesting birds. The result: only a very small number of ancient murrelets survived the rat attack. All other species were wiped out.

In an effort to restore the island's nesting seabirds, the Canadian Wildlife Service established a rat removal program. Beginning in 1995 and continuing for several years, a systematic poisoning and trapping program successfully purged the island of the vermin. In 2004, researchers returned to determine if the rat extermination had been beneficial to the birds. The results were heartening.

Estimates of nesting ancient murrelets indicate that the breeding population has doubled in size from about six thousand pairs in 1999 to over twelve thousand pairs five years later. Also, a small pocket of nesting Cassin's auklets was discovered on the north shore. Both of these very positive signs suggest seabird nesting success has increased and the colony is in much better health.

Despite the remoteness of Langara, civilization has upset its cultural and biological balance. Much was lost before we were able to fully understand and appreciate this place. Langara Island still offers us its beauty, resources, and spirit. Knowing now the island's fragility, we must continue to act responsibly and preserve or restore the natural attributes of this outstanding wilderness area.

GETTING THERE

Langara Island is remote and accessible only by boat or aircraft. The venturesome can charter air or water craft from Masset. Helicopter travel must be prearranged at the Sandspit Airport. Mooring buoys for yachters are located in Pillar Bay, Bruin Bay, Henslung Cove, Beal Cove, Cloak Bay, and in front of Kiusta village. For details on accommodation and camping, see Part 3: Planning Your Trip.

FISHING ON HAIDA GWAII

The waters surrounding these islands supply the traditional protein source for islanders, offering, as they do, the very best in fresh seafood. The rod-and-reel recreation is renowned, access is easy, and the fish are abundant. In recent years, however, salmon fishing has come under such immense pressure that closures are now common in all BC coastal areas. Be sure to consult the latest fishing regulations before wetting your line.

Fishing can be divided into lake, stream, and saltwater categories. Steelhead, salmon, and halibut are of greatest interest to most anglers, but rockfish and cod also live in the waters around Haida Gwaii. On the freshwater side, there are rainbow and cutthroat trout as well as Dolly Varden char in most streams and lakes. Small boats can be launched at Mayer Lake in Naikoon Park, and at Mosquito and Skidegate Lakes on Moresby Island. The latter two offer trout up to 1.4 kg and Dolly Varden weighing in at 0.5 kg. If you don't have a boat, you can still dangle your line along the lakeshore or head to the nearest river and cast for steelhead or sea-run trout.

Former US president Jimmy Carter includes a chapter on Moresby fishing in his book *An Outdoor Journal* describing his steelhead experiences and heralding this fishing as among the best in North America. The season for these fighting fish starts in November, climaxes during the Christmas holidays, and then declines toward spring. The timing of the runs varies somewhat from river to river, and techniques vary according to the angler and the nature of the water. The Yakoun and Tlell Rivers on Graham Island, and Pallant Creek on Moresby Island, are among the best producers.

Mid-September is when coho salmon aficionados arrive for stream fishing, so accommodation and vehicle rentals can be scarce at that time of year. Coho return to fresh water when fall rains raise river levels to a point where the fish can swim up from the ocean to spawn. The Tlell, Yakoun, Copper, and Deena Rivers offer good water. Since their stream gradients are low, they have tidal action as far as 1 kilometre upstream. Check for triangular markers indicating the boundary of tidal fishing. Here,

A winter steelhead caught on a fly. Such superb fishing attracts anglers from around the world. LANGARA LODGE

as throughout BC, separate fishing licences are required for salt and fresh water.

Saltwater fishing is a year-round activity if you can tolerate the winter weather. We have detailed some specific locales in the sections on Tow Hill, Langara Island, Louise Island, and Skidegate Inlet.

There is great fishing for salmon and bottom fish in many other locations as well. Bottom fish include halibut (easily as desirable as salmon from a culinary point of view), ling cod, and red snapper. These species can be caught by jigging on simple handlines: reef raiders and buzz bombs are popular lures. Bottom fish aren't always that easily caught, and you really have to know what you're doing to land a large halibut. Counting on fresh fish for an expedition menu has meant going hungry for more than a few intrepid travellers.

Small boats can be launched on both sides of Skidegate Inlet. This area is within the boundaries of the popular annual Sandspit coho derby.

In the last decade, numerous floating lodges, land lodges, and roaming ships have attracted fly-in clients for extended salt-water fishing. Most of these fancy facilities are on the west and north coasts of Graham Island. Coho and spring salmon are the major attractions, but halibut is also high on the list. All bookings must be made in advance through companies in Victoria or Vancouver. Consult the *Saltwater Fishing Guide* (free from almost any fishing store) for their locations, or look in recent fishing magazines for their ads. Inquire locally for the names of people who have smaller boats available for casual charter fishing. The Village of Queen Charlotte website lists local charter operators. Visit queencharlotte.ca, then click on "Directory," then on "fishing charters."

If you don't have a boat or the budget for a guide, you can still catch saltwater fish from shore. Surf-casters have brought in halibut from the rocks at the foot of Tow Hill in Naikoon Park, although there's an equal chance of landing dogfish—a small, undesirable shark. Other anglers report success catching young coho and pink salmon from the spit at Sandspit, from southside beaches in Skidegate Inlet and in Rennell Sound.

Once spawning starts, the local salmon derby gets underway as salmon begin to concentrate at the mouths of their home streams. On the four September weekends each year, the Sandspit Rod and Gun Club sponsors a coho derby. To be eligible, fish must be caught between Gray Bay and the Deena River on Moresby Island. The coho, though much smaller than spring (also called king or chinook) salmon, has a reputation as the wildest fighter of the salmonid family. A fish in the 3- to 5-kg range can create tremendous excitement when caught on light tackle. Many anglers concentrate on the Copper River estuary, where a sizeable encampment of the devoted suddenly appears during the derby. The competition is open to visitors and residents alike, and prizes are awarded in various categories. The largest coho caught is usually in the 9-kg range.

Saltwater fishing also includes shellfish, but as with finfish, you need a licence before you can set a crab trap or dig for razor clams. Remember that the islands are under a permanent closure for all other bivalves due to the paralyzing toxins found in some molluscs. Thankfully, shrimp, prawns, and crabs aren't affected. Dungeness crabs are the favourite (or should we say "flavourite"?). A collapsible crab trap baited with any smelly fish or tinned meat should produce a cracking good meal off North Beach, in Naden Harbour, or in Masset Inlet. The key is to find sandy ocean bottoms, preferably with eelgrass as cover for the crabs.

Licences and regulations are available from most sporting goods stores or the government agent's office in the Village of

74

Queen Charlotte. We further recommend having a copy of *Fishing the Queen Charlotte Islands,* by former resident Bob Long. (See "Further Reading," page 297.) His book has numerous maps giving away the best fishin' holes on the islands.

DELKATLA WILDLIFE SANCTUARY

Every spring, millions of shorebirds and waterfowl leave their wintering areas and fly north to nesting grounds in the Arctic. One migration route lies along the western edge of North America—the Pacific Flyway. Birds making this trip almost always stop for rest, shelter, and nourishment. Favoured locations spaced along their flyways supply these requirements. Delkatla slough is one such location and is an excellent place to see birds during spring and fall migration.

A border of dense conifers, several roads, and Masset townsite rim the sanctuary's marsh. Ponds of varying sizes, separated by ditches and dikes, cover most of the sanctuary. In 1977 a tidal gate was installed, which allows seawater to flood the largest basin. The present bridge, finished in 1995, allows normal tidal action within the sanctuary. Water levels on the largest pond fluctuate four times a day, revealing extensive mud flats at low tide. Above the water line, lush grass, wildflowers, and small trees grow in the dark soil. Birds use all these habitats.

A short trail from the parking area along Cemetery Road leads to a viewing tower. This is an excellent vantage point for scanning the entire marsh with binoculars, but the best birding begins as you return to ground level. Three trails lead to the waterways.

Simpson Trail, marked by a driftwood sign at the Cemetery Road parking lot, winds pleasantly along the treed side of the sanctuary. Rustic benches provide an opportunity to sit quietly

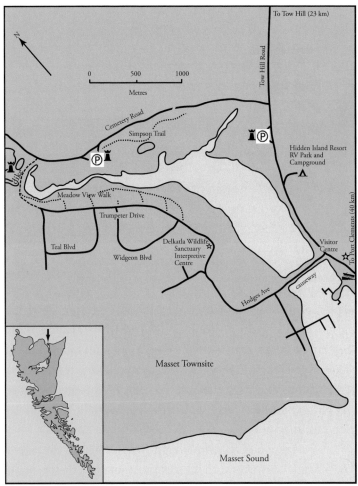

To Tow Hill (23 km)

Tow Hill Road

0   500   1000

Metres

Cemetery Road

Simpson Trail

Ⓟ

Ⓟ

Hidden Island Resort
RV Park and
Campground

Meadow View Walk

Trumpeter Drive

Teal Blvd

Widgeon Blvd

Delkatla Wildlife
Sanctuary
Interpretive
Centre

Visitor
Centre

To Port Clements (40 km)

Hodges Ave

causeway

Masset Townsite

Masset Sound

listening for calls. Through the dark foliage you may glimpse a shy varied thrush or a chatty Pacific wren. The Steller's jay and hairy woodpecker also prefer wooded areas. Both of these birds are particular subspecies endemic to Haida Gwaii.

At several spots the trail emerges at meadows and ponds. Skulk along the edge of a ditch, staying alert for waterfowl. A fanfare of discordant trumpets will announce the arrival of the

Viewing towers and platforms are easily accessible on both sides of the sanctuary. They provide unobstructed views of the waterways and meadows.

largest species—swans and geese. Mallards, American widgeons, and teal may be feeding with their tails turned up in the shallows. They can execute a near-vertical takeoff, which allows them into confined ponds and ditches. If a bald eagle or peregrine falcon suddenly appears, these smaller birds will scatter. An alarmed snipe may burst out, while Lincoln's sparrows furtively flit between the grass hummocks.

You can take a second route along a dike that bisects the marsh. It begins 300 metres past the first parking lot on Cemetery Road. Midway along, a second viewing tower provides a platform to set up a spotting scope and observe distant waterfowl. Wade through thigh-high grass near the ponds. This open portion of Delkatla is the best area to see sandhill cranes performing their spring courtship dance. You'll need patience and stealth to see these elegant birds as they leap repeatedly skyward, then drop awkwardly to earth, all the while flapping, trumpeting, and bowing.

Sandhill cranes nest and forage among the meadows of Delkatla. They are seen regularly from April through to September.

Sandhill cranes are but one of more than 130 species of birds recorded at Delkatla. The high number of sightings is mainly due to the dedication and commitment of local naturalist Margo Hearne. (See page 269.) For three decades she has recorded migration patterns and numbers, details that are vital to research on breeding species Past studies focused on the least sandpiper, a tiny shorebird that normally breeds on the Arctic barrens. Biologists recorded up to ninety pairs nesting at Delkatla, the highest breeding density in North America. A coloured leg banding initiative also yielded some interesting results. By late summer, only the immature sandpipers remained. Their parents had left for Central America, leaving the juveniles to find their own way south.

Unfortunately, these and other ground-nesting birds have to contend with obnoxious neighbours. Hereford cattle graze within the sanctuary because border fences are not maintained. These

Northern Pintail can be seen year round on Haida Gwaii especially during migration periods and throughout the winter.

lumbering beasts create havoc by disturbing incubating adults and squashing ground nests. Since Delkatla is only a municipal sanctuary, it lacks environmental protection.

From Trumpeter Drive at the eastern edge of Masset, Meadow View Walk offers unobstructed views over the open water. In late April and early May, chocolate-coloured dowitchers probe the muck, black-banded killdeer cry plaintively, and flocks of tiny shorebirds zoom over the water's edge like jets in formation. More than twenty species of shorebirds have been recorded here.

While on this side of the sanctuary, you will be pleased to discover the interpretive centre complete with a viewing platform overlooking the meadows. The centre is a showpiece for interpretive centres. Margo Hearne and Peter Hamel have devoted endless amounts of time ensuring the centre and the sanctuary lands continue to serve both the migrant birds and island visitors.

Most birds that stop at Delkatla are common along the Pacific Flyway. Rare species, however, do drop in from distant locales. A warm-weather cattle egret was spotted during one Christmas bird count. Marbled godwits, which rarely stray east of the Rockies, have also made a surprise appearance. Wood sandpipers and ruffs, which regularly migrate beyond the outer Aleutian Islands, caused quite a sensation when they appeared in Delkatla. All these birds are rare in BC.

Since it's on a major migration route, Delkatla will always be a good place for birders to visit. Spring and fall are the best times, but a storm may yield a few surprises. Who knows? You might spot a transient from Siberia, or witness the spectacular dive of a peregrine falcon.

GETTING THERE

This 553-hectare lowland refuge lies adjacent to the Village of Masset. Delkatla is accessible by car and trail, and has three viewing towers. For a visit, follow Tow Hill Road east past Masset, turn left onto Cemetery Road, and drive 1.7 km to a gravel parking lot. Begin your walk at this location or along a dike, 300 m farther on.

The Delkatla Wildlife Sanctuary Interpretive Centre is located along the opposite side of the sanctuary. To reach it, cross the causeway leading into Masset. Once across, continue along Hodges Ave. A short distance along, turn right on Trumpeter Drive and watch for the gate marking the entrance to the interpretive centre.

2.4 NAIKOON PROVINCIAL PARK

If you've ever stood in wonder before the monumental *Raven and the First Men* at the Museum of Anthropology at the University of British Columbia in Vancouver, you've been touched by Naikoon.

This world-famous cedar carving by Haida artist Bill Reid interprets the myth describing the creation of humans at Rose Spit in Naikoon Provincial Park. That such artistry was inspired here is indicative of the special nature of this landscape. Within the boundaries of Naikoon Park lie 72,600 hectares of beaches, sand dunes, bogs, and lakes. With the exception of two bedrock outcrops, more than 100 kilometres of unbroken beach form its oceanic perimeter. Extensive sand deposits are continuously blown into shifting dunes behind the driftwood. The park's interior is largely a boggy lowland interspersed with a few lakes. This is the Argonaut Plain, a landform created by glacial action thousands of years ago. Some significant geological discoveries have been made here, but they have little commercial value.

Amazingly, the provincial government promoted development of this plain in the early 1900s by issuing homestead permits. Although none of these settlers managed to establish a permanent residence, private property still exists within today's park boundaries. Modern homes along the northern beaches and the Tlell River have replaced some old homesteads.

The BC government made a wiser land-use decision in 1973 when it declared Naikoon a provincial park, an excellent choice for the preservation of landforms and lowland typical of BC's coast. A park also served to protect the habitat of some unusual plants, birds, and fish—including the 5-centimetre-long, three-spine stickleback mentioned on page 266, which has evolved into specialized subspecies in some of the park's lakes. Three Provincial Ecological Reserves near the park boundaries protect additional areas with environmental significance.

Seasonal visitors can enjoy a wide range of recreational opportunities that the park has to offer. Naikoon has something for everyone—from four-wheeling on the beach to quiet

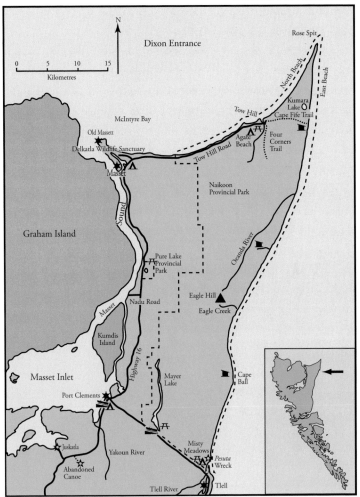

contemplation of nature. It has a coastal trek for experienced backpackers, forest trails for families, and limitless beachcombing. The fishing is a big draw for anglers, particularly in the fall, when salmon and steelhead enter the park's rivers. Both sea-run and resident cutthroat trout can be fished in the Tlell and Sangan

Haida Gwaii, Region by Region

Rivers, as well as in Mayer Lake, which is great for canoeing and has a launching ramp for boats.

The park's headquarters is located on the Yellowhead Highway just south of the Tlell River. Facilities include Agate Beach and Misty Meadows, serviced campgrounds at the north and south ends of the park. Neither of these campgrounds has hot water, hookups or sani-dumps, and the campsites are available on a first-come, first-served basis. A fee is charged from May to September.

There are picnic areas in a satellite provincial park called Pure Lake, and at Tow Hill, Mayer Lake, Tlell River and Misty Meadows, all within Naikoon. Most stores and commercial services are in the nearby villages of Masset or Port Clements. A regular provincial fishing licence is required for anglers within BC provincial parks. Hunting is permitted within Naikoon Provincial Park; see Appendix 4 for more details.

For brochures and current information, contact the area supervisor at:

Naikoon Provincial Park
Box 19, Tlell, BC V0T 1Y0
Phone: 250-557-4390
Website: env.gov.bc.ca/bcparks/

TOW HILL AREA

The rounded dome of Tow Hill is the dominant landmark and a must-see for visitors to Naikoon Park. There are picnic facilities at the hill, a short trail to its summit, and a grand view of Dixon Entrance. From its base, anglers may cast into a river or the sea, jig offshore for halibut, or catch crab beyond the surf. Hiking routes lead inland in both directions along the extensive beaches. This is a pleasant place to picnic for a few hours or to linger for several days of camping, fishing, crabbing, and exploring.

Agate Beach is named for the translucent stones found all along this shore. They're a form of quartz, washed from glacial deposits by the waves and tumbled in the saltwater swash until they gleam. They have no commercial value but don't try telling this to a child—for young castaways these are diamonds for their treasure chest.

The pebble beach gives way to soft sand at low tide. If the surf is down, inflatable boats can be launched from the beach. The water averages 4 to 10 fathoms offshore, ideal for jigging bottom fish. Buzz bombs, cod jigs, or baited hooks are popular for halibut. If you don't have a boat, try bait-casting for groundfish from the base of Tow Hill. The Hiellen River also supports cutthroat trout and Dolly Varden, and commercial fishers work offshore for Dungeness crab, which are abundant. You can set out crab traps as well if you have a boat and the surf stays calm for a few hours.

A more popular method of crab fishing is to wade through the surf at low tide. You will, however, need a net and chestwaders. Hardy (or hungry) souls sometimes brave the cold water and wade out in only their bathing suits. You need a licence to harvest crab: be sure to check the saltwater fishing regulations for sizes and limits.

From the campground, Tow Hill is a fifteen-minute walk along the beach, or a 2-kilometre ride along the road. From its ocean side, the distinctive character of Tow Hill can be easily observed. The cliff is composed of hexagonal columns of rock that fit together like six-sided cells of honeycomb. This is basalt: an igneous (fireformed) stone that long ago flowed into cracks of sandstone that were already in place here. When the molten basalt cooled, it cracked into metre-wide columns.

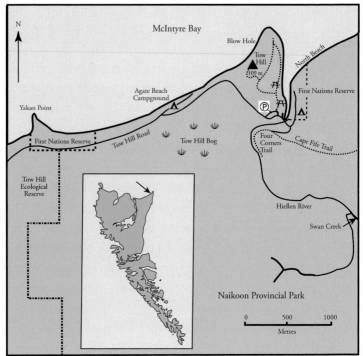

Tow Hill was further sculpted by glaciers during the last ice age. Viewed from North Beach, the gradual, inland slope of the hill lies in contrast to its fluted face. A wall of ice pushed down from the Queen Charlotte Mountains, depositing gravel against the back side of the hill before rising over it and moving out to sea. On the seaward side, bedrock was plucked away. This left an excellent example of a landform known as a *roche moutonnée*.

From the parking lot at the base of Tow Hill, a loop trail system ensures that visitors experience all angles of Tow Hill. After leaving your car, follow the gravel path to the picnic site at the trailhead. From this location a wheelchair-accessible gravel trail and boardwalk meanders alongside the Hiellen River way to a viewing platform adjacent to the beach at the base of Tow Hill.

Part of being touched by Naikoon is searching through the drift line. With each tide, the beach renews itself and something new appears as if by magic.

A second boardwalk trail gradually inclines to two more viewing platforms. The first platform looks over sickle-shaped North Beach, and the second platform sits atop the 109-metre summit of Tow Hill.

From this vantage point on a clear day, islands in the Alaska panhandle can be seen to the north, 72 kilometres away across Dixon Entrance. To the west, Agate Beach campground is visible and in the distance beyond is the ridge of the Queen Charlotte Mountains. Directly below the lookout the cliff drops to a rocky point, where pelagic cormorants sometimes gather before roosting overnight on the cliff face. This edge is concealed—do not leave the established trail, and make sure to supervise children at all times.

After taking in the vistas and crashing surf around the hill, you may want to investigate the forests behind it. Here, the pale

It's chilly, but wading the surf is a popular way to catch crabs. A forked stick or, better yet, a dip net will lift the crabs off the bottom.

HAIDA GWAII

A popular way to cruise the beaches is with ATVs. They can get you to your favoured spot in a hurry and there is little chance of being caught by the incoming tide.

beauty of a single flower and the whistle of a shy varied thrush are contrasting pleasures on a micro scale. Among these trees, a general store, a post office, and a clam cannery once operated. A rusting boiler and concrete foundations in the trees downstream from the bridge are all that remain. This property belongs to the Old Massett Village Council. They have built Haida-style cabins and a longhouse in the shade of the spruce and hemlock forest. See Part 3: Planning Your Trip for details about overnighting in these stylish cabins.

In the early 1900s an ill-informed government in Victoria promoted vast tracts of Graham Island for agricultural settlement. Immigrants found themselves trying to locate unsurveyed land that had no access. Later they discovered there was no export market for the produce they grew. At first only a few determined settlers used the beach as their road, but by 1912 there were about a hundred people dealing at the Tow Hill store. World War I and

North Beach bounty. A low-tide catch of crab and clams guarantees a great meal back at camp.

From atop Tow Hill you can view the beaches below and glimpse Alaska across Dixon Entrance.

Haida Gwaii, Region by Region

the subsequent Depression ended their efforts. Today their wagon routes are walking trails from Tow Hill to East Beach and the park's interior. To explore them is to gain an appreciation of the work ethic of these pioneers.

GOLFING ON HAIDA GWAII

If packing for a trip to Haida Gwaii includes making room for your golf clubs, then you will be pleasantly surprised that both of the courses found on the islands welcome visitors.

The Dixon Entrance Golf Course can be found 5 km east of Masset along the Tow Hill Road. You won't have any trouble locating the fairways as they surround a curious circular antenna. This high-wire structure belongs to the Armed Forces and dominates the skyline. It makes for a great conversation starter. One might imagine listening to foreign ships or submarines while lining up your next shot. The course runs on the honor system. If no one's there, sign in and head straight to the first tee. The gate's open April through to October.

While visiting Sandspit, visit the Willows Golf and Country Club. This area was once the Mather family homestead. They operated a dairy on the flats, complete with their own cattle. Today, the only four-legged animals likely to graze on the greens will be the prolific island deer. The fairways follow the shoreline and blend into the neighbouring forest offering a bit of shelter should the weather change. Between rounds, consider resting your feet while chatting with some locals in the clubhouse restaurant.

Both courses offer the challenge of eighteen tees with nine greens. Eagles and birdies are a common occurrence, both soaring overhead and on the greens. Tee-off times are almost always at your convenience. If this is your sport, you'll enjoy the courses' unique history, local wildlife, and the feeling of sinking your ball along the sandy shores of Haida Gwaii.

Dixon Entrance Golf and Country Club
PO Box 68 Masset, BC VOT 1MO
Phone: 250-626-3500

Wiillows Golf and Country Club
342 Copper Bay Road
Box 216 Sandspit, BC, VOT 1TO
Phone: 250-637-2388
Email: bcharman@qcislands.net

FOUR CORNERS AND CAPE FIFE TRAILS

The departure point for both the Four Corners and Cape Fife trails is on a marked side road on the immediate east side of the Hiellen River. Vehicles are best left nearby at the Tow Hill parking lot. Both trails are suitable for small children along the initial portions.

The Four Corners Trail originally led south for nearly 5 kilometres. Today, only the northern end can be easily walked. We followed the trail for about forty-five minutes but were impeded by several blowdowns and rotten planking. We turned back after reaching a washed-out bridge and a deep creek. Anyone wishing to follow this settler route to its extremity should be equipped with waterproof boots, GPS, a 1:50,000 topographic map, and previous wilderness hiking experience.

The first part of the trail, however, makes a short, pleasant walk. The mossy road is now fringed with tall trees and edged in some places with drainage ditches—all dug with pick and spade. With some imagination, one might envision horse-drawn wagons jostling along with the driver carefully navigating the rutted road. The pioneers who once lived here did not have an easy life. The eventual abandonment of the area must have been heart-wrenching. Apart from the road, a few posts and the remains of old bridges, all other signs of human habitation have been either overgrown with moss or rotted away into the humus.

You will not need your imagination to investigate the forests and bogs alongside the road. Here you might surprise a cock-eared deer or a black bear munching on the green grass. If you're lucky, sandhill cranes may pass overhead. Their guttural, vibrating "gar-oo-oo-oo" calls are distinctive. Judging from the names Swan Creek and Cygnet Lake, trumpeter swans may have once nested in nearby lakes all but invisible from the road.

The Cape Fife Trail leads to East Beach, winding 10 kilometres through rainforest and open woods before reaching sand dunes just south of Kumara Lake. The route is level and in good condition, with cedar timbers spanning the wet and muddy portions. At about the halfway point, the dark woods are left behind as open marshes and meadows appear.

A hiking shelter constructed using Haida building techniques marks the eastern end of the trail. It is available on a first-come, first-served basis. You will find a wood stove inside and enough room to sleep five people. You can complete a circle trip by following East and North Beach back to Tow Hill, but this makes for an exceedingly long day. Try to have a vehicle pick you up at North Beach, or camp overnight to make this an easier option.

From a base at Agate Beach, anyone curious about the natural environment or seeking some quiet relaxation can happily spend three or four days in the Tow Hill vicinity.

GETTING THERE

From Masset, a well-travelled, partially paved road leads east past the old Canadian Forces base toward Naikoon Provincial Park. It passes beachfront homes and an ecological reserve before reaching Agate Beach Campground at 25 km.

Beyond the campground the road rounds Tow Hill, crosses the Hiellen River, then heads north toward North Beach. Trailers are best parked at the Agate Beach campground or at the Tow Hill parking lot.

Park your vehicle in the Tow Hill parking lot if you are headed for Cape Fife or the Four Corners trail. Walk across the bridge and follow a side road immediately to your right. A short way along this road, the Cape Fife trailhead branches left, leading toward the eastern beaches. The wagon road can be walked for about forty-five minutes.

TOW HILL BOG

Bog communities have their own beauty and points of interest, but sometimes the name puts people off. "Who wants to stomp about in a sodden swamp?" some may think, but those who venture farther will be well rewarded.

Bogs are a major feature of BC's coast, and Canada has more bogs than any other country. Preserving this bog on the Argonaut Plain was a major reason for the park's creation, and an ecological reserve has been created nearby to give this vegetative resource additional protection for research purposes.

This peaty plain was formed, and is maintained, by high rainfall and poor drainage. The water table is close to the surface, indicated by the numerous small pools. Few plants can tolerate such a root-soaking habitat. Stunted conifers, sphagnum moss, and evergreen shrubs, such as salal, are dominant and easily recognizable. Ten species of sphagnum, which forms peat moss, have been identified here.

The solid strata of moss, capable of filling shallow bodies of water, functions much like a sponge—and indeed feels like one underfoot. Inhibiting the water's flow and preventing oxygenation, the moss also turns it acidic by releasing tannin, a natural plant by-product. This chemical accounts for Naikoon's brownish streams. Tannin is also a component of tea; you might imagine you're walking across a gigantic tea bag!

These chemical conditions are typical of peat bogs and necessary for their development. A bog is defined as a deposit of partially decomposed organic matter. The sphagnum moss and other plants that grow here are not broken down into soil when they die, as happens in most plant decay. Bacteria and microscopic organisms that normally carry out the task of decomposition are deficient in bogs due to the acid and lack of oxygen. Thus each year's growth is established on layers of previous plants.

Bogs often evolve to many metres deep and can date back to the end of the ice age. Although their lowermost layers become black and oozy, laboratory analysis will reveal woody pieces and microscopic pollen grains released by flowers each spring. Most pollen is scattered on the ground, so peat bogs function like a bank, containing extensive deposits undamaged by decay. Since each species' pollen looks different, scientists can tell what plants once grew in this vicinity.

Researchers recently discovered a species of fir tree that grew here thirty thousand years ago. Even more remarkable is the fact that no firs grow naturally on Haida Gwaii today. They were evidently removed by the ice sheets and have not returned, although

A flying insect, attracted by the sundew's deceptive leaf, has been snared by the sticky hairs. The bug will dissolve and its proteins will become additional food for the plant.

this conifer is found in abundance on the adjacent northern mainland. In other instances, some plants that grow on these islands are found nowhere else in BC, or have their closest counterparts in Asia. Such unusual distributions, and the changes to the earth's climate they imply, are the subject of considerable debate among scientists.

Additional discoveries in ancient deposits at Cape Ball on East Beach provided some of the evidence for refugia on Haida Gwaii. For years, geologists balked at the notion of isolated pockets of vegetation surviving during the ice age. Botanists and zoologists have argued otherwise because the odd distribution of plants and subspecies of animals found on the islands can be explained by survival within a refugium.

If the depths of a bog are so revealing, the surface can hardly be dull. A quick examination on your knees soon demonstrates this. If you visit Tow Hill Bog in early July you'll find two inconspicuous plants in bloom. Even if they're not flowering, the

Dwarf shrubs of the bog. Labrador Tea (left) produces white flowers while Western Swamp Laurel blossoms have a rose-pink hue. SHEILA DOUGLAS

adaptations of the round-leafed sundew and the common butterwort will boggle your mind.

These plants are insectivorous—they supplement their nutrition by capturing and digesting insects. They do this because their habitat is deficient in minerals and nitrogen. Both have mechanisms for capturing small prey on their glandular leaves. Once trapped by sticky hairs, bugs are dissolved by enzymes and absorbed. It's challenging to capture this detail on film but a good close-up will amaze those who believe such oddities grow only in tropical jungles.

After walking around a bit you'll discover there are wetter and drier areas within the bog, and that plants tend to favour particular micro-habitats—localized conditions beneficial to a particular plant's needs. Along with the insect-digesters found in wet areas are beauties such as cotton grass and tall shooting star. Even without a field guide, their descriptive names should help you identify these white and pink species.

Around the perimeter of the bog, the peat moss forms hummocks. On this drier ground grow several species of the heather family. Look for bog cranberry (like a miniature shooting star), Labrador tea (with fuzzy rusty underleaves), and swamp laurel (bright pink flowers). Here, too, survive stunted shore pines and dwarf juniper. They look like bonsai, the dwarfed, potted art trees of Japan. It may have taken them several hundred years to reach this size under such difficult growing conditions.

While searching for these plants, don't be surprised to see small frogs leaping away from just in front of your feet. Pacific treefrogs have sticky pads on their toes, enabling them to climb shrubs and trees. For the most part, they are content to clamber in the moss and low bushes. Like many land creatures on these islands, this frog was introduced. Fortunately, they have not become a problem like other non-native creatures.

For simple majesty, Tow Hill Bog can't compete with the coastal features of Naikoon Park. But for those that enjoy wildflowers and investigations on a micro scale, bogs have a lot to offer. All of this is within easy grasp of anyone willing to spend an hour or two examining this unique landscape.

GETTING THERE

Follow the road from Masset to Agate Beach Campground (about 25 km). Across the road from campground, look for the deer trails leading through the thick salal up the embankment. Once through the bushes, visually mark your position so you can return via the same route. Using a well-travelled deer trail, you will reach the bog in under ten minutes. Gumboots will help keep your feet dry.

The summit of Tow Hill (see preceding section) is a good place to get an aerial view of this bog.

NORTH BEACH

North Beach is one of the most popular attractions on Haida Gwaii. The foreshore is remarkably wide, firm and beautiful. This expanse of sand stretches 15 kilometres from the Hiellen River to the base of Rose Spit. It's a great place to enjoy the surf and sand, ride along the beach, beachcomb, dig for clams, or catch crabs.

The extensive beaches on Haida Gwaii owe their existence to glacial and water action. Sheets of ice hundreds of metres deep once slid from the Queen Charlotte Mountains carrying millions of tonnes of sand, gravel and rock. This ice melted slowly, depositing its cargo over what are now the lowlands of Graham Island and the surrounding sea.

Since the ice age ended, Hecate Strait and Dixon Entrance have had a dramatic effect on these glacial deposits. Nearshore currents and waves in Hecate Strait wash northward, eroding the deposits along East Beach. Similar patterns circulate the fine material in Dixon Entrance. All these materials move eastward toward Rose Spit. Ocean currents, combined with onshore wind and waves, transport this sand onto the gentle slope of North Beach. In places the beach is more than 200 metres wide.

Think twice before driving your vehicle straight toward the surfline. The tide can come in with deceptive speed. A friend discovered this the hard way. He drove his brand-new truck out to the water's edge where he parked for a few moments to photograph the surf and foaming froth on the beach. In no time at all,

Large-headed sedge prefer the higher, drier areas of the beach or sand dunes. Their club-like head is easily recognizable among the driftwood and other vegetation.

Shells abound on North Beach. Who can resist not picking up at least a few for souvenirs? Naikoon touches everyone who visits this beach.

the incoming waves began to lick the tires. Before you could say "pass the towrope," the sand softened and the vehicle settled into the beach like a nesting duck. There was no choice but to abandon the truck, head for higher ground, and watch in horror as the incoming surf turned it turtle, filled the cab with sand, then flattened the vehicle into the beach.

Signs at the beach entrance advise all 4 × 4 vehicles to cruise just below the high-tide line. ATVs and bicycles provide more flexibility so you can wander closer to the breaking waves. We found cycling a relaxing way to explore the beach. A leisurely trip along the beach can be completed in half a day. The hard-packed sand allows young riders to also enjoy this special place. Carry side bags and some light line so you can return with your beachcombing treasures strapped to your bike. Afterward, thoroughly rinse your bike in the nearby campground to prevent corrosion.

If you have an ATV, the ride along the beach from the Hiellen River to the spit takes about thirty minutes. As you cruise along the beach, keep an eye open for drift logs, kelp, and other hazards.

After twelve years of being pounded by surf and sand, little remains of this commercial fishing boat. Mariners give this area a wide berth as its currents and tides can catch you with little warning.

It will take another fifteen minutes to cross Rose Spit and, if conditions allow, to continue down East Beach.

Whether you are travelling by car, ATV, or bicycle, plan to start your beach explorations on a falling tide. This will allow ample time to stop and beachcomb. After every tide the beach looks different. On occasion it will be washed clean. At other times you will have to navigate through every sort of international flotsam imaginable. After most storms, serious beachcombers race along the tide line seeking their most cherished prize—spherical glass fishing floats. These balls, which can be as large as basketballs, break away from Japanese fishing nets.

Other interesting debris includes sponges, jellyfish, shells, and unusual fish. Even a great white shark has cast up on this beach. Once we found a large skate. On another visit we discovered a peculiar leathery pouch within a tangle of kelp. It was later identified as a mermaid's purse. This pouch protects the skate's embryo until it is strong enough to swim free.

Besides beachcombing, there are lots of other activities to occupy your time at North Beach. The shallow water offshore

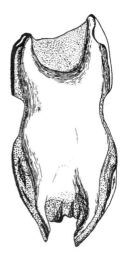

The egg case of a skate can be over 20 centimetres long. Skates reach sizes exceeding 2 metres and are sometimes caught commercially.

makes first-class habitat for Dungeness crab. Bright orange floats mark crab traps set by commercial boats from Masset. As the tide falls, a quick dig in the sand may expose equally delectable razor clams. In BC, these olive-coloured shellfish occur only here and at Long Beach on Vancouver Island. Razor clams seldom accumulate biotoxins such as PSP (paralytic shellfish poisoning). To be on the safe side, check with the local DFO office or visit their website to learn about any shellfish closures in the area.

Razor clams are concentrated along the low-tide line. They bury themselves 15 to 20 centimetres beneath the sand. A shallow dimple marks their "show." The ideal tool for digging them is a narrow-bladed shovel called a "clam gun." Various techniques are effective, but all require speed and care because the clams can move quickly and fracture easily. You must have a tidal-waters licence to dig for them; check the saltwater fishing regulations for bag limits.

Between 1923 and 1931, a cannery on the Hiellen River processed the razor clams harvested at North Beach. You can find an

North Beach is lined with driftwood. Drive your 4 × 4 vehicle close to the logs and resist the temptation to wet your wheels in the surf.

old boiler and concrete foundations from this cannery hidden in undergrowth on the east bank just downstream from the bridge. After the cannery closed, the clams were taken to Masset for processing.

Summertime is not the only time to have fun on these beaches. For many years, kayakers have launched their small craft from the beach and frolicked in the large winter waves. Recently, the northern beaches have also been discovered by surfing enthusiasts eager to catch a wave, even if it means having to don a dry suit and hood. Midway between Masset and Tow Hill, and off the mouth of the Hiellen River have become favourite spots. Surf's up!

Experiencing North Beach will be a highlight of any visit to Haida Gwaii. It's a place to walk alone when the surf is pounding and the salt spray stiffens your hair, a place to build castles of sand on sunny days, to relax around an evening campfire sharing tall tales, or to cruise along the hard sand in an ATV. It's hard to imagine anyone not enjoying this special environment.

GETTING THERE

North Beach stretches along the northeastern edge of Graham Island from the village of Old Massett to Rose Spit. It is accessible from various unmarked side roads along its entire length. This chapter covers the portion east of Tow Hill that lies within Naikoon Park. A 25-km road from Masset ends just after crossing the Hiellen River. Here, 4 × 4 vehicles and ATVs can be driven directly onto the hard-packed beach sand. All drivers must keep their motorized vehicles between the low- and the high-tide line. It is permissible, however, to cross from North Beach to East Beach via a connector road across the base of Rose Spit. Driving on the dunes or Rose Spit meadows is strictly prohibited.

CAUTION Crossing Rose Spit or following East Beach is recommended for experienced off-road drivers only.

MOUNTAIN BIKING

On almost all our trips to Haida Gwaii, we took our mountain bikes along. Our main purpose was to ride North Beach (Hiellen River toward Rose Spit), almost 10 km of hard, smooth sand that is suitable for bikers of every age and ability. This is an excellent way to beachcomb and explore this section of Naikoon Provincial Park. Be extra careful to keep the sand out of your gears and chain. Afterwards, you can wash your bike with tap water in Agate Beach Campground.

Back at the beginning of time, when the water that once covered the earth subsided, only a raven survived. In his loneliness the bird combed the islands that broke the surface of the great sea, seeking companionship. Finally, while soaring over a long sandy beach, he heard faint cries emanating from a clamshell that had washed up on the shore. The raven swooped down and pried the shell open. To his great wonder, the sounds grew louder and louder, and the startled bird watched in amazement as several men clambered out.

This Haida myth of human creation has been retold for centuries and has parallels with the Biblical story of the ark on Mount Ararat. The event occurred at Nai-Kun, the long nose of Nai, which today is known as Rose Spit. Natives and visitors hold the spit in high esteem as one of the most interesting places in Haida Gwaii.

The spit has undergone several name changes over the last two hundred years. The present title gives undeserved recognition to a British politician who never visited this place. Fortunately, the original name is preserved by adjacent Naikoon Provincial Park.

Rose Spit is located at the junction of North and East beaches. Waves and currents that move along these shorelines have built an elongated neck of sand and gravel. The base is 1 kilometre wide at the forest edge, and the spit hooks 3 kilometres out to sea. An additional 3-kilometre bar continues beneath the water's surface. Portions of this submarine section are sometimes visible as offshore sandbars. This is the largest such formation in the province.

The best overview of the spit is gained from atop the sand dunes at the forest edge. Prevailing winds from the southeast have shaped sand into dunes exceeding 10 metres in height. In the process, large trees have been partially buried. Many plants that grow here have thick waxy leaves or special root systems. Both represent adaptations to the brutal conditions—plants are washed by salt spray, dried by the sun, pelted by drifting sand, and blown by wind. (See page 115 for more about the difficult plant colonization of dunes.)

From this vantage, other features of the spit are also visible. Rose Spit is bordered on both sides by compacted driftwood. The amount of wood appears to be increasing, as photos from 1960 show considerably fewer logs. In places it is possible to walk across the mass of tangled wood for 50 metres before touching the shore.

Between the lines of logs the spit is covered by a lush meadow. Botanists have recognized three distinct plant communities containing rare species. One, the sea bluebell, is found nowhere else in BC. Others, such as bighead sedge and western dune tansy, are found only on shore sand. Flowering patches of yellow paintbrush and blue lupines are so fragrant that you might smell them downwind.

Plants are but one of many specialties of the spit. Upwelling currents concentrate plankton and fish near the surface, attracting many birds: more than one hundred species have been recorded here. Expect to see shearwaters, ducks, sandhill cranes, and many species of gulls. During migration, the area is also a haven for shorebirds, which stop here to rest and feed. Occasionally, a peregrine falcon will ambush migrating peeps and plovers.

While keeping a constant watch for wildlife, a walk to the tip of the spit is a must. The merging of Hecate Strait and Dixon Entrance creates spectacular displays. When the surf is up and the tides are changing, opposing waves smash against each other in a spuming wall of water. Turning your back to the waves creates an exhilarating sensation. The boiling sea wraps around you on three sides, leaving only a narrow line of retreat.

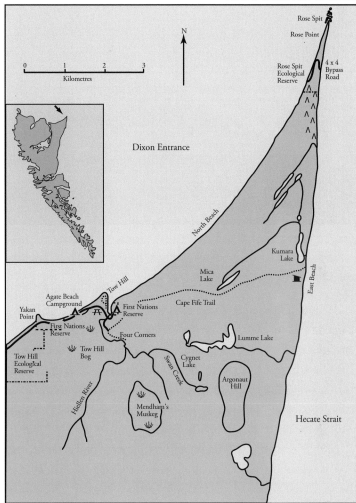

The erratic water movements have formed an offshore sandbar that is a favourite haul-out for both seals and sea lions. If you have binoculars, you should be able to spot their large brown and grey shapes on the lee side. As an added bonus, a walk out on the spit may yield a glimpse of either grey or killer whales.

Haida Gwaii, Region by Region

Northward flowing currents have shaped Rose Spit into a sandy hook extending several kilometres out to sea. The ridges parallelling North Beach are old shorelines formed during the ice age. ANDREW DEJARDIN

Although Rose Spit is a mecca for wildlife and recreationists, it can be a death trap for mariners. Boats are advised to stay well out from this menacing crooked finger. Those who are unfortunate enough to be swept into the grasp of the vicious currents that swirl around the spit often capsize. Over the years, many lives have been lost. In some cases, even those who were lucky enough to reach the beach still died of exposure.

In 1971 the unique features of the spit were protected by the BC government under the Ecological Reserves Act. The purpose of the act is to secure such places for scientific research. Visitors are welcome, but should be aware that it is illegal to camp, have a fire, hunt, or otherwise disturb or remove plants and animals. Hikers and motorized vehicles are directed to stay on designated roads or beaches in this area.

When you stand alone at the very tip of Rose Spit, you feel like the first person on earth. One experiences what it might have been like stepping out of the clamshell after the Great Flood. The

Lupines and yellow paintbrush flourish in the meadows past the tree line.

immense power of the sea wrapping around you is simultaneously humbling and rejuvenating. Behind lies a whole new world.
You return to it with renewed appreciation and a sense of having
been touched by the spirit of Nai-Kun.

GETTING THERE

Rose Spit extends into Dixon Entrance from the extreme northeastern corner of Graham Island. The quickest approach is via
Masset, or alternatively, East Beach. From Masset drive the
25-km road to Tow Hill. From here it's a 15-km hike, bicycle
ride, or drive along North Beach to where the trees end at the
base of the spit. The meadows extend another 3 km. Vehicles
must stay on the road and are prohibited in all other areas of
the reserve.

The weather-beaten remains of the *Pesuta*, an 80-metre log barge that grounded during a fierce gale in December 1928. The trail leading to the wreck begins at the Tlell River picnic site. GUY KIMOLA

EAST BEACH

At 90 kilometres, East Beach is one of the longest beaches in western North America. A four- to seven-day trek along its length has been gaining popularity ever since the park was created. Though the route is flat, it can still be a challenge to backpackers. The trek offers that wonderful sense of shoreline solitude that humans find so soothing to their psyche. Many hikers familiar with more rugged terrain have proclaimed this a highlight of their outdoor experiences. The beach is also travelled in more leisurely style by people in four-wheel-drive vehicles.

The trail begins at the Tlell River bridge just north of Misty Meadows Campground. From the picnic site at the bridge, a 2-kilometre trail follows the river through the forest to the beach. A faster route is to follow Beitush Road along the river's edge, then wade the river at low tide. It's only knee-deep at a stony ford. By walking northward from this point, you keep the prevailing wind, rain, and sun at your back.

Before heading out on this adventure you should prepare for all kinds of weather—even in summer there can be fog, rain, and cool temperatures. It's also essential to carry a watch and up-to-date tide table. You'll need these to time your crossing of unbridged tidal rivers.

From the mouth of the Tlell River the beach is beautiful. To seaward, an unbroken but ever-changing expanse of cloud and waves stretches from horizon to horizon. In the foreground, semi-palmated plovers scurry down the beach, which fades to infinity. On the left stretches a continuous line of sand cliffs or dunes, topped by spruce forest. A few days of such spectacular scenery satisfies some; others take seven delightful days to reach the end of this magnificent trip.

Five kilometres from the picnic site is the bow remnant of the 1928 shipwreck *Pesuta*. This wooden barge was under tow in Hecate Strait when its line parted in a winter storm. The barge and its cargo of logs became driftwood. When looking at the innumerable drift logs on these islands, note how few are of natural origin. Virtually all have sprung loose from log booms over the past five or six decades. Driftwood, at least on Haida Gwaii, is largely a human-made phenomenon.

A couple of hours' walk north of the wreck will bring you to Cape Ball River, a good overnight location. Please respect the private property here and pitch tents near the driftwood. Private holdings, such as lots 1357 and 1358, still exist within the park and are noted on topographic maps of 1:50,000 scale.

The tide floods the mouth of this river, as well as the others along this route. Fresh water and a crossing can be gained only at low tide. You also need a receding tide to pass under the 60-metre sand cliffs at Cape Ball. The trek north around this headland to Eagle Hill may take as long as five hours. Eagle Creek is the only break in this wall that will allow a retreat from incoming waves.

Haida Gwaii, Region by Region

Some exciting research on these cliffs and on the plain beyond resulted in discoveries that are altering our perception of geologic events in British Columbia. Other fields of research are now reforming their theories based on the biological, climatic, and cultural history of the Haida Gwaii.

This site was chosen for investigation because the uncompressed sediments were deposited in chronological order during and after the ice age. Researchers have determined that melting of the provincial ice cap throughout most of BC began about ten thousand years ago. However, geologist John Clague of the Geological Survey of Canada and biologist Rolf Mathewes of Simon Fraser University have discovered plant remains in these cliffs dating back sixteen thousand years.

There were actually trees and peat bogs here when continental Canada was still as stiff as an icicle. This evidence strengthens the theory that there was an oasis or refugium during the last big chill. If all these features were in place, could there have been animals or people present? Equally intriguing has been the discovery of high concentrations of fungi spores associated with dung from mammoths and mastadons. Did these hairy beasts roam Haida Gwaii some 57,000 years ago? Finding an extruding tusk from the cliff faces might provide definitive proof. Stay tuned as the leading edge of science probes these possibilities.

Moving north along the beach, there are good camping spots at Eagle Creek, Lot 114 A, the Oeanda River mouth, and Kumara Lake. The availability of fresh water determines where you camp each night. Rivers are either tidal, of periodic flow, or enter the ocean beneath the beach, making it difficult to obtain drinking water. Topographic maps will help you locate the streams on this featureless coast.

In a pinch, you can take water from ponds behind the beach, but we highly recommended that you carry additional water and a portable water purification system. All surface water in the park is tea-coloured, having drained through peat. The Scots may claim it makes better whisky, but we advise boiling or otherwise purifying this water before drinking it. Flavoured juice crystals make it more palatable. Alternatively, a plastic tarp can serve as both a cooking shelter and water-catcher. It will funnel rain into a water bottle when used as a flysheet or when spread across a sandy depression overnight.

Nearing Kumara Lake, sand dunes become prominent. Look for places where sand-buried trees have been uncovered by high waves during recent storms. In other areas you can find marine shells embedded in the mud banks above sea level. Obviously, this land has not always been the way it appears today. The landscape is in a constant state of transformation.

Dune formation and erosion are natural processes, but they are accelerated by the removal of stabilizing plants. (See "Sand Dunes, Tlell River, and Vicinity," page 115.) Regrettably, in places around Rose Spit, 4 × 4 vehicles have damaged plants and their supporting dunes. According to the park master plan of 1983, these "infernal combustion" machines are supposed to be prohibited from this wild beach. For a time they were, but politicians reversed this policy under local pressure.

There is a hiking shelter at Cape Fife, where a trail leads past the southern end of Kumara Lake directly to Tow Hill. (See "Tow Hill Area," page 82, and "Four Corners and Cape Fife Trails," page 91.) Hikers exiting via Cape Fife will arrive home earlier but miss seeing Rose Spit, one of Naikoon's most memorable spots. If possible, allow time to visit the spit, or make plans to return to Haida Gwaii with a trip to the spit at the top of your list.

GETTING THERE

East Beach in Naikoon Park stretches continuously from the Tlell River in the south to Rose Spit on the northeast tip of Graham Island. You can hike it from the north at Tow Hill but most hikers prefer to begin at Tlell. Get advice and current information from the park headquarters located near the campground entrance. Refer also to the sections on Rose Spit, North Beach, and Tow Hill in this book to complete your picture of this 90-km hike.

CAUTION This is an unpatrolled wilderness. You cannot be assured of a speedy rescue if you run into trouble.

TOPOGRAPHIC MAPS

The following topographic maps (NTS 1:50,000 scale) cover the entire hike and may be purchased from commercial online websites. They are offered free for personal use from geobc.gov. bc.ca/base mapping. After launching the Topographic Map Viewer, follow the directions to download and print maps of your choice.

103 G/12 West Tlell   103 G/13 West Eagle Hill
103 G/13 East Eagle Hill   103 J/4 West Tow Hill
103 J/4 East Tow Hill

Tide tables for the islands are found online or in *Canadian Tide and Current Tables, Volume 6: Barkley Sound and Discovery Passage to Dixon Entrance*. (See page 230 for ordering information.)

The Sand Dunes

Coastal sand dune ecosystems are relatively rare in BC. They occur sporadically on Vancouver Island and on a few islands in the Strait of Georgia. The most spectacular concentration of dunes, however, occurs along the northeast coast of Graham Island. Large, high, and accessible dune formations occur at Rose Spit, along East Beach and at Tlell. The remarkable dune system at Tlell is easily accessed and allows visitors to comfortably complete a looped stroll among the dunes in about an hour. You might find yourself taking longer as the plant life and dune formations entice many visitors to walk slowly, examine the unusual plants, and take plenty of photographs.

A return walk to the dunes begins near the Haida-style picnic shelter. After parking, walk back along the pavement toward the highway. The marked trailhead begins opposite the campground entrance. For the first ten to fifteen minutes, you will be walking through trees. It seems an unlikely beginning to a dune walk, but you will soon leave the forest behind and break out into the open. In this initial section, take a few minutes to peruse the interpretive plaques. They help explain how dunes are formed and identify most of the plants that have colonized the ridges and mounds of shifting sand. Once you are through the trees, take note of two tall wooden posts placed there by park staff. They will help you find the trail should you choose to leave the dunes and walk farther out on the beach. Once most of the trees are behind you, follow the faint but discernable path. When it comes to a Y, you have two choices. The wooden markers direct you toward the beach. If you take the trail left or northward, the route continues through the dunes and will ultimately lead you back to the parking lot where you started.

As you turn left, the route winds up and through the dunes. Do your best to follow the pathway as extensive foot traffic on the dunes causes instability among the plants. The first thing you might notice, however, is the wind rather than the plants. If the gusts are strong and tussling your hair, it is probably coming from the southeast. Sou'easterlies are the most prevalent and strongest winds on Haida Gwaii. Without them there would be no dunes.

Along this section of Graham Island's coast, massive sand deposits are being eroded and re-deposited onto the beaches. Where the ground behind the beach is low-lying, windblown sand forms dunes. These moving mounds often reach an impressive size. Active dunes are sparsely vegetated.

When you arrive where the dunes are advancing, note the parallel zones that characterize this area. At the front is the surf zone, whose limit is defined by fresh drift logs. Behind them is a narrow zone of older driftwood, often partially buried. Behind that is a transition zone. This is an ecological no man's land where sand dunes and plant life fight one another for supremacy. The final zone is the fringing forest. This is the plants' ultimate defence in stopping the dunes' advance.

As you walk through these zones you'll witness the force that moves this sand. On the windward side of old fence posts, the blasting and chiselling action of windblown sand has raised the grain. In the transition zone you might find a ventifact. This is a stone with glossy surfaces and sharp ridges that have been sand-blasted by the wind. Finally, on the dunes, you will see dead trees. Large branches protruding from trunks at ground level show that some have been smothered by sand to depths of 10 metres.

These dunes actually start at the driftwood. Sand picked up here by the wind shifts until it meets an obstruction. In this way, small dunes accumulate around rocks, driftwood, or even plants. As the dune grows it acts as a windbreak. The sand rolls

The sand dunes on Haida Gwaii are some of the largest and most extensive in the province. They form along the east side of the islands from Tlell to Rose Spit.

up the windward slope, then drops over the lee side. By tiny granular increments, the dune continues to grow as it is pushed before the wind. Small dunes travel faster than large ones, so they ultimately merge with others. You will notice that the landscape features here are all aligned in the direction of the prevailing wind.

As dunes travel across the transition zone, plants attempt to cover them. Grasses and sedges are particularly suited to this type of colonization. As sand piles around their stems, they send up new leaf shoots. They can grow rhizomes (horizontal subterranean stems) very quickly, and green leaves pop up all along this system. In this shifting environment, this method of rapid reproduction is much more effective than the seeds spread by the wind. You might recognize species such as bighead sedge or wild strawberry.

These plants are pioneers, trying to stabilize the dune with their rhizomes and runners. If they succeed, other plants like

Living on the dunes is tough. Beach silver-top (*Glehnia littoralis*) has thick leaves, a water storing taproot, and deep roots. These features help it survive salt spray and extreme desiccation on the dunes.

dune tansy and beach lupine can get a start. If they fail, the wind may resume the dune's progress, or a blowout, an erosional hollow blown out of a disturbed dune, may occur. This happens when root systems are damaged by drought, grazing cattle, beach buggies, or human trampling. Each plant is important. Walk carefully and avoid crushing plants or making a rut.

Generally, dunes at the forest edge are fully vegetated. The trees prevent further progress. On the forest side of these dunes, mosses and shrubs have formed a stable plant community. At some places along the way, note how grasses have successfully covered the dunes.

About an hour after starting out, you should find yourself back close to the parking lot. Although overall it is a short, modest walk, such places are rare in BC. The dunes are a major coastal feature of Haida Gwaii and Naikoon Park was created, in part, to preserve them. They are small but very important pieces of the island mosaic and help make Haida Gwaii such a special place.

Fly-casting on the Tlell River can be enjoyed year round. It is famous among fishers for steelhead and coho salmon runs.

Tlell River

The other walk from the campground takes you in the opposite direction. If you're an angler, you probably headed this way first—never mind the sand dunes. The Tlell River bridge is just a short walk along the highway north of the campground. There are good access points to the river's lower reaches from Beitush Road, which parallels the east bank. Many people head downstream from the bridge in order to cast first at the fish swimming with the flood tides.

The main species of interest here is coho salmon, which run from the first week of September to mid-October. Timing is dependent on fall rains; the fish mass offshore until river levels are high enough for successful spawning. They peak midway between these times, with fish ranging from 5 to 9 kilograms. Green krocodile lures are a favourite.

The Tlell River is also known for steelhead, although this run isn't as good as it used to be. These seagoing trout grow to

A frosty March morning is a great time of the year to enjoy the Tlell Anvil trail.

4.6 kilograms and enter the river from early February through April. Fishing is good on both the upper and lower sections.

If you miss these times, take heart. The Tlell also offers good cutthroat trout fishing in the spring and early summer. These fish go to sea and are caught on their return. Dolly Varden weighing up to 2 kilograms can also be caught in midsummer. Be certain to check the tidal and non-tidal fishing regulations, as they change from year to year. Fishing licences are not available from park staff, but are available in Masset or the Village of Queen Charlotte.

Continue your walk along the east bank past the trees at the end of Beitush Road. Notice how the river heads north, paralleling the beach. The north-flowing ocean currents that created Rose Spit have also formed a small spit here.

On the open dunes you can view the remains of two teepee-like structures. These are Haida fishing stations that were apparently still active in 1884 when Captain Newton Chittenden explored this area. The wreck of the *Pesuta* is visible in the distance. (See "East Beach," page 110.) If you return to the campground via the beach, allow three hours for the round trip.

Tlell Anvil Trail

If you have had enough of beach, surf, and sand, then a pleasant forest walk awaits you a few kilometres south of the Misty Meadows campground.

The Anvil Trail loops through a typical island rainforest. You'll walk beneath towering spruce, hemlock, and cedar. Trees such as these are among the most massive living things on earth. By contrast, delicate single white blossoms emerge shyly just above the forest floor. In spring, fairy slipper orchids add splashes of soft mauve to the green of prolific mosses and ferns. While walking near the river, you may see salmon spawning in late summer or watch eagles careening overhead.

Begin your hike at the trailhead directly across from Mariners Point pullout, 4.5 kilometres south of the Misty Meadows campground. A narrow, meandering trail leads you in a 5-kilometre loop through the forest and beside the Tlell River. Allow two hours to fully enjoy the cool air, solitude, and soft sounds.

We recommend waterproof footwear for boggy sections. Reschedule your hike if high winds are forecast.

GETTING THERE

Tlell is an unincorporated hamlet scattered around the southern edge of Naikoon Park. Tlell is 42 km north of the Skidegate Landing ferry dock and 21 km south of Port Clements. The Yellowhead Highway crosses the Tlell River via a wooden bridge.

The park headquarters and Misty Meadows Campground are located about 1 km south of the bridge. If you wish to walk on the dunes, turn off the highway at the campground sign and drive to the Haida-style picnic shelter. Begin the walk from the parking area.

If you packed a rod and reel, watch for Beitush Road, immediately south of the wooden bridge. This road parallels the Tlell River and offers numerous access points to cast from the river's edge.

The Tlell Anvil Trail begins 4.5 km south of the Misty Meadows campground sign. You can park at the Mariners Point pullout. The trailhead begins across the road.

2.5 NORTH MORESBY ISLAND

GRAY BAY

Alders and hemlock overhang the bumpy, one-lane Spur 20, which you drive along after turning off Copper Bay Road. A small bridge crossing Gray Bay Creek marks your entry to Gray Bay and a recreation site within the new Kunxalas Heritage Site/Conservancy. Twenty spacious campsites have been cleared along the road paralleling the beach. Within a few paces of each site lies one of the best beaches on the islands. Soft grey sand arcs around a gentle bay reminiscent of a tropical paradise. Low tide exposes sand flats stretching well out from shore. Throw off your shoes and titillate your toes in the bubbling surf.

When you're ready to explore beyond the beach, there are three hiking options nearby. The shortest trail begins about 100 metres back from Gray Bay Creek. A 15-minute walk on a sandy path through the trees ends at Secret Cove. In this quiet spot, cast your worries out with the receding tide. Let your eyes wander the expanse of Hecate Strait, and allow the music of songbirds to soothe muscle and mind.

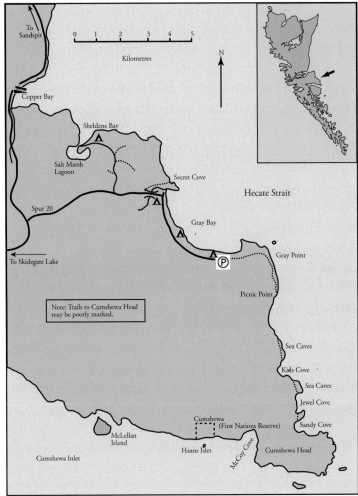

To
Sandspit

Copper Bay

Sheldens Bay

Salt Marsh
Lagoon

Secret Cove

Spur 20

Hecate Strait

Gray Bay

To Skidegate Lake

Gray Point

P

Picnic Point

Note: Trails to Cumshewa Head
may be poorly marked.

Sea Caves

Kids Cove

Sea Caves

Jewel Cove

Sandy Cove

Cumshewa (First Nations Reserve)

McLellan
Island

Haans Islet

McCoy Cove

Cumshewa Head

Cumshewa Inlet

N

0   1   2   3   4   5

Kilometres

You'll need more time to walk or cycle the road that runs along
Gray Bay. The road south ends abruptly at a small turnaround
where a footbridge allows easy crossing of a salmon-bearing creek.
A trail continues on the other side and soon ends at the foundations of an old LORAN (LOng RAnge Navigation) station. GPS has
made such land-based structures obsolete.

Haida Gwaii, Region by Region

Trails lead from there to Gray Point and south to Cumshewa Head. The trip to Cumshewa Head and back involves at least a full day's hike. For the first portion, a minimal trail parallels the beach. Families with small children might find this to be a long walk. Beyond that point, the trail deteriorates into a flagged route along beaches, deer trails, and awkward rocky scrambles.

Keen hikers may wish to tackle this trail during the long days of summer—this latitude enjoys seventeen hours of light at the solstice. A round trip to the Head takes twelve to fourteen hours. Plan to leave Gray Point just after a high tide to avoid being caught by the rising tide. Sea caves, rocky outcrops, and tidepools are the main attractions. Also watch for seals and river otters in the surf. Take a marine chart and topographic map to track your progress, as well as plenty of snacks and drinking water. This is one of the few hikes mentioned in this book where hiking boots have a definite advantage over gumboots.

If Cumshewa Head is beyond your ability, try hiking, cycling, or driving to Sheldens Bay. From the bridge at Gray Bay Creek, travel back toward Sandspit 3.4 kilometres. A spur to the right leads to Sheldens Bay, 7.6 kilometres farther on. Ambitious mountain bikers may wish to cycle this bumpy, hilly, gravel road.

About midway along, the road climbs a small hill overlooking a lake and most of Hecate Strait. The road then descends to a picnic area with tables, four campsites, and pit toilets. There is room for parking, but people with motorhomes or trailers are advised to leave them at Gray Bay. An additional road leads from the picnic area to Dogfish Bay. This road is best walked or cycled. Allow about thirty minutes walking one way.

Several homesteaders lived in the Sheldens Bay area in the early 1900s. Now it is a haven for deer and migrating waterfowl. Look for dabbling ducks, shorebirds and great blue herons. You may be lucky and spot trumpeter swans or sandhill cranes.

The gentle arc of Gray Bay is one of the largest beaches and most popular camping sites on Moresby Island. What a place to soak in the solitude of Haida Gwaii.
JIM THORNE

Gray Bay is typical of Haida Gwaii: many of the islands' best qualities are found here. Sandy beaches are sheltered by rough volcanic headlands. Scattered beneath giant spruce and hemlock, the rustic campsites ensure privacy, yet link to nearby roads and trails. Relaxing, walking, wave watching, or birding will easily fill your time for several days. You'll find Gray Bay to be a pleasant introduction to this island archipelago.

GETTING THERE

The 4-km crescent beach at Gray Bay is located south of Sandspit on the northeast side of Moresby Island. From Sandspit, allow an hour to drive via Copper Bay Road. This partially paved road heads south, passing the airport and numerous seasonal

The Cumshewa Head trail begins at the south end of Gray Bay. Along this rugged 10-kilometre route, be prepared for rock scrambles, deer trails, sea caves, and hidden beaches. Check a tide table and carry a sizeable container of water.

dwellings at Copper Bay. After 19 km, turn left off Copper Bay Road onto Spur 20, which leads east for an additional 7 km to Gray Bay.

A much longer alternative route from Alliford Bay also leads to Gray Bay, but you have to travel entirely on gravel roads that are open to the public. Logging trucks travel from various locations along these roads at unscheduled intervals. During working hours visitors should contact the Ministry of Forests for information on current logging activity. Watch for signs on the logging roads and follow their directions. (See page 227 for contact information.)

LOUISE ISLAND CIRCUMNAVIGATION

Louise Island is the third-largest island on Haida Gwaii. If your time is limited, the circuit around it will provide a taste of the wild archipelago farther south. Louise Island has ancient archaeology, recent relics, and natural history, and it gives you the opportunity to see the Moresby region from its maritime aspect. We have divided the trip into two sections: Cumshewa Inlet and K'uuna Llnagaay (Skedans) through to Louise Narrows.

For anyone wanting to spend several days fishing or adventuring in the inlet, good camping sites exist at Moresby Camp and nearby Mosquito Lake. (See "Part 3: Planning Your Trip.")

Waterways around Louise Island are generally protected, but some open directly onto Hecate Strait. Small boats and kayaks do venture out that far, though they need to beware of the wind and waves. The exposed waters can be rough. On one occasion we waited five hours for high winds to calm down enough to allow us around Skedans Point. Our inflatable made the trip successfully, but as we rounded the point we couldn't help but notice a double kayak drawn up on a boulder-strewn beach with everything laid out to dry.

VOLUNTEER AT A MARINE RESEARCH STATION

If you're planning a visit to Haida Gwaii in the spring or early summer you will have the opportunity to volunteer as a citizen scientist. Laskeek Bay Conservation Society is a non-profit organization that researches and monitors marine wildlife on Haida Gwaii. For more than two decades, the research station on East Limestone Island has been the operations base.

From May to early July volunteers spend a week on East Limestone monitoring ancient murrelet chicks as they move to the sea, checking Cassin's Auklet nest boxes and documenting marine or terrestrial wildlife. It's a first-class opportunity to be

A rusting fuel cistern and a wheel-less Chevrolet slowly succumb to the elements at Aero. Lanes of emerald grass and thick moss hide evidence of the only railroad logging operation on Haida Gwaii.

a scientist while enjoying the wilderness environment of Haida Gwaii. For more information, check out laskeekbay.org or call 250-559-2345.

Cumshewa Inlet

Cumshewa Inlet, a deep channel with Moresby Camp at its head, is the launching point for boaters heading to the southern islands and passages. From here, Cumshewa Inlet can be explored by motor boat in one day. There is a kitchen shelter, a small dock, and a concrete boat ramp suitable for virtually any trailered craft.

As you motor away from Moresby Camp dock, you can see evidence of logging on the south shore of the inlet. Some visitors may find the regenerating cutblocks detracting. It's easy to agree with that sentiment if landscapes have suffered irreparable damage. In

At the village of K'uuna Llnagaay (Skedans) ancient poles still stand, but for how long? Trees have been cut or cleared to help extend the poles' longevity. JIM THORNE

other instances, we've walked in forests that at first looked virgin, only to be surprised later by stumps. Logging has gone on here for

Haida Gwaii, Region by Region

Raven House was the largest house in the village of K'uuna Llnagaay. It had platforms or steps inside which increased its internal size. It was known as "Clouds Sound Against It (as they pass over)."

decades, and most cut areas are regenerating nicely. Nature knows its business!

During the Second World War, as many as ten logging camps existed on this inlet. Crews bundled logs into heavy rafts, known as Davis rafts, that were towed south to mainland mills at a speed of 2 or 3 knots. There was enough wood in some rafts to cut more than two million board feet of lumber. Such huge rafts were expensive to move, but saved the high log losses associated with unbundled booms. Today's self-loading, self-dumping, self-propelled log barges are some of the more interesting vessels plying these inlets.

The biggest logging operation in this area was Aero, named for the airplane (Sitka) spruce. Aero had the only logging railroad on Haida Gwaii, and track ran from the ocean over the hill to Skidegate Lake. Steep hills required the use of geared-drive locomotives that sounded like they were going 90 kilometres per hour, but actually crawled up the steep grades with massive

The ultimate fate of every pole will be to return to the earth from where they came. This is Haida tradition.

loads—sometimes only one log to a car. In the bush at Aero what remains of the railroad has been covered with thick layers of green vegetation. The old roadbeds have grown over with emerald grass to form cultivated paths through tunnels of second-growth alders. Spikes of flowered foxglove and lupine are healing the embankments. Today it's hard to imagine the steaming shriek of the locos and the roar of two-man chainsaws used here in 1945. Since the site, however, was not cleaned when the logging activity ceased in 1967, the remains will help you visualize life and work here.

Invisible from the water is a collapsed fuel storage tank that once rose to the height of the forest canopy. It is accompanied by remains of old cars and a Fairbanks Morse power plant of WWII vintage. Plenty of rusty metal and collapsed buildings prove the place was once a busy hub. Aero is one of the more interesting abandoned European sites to explore on the islands because its ruins are widely distributed, not extensively overgrown and easily accessible.

This donkey engine at Mathers Creek would have provided power to drag large logs to a marshalling area. Imagine hearing shrieks from the boiler and watching cables drawn tight by the winch.

A very different kind of logging activity can be found at Mathers Creek, farther east and across the inlet from Aero. This site is also known as Church Creek, after the place of worship that once stood here. This watershed was also first logged during the war years, but hauling here was done on ingenious log roads. Trucks with hard rubber tires ran on flattened log "rails." A number of these vehicles remain in the second growth a few minutes' walk west of the creek. The lack of light beneath the dense foliage makes them a challenge to photograph. You may want to have a camera tripod handy. Old machinery also lies farther along the trail and in the tidal zone. Boaters should use caution when approaching the beach.

Mathers Creek was the location of the former village of New Kloo (also spelled Clew). This short-lived Haida settlement was built in 1887 in contemporary style. People came here from T'aanuu Llnagaay (formerly Tanu) after that village deteriorated

The new and old Pacofi Bay. A modern lodge provides a backdrop for the intertidal remains of the Pacofi cold storage and reduction plant. It was in operation for about fifty years, ending around 1950.

due to contact with a European culture counter to its own. Reverend Thomas Crosby helped build the new town, including a plant for extracting oil from dogfish livers. The oil was sold for lubricating machinery and burning in lamps.

Despite the brave effort, New Kloo was abandoned in 1897 in favour of Skidegate. The concentration of community facilities at the latter location made it sensible for scattered villages to amalgamate. The experience humiliated the survivors of T'aanuu Llnagaay. Only twenty years earlier their original village held 547 people, one of the largest populations in this archipelago. Their headstones along Mathers Creek bear many familiar surnames—Clew, Ninstence, and Skdance. As you motor away from the beach and look back at the burgeoning forest growth, there is nothing to suggest this location supported so many different enterprises.

Moving down the inlet toward Hecate Strait, don't be surprised to encounter porpoises. Of the two species common on

Cumshewa Inlet's east–west orientation means some protection from the prevailing winds. Early morning departures will often have calm waters pleasing for young paddlers. KAREN CARTER

Haida Gwaii, harbour porpoises are most likely to be seen within such fjords. They are shy and will not tolerate pursuit. Be on the lookout for their grey backs and triangular dorsal fins disappearing into the distance. Occasionally porpoises are caught in gillnets, especially when commercial boats are going after salmon returning to spawn in Pallant and Mathers Creeks.

Cumshewa Inlet and Gillatt Arm are popular for sport fishing, too, as anglers try for coho salmon between mid-August and September. Several ships have anchored here to serve as floating lodges for well-heeled clients. They troll herring, a very effective bait, but the locals like green buzz bombs and pink hoochies. Try your luck. Good fishing is almost assured in these waters because the salmon are concentrated as they pass up the narrow inlet.

The steep sides and plunging depths of this marine valley are characteristic of routes once gouged by glaciers. All along British Columbia's coast there are fjords like this, which were enlarged during the last ice age. Geologist A. Sutherland Brown

A family kayak trip will be more enjoyable if you are well organized. Plastic bags help keep everything dry and in its place. TRAVIS CARTER

has found evidence to suggest that this area was covered by 1,000 metres of ice. This frozen flow originated in the mountains to the west and ground slowly toward Hecate Strait. Imagine it as Nature's earth mover, scraping soil from the hills and pushing a ridge of rubble before it. When the ice melted, it left a mound across the mouth of this inlet. Marine charts label this Fairburn Shoals, and it marks the terminus of the former ice front.

Fairburn Shoals is covered by a huge bed of bull kelp, which can be a significant barrier to navigation, especially at low tide. When the tide is high, you might find a narrow passage along the shoreline. This route saved our skins one day when a heavy swell, topped by whitecaps, made the inlet dangerous. Sneaking our inflatable into the lee of the kelp, we found calmer water.

Near here is the village from which the inlet draws its name. Very little remains at Cumshewa. However, it still has a pleasant, serene atmosphere. Several totems and some leaning house planks have been all but overtaken by the trees. At low tide you

Those born at K'uuna left or died long ago. Many of their remarkable poles have now leaned or fallen back into the earth. Of these two poles, only the left—an eagle mortuary—tentatively remains upright. ROYAL BC MUSEUM PN 5555-B

can walk out to Haans Islet, a former burial site in front of the village. Recently, a modern dwelling with Haida architecture was constructed at the edge of the former village. If you want to land here, it is best to seek advance permission from the Skidegate Band office.

K'uuna Llnagaay (Skedans), on Louise Island, is probably the most famous abandoned village on Haida Gwaii. In 1878 the Canadian geologist George Dawson photographed fifty-six totems standing here before a row of twenty-seven houses. A more recent book, *Those Born at Koona*, by John and Carolyn Smyly, describes these totems in detail and is a useful onsite guide.

Sadly, most of the totems here have succumbed to rot and gravity. Each time we've visited, inevitable deterioration of the remaining poles has been noticeable. The few left will soon succumb and join others covered by leaves and moss. How inspiring it would have been to have visited here with painter Emily Carr in 1912, before the superior totems rotted or were collected by museums.

Today, one remarkable specimen is nearly indistinguishable from a rotting log. Beside a path at the western edge of the village sits the carved figure of a wolf. It crouches horizontally, a memorial to a deceased authority. A large tree now grows from its back, and moss obscures the figure's minor defining lines. When you suddenly recognize its form, the feeling of surprise is akin to being startled by a live beast in the grass. More than a century has passed since this carving was released from its bondage in a cedar log. Now it is returning to the earth that claimed its carver and his village. This wolf's supernatural ability to snap our vision is not unlike the Haida belief in transformations. It demonstrates the power in Indigenous art and is indicative of Haida kinship with nature.

Landing at K'uuna Llnagaay is best accomplished from the south side. A sandy, sheltered beach and small float offer easy landing for small craft. Skedans Bay, located to the southwest of Skedans Point, offers temporary anchorage and a place for kayakers to camp, should you want to stay longer.

K'uuna Llnagaay through to Louise Narrows

From the village of K'uuna Llnagaay a collection of smaller islands, including Reef and Skedans, can be seen. The far side of these islands is frequented by northern sea lions. As many as a hundred of these animals can be seen here, although their numbers have declined—despite being protected since 1970 under the federal Fisheries Act. Haida were known to kill these marine behemoths. The figures of sea lions appeared on totems that once stood in the village of K'uuna Llnagaay.

Head south for Limestone Islands and Vertical Point. The Haida once had a small village at Vertical Point, but no evidence of it remains today. In wet weather, paddlers will be pleased to come upon a tiny cabin here. It was the studio of a New York artist in summers past. Vertical draws its name from the upturned limestone beds at the point.

You can pass a quiet evening in Rockfish Harbour on the southwest corner of Louise Island. It didn't live up to the angling expectations suggested by its name, but the bay does offer fair-weather anchorage and fresh water for campers. From Rockfish Harbour, you may wish to explore three sites adjacent to Louise Island—Pacofi Bay, Sewell Inlet, and Lagoon Inlet. Like us, you may find these two industrial settlements and the tidal rapids almost as interesting as old Haida villages.

Pacofi is an acronym for the Pacific Coast Fisheries plant that began operation in 1910 in the bay of the same name. Many rusty remnants are still visible. Over the years a packing plant, a saltery, an oil and fertilizer reduction plant, and a plant for making potash from kelp operated here periodically. In the next millennium, archaeologists may be unearthing places such as Pacofi to reveal clues as to why white, Asian, and Indigenous men worked in the same building, but resided in separate quarters.

BC Packers demolished most of the buildings in 1949, but machinery still remains in the woods and on the beach. Use caution when approaching because submerged concrete blocks and metal are scattered along the shoreline. In recent years, this property was purchased and a large, attractive lodge was built above the packing plant ruins. An onsite watchman controls all visitor access. You may have to be content to motor slowly along the shoreline before moving on toward Sewell.

In nearby Sewell Inlet, Western Forest Products Ltd. once ran a small company town. Visiting this town was like taking a walk back in time. In its heyday, fifty-two families lived here. They made good use of a driving range, tennis courts, bowling alley, post office, and pub—the Full Boar Inn. Today the hustle and bustle of this lively coastal community is long gone. Even the generator is silent. The remaining buildings have been moved or demolished.

The demise of such towns is perhaps inevitable as cutblocks for logging are withdrawn or reduced. Some blame forest companies for overcutting, but residents point directly to the formation of the national park reserve for their lost livelihood. Soon after the park boundaries were announced, one very frustrated longtime resident declared: "I wouldn't want to be an environmentalist in there [the pub] on Friday night. That's what you'd call livin' dangerously."

If the suggestion of bottled fluid and suds is appealing, you may want to make Lagoon Inlet one of your last stops. Here, a bedrock bottleneck squeezes the foaming tide in and out of a shallow basin. Levels between the inlet and lagoon may vary by a metre, creating lots of froth as the water races to catch up. River otters often play in the reversing rapids, and deer and bear graze along the estuary. Camping is good inside the "bottle," but plan your departure so you're not left high and dry when its contents drain. Remnants of a cannery built here in 1918 are scattered above and below the tide line. Look for pieces of china or other artifacts while exploring the site. Fire destroyed it in 1941.

Return to Moresby Camp via Louise Narrows, a dredged channel. It provides easy passage on a rising tide between Louise and Moresby Islands. Moving through during tidal changes is similar to running a river. Paddlers will be challenged to make progress "upstream." Prior to their excavation in 1967, these narrows resembled the more southerly Burnaby Narrows, where the flushing action draws an abundant supply of nutrients for marine organisms.

Circumnavigating Louise Island by kayak is well worth considering if a trip to Gwaii Haanas stretches your time or pocketbook. Completing the trip will take about a week to ten days. You can explore five historical sites, visit K'uuna Llnagaay (Skedans), and enjoy beach camping at its best. In most places, the waterways are sheltered, making this an ideal trip to bring along younger family members.

If this kind of adventure appeals to you, Moresby Camp is your best starting point. Point your bow east taking advantage of calmer waters and narrow end of Cumshewa Inlet. Aero will likely be your first stop, then you can criss-cross the inlet to Mathers Creek and possibly Cumshewa Village.* Extensive beaches with good approaches are on both sides of the waterway. Many have freshwater streams, ample beach firewood, and flat tent spots. After a few days of easy paddling, you will approach the wide entrance onto Hecate Strait. Most kayakers leave the inlet in the morning, passing Skedans Point before afternoon winds increase.

Visiting K'uuna Llnagaay is a must, but be sure you make arrangements at the Gwaii Haanas office before leaving. (See "Gwaii Haanas National Park Reserve and Haida Heritage Site—Reservations and Orientation," page 217.) Campsites on the south side of Louise Island will be harder to find as steep, rocky shorelines dominate the topography. As you paddle past Rockfish Harbour, you can explore Pacofi Bay, Sewell Inlet, and Lagoon Inlet, all former canneries or logging communities. On your final homeward stretch, time your arrival at Louise Narrows on an incoming tide. Your kayak will zip through the narrows much like running a river.

If you plan to take children on this trip, the variety of experiences along the entire route will keep young minds and muscles active. Four to five hours of daily paddling, beachcombing, exploring tide pools, rope swinging, building sand castles, and walking on the beach at sunset will fill your photo file, giving you many memorable moments.

* Arrangements to land at Cumshewa Village should be done in advance by contacting the Skidegate Village Office. Landing in front of Cumshewa Village can be difficult at low tide.

Band Office: Box 1301 Skidegate V0T 1S1 Haida Gwaii
Phone: 250-559-4496

GETTING THERE

Louise Island and Cumshewa Inlet, located in the North Moresby region, are accessible by boat, helicopter, and floatplane. Trailered boats are best launched at the concrete ramp at Moresby Camp. This is a former logging encampment on Gillatt Arm of Cumshewa Inlet.

It can be reached by gravel roads leading from the ferry dock at Alliford Bay on Skidegate Inlet, or from Sandspit. The route is marked, but may have active logging. Check with the Ministry of Forests before driving on these roads. (See Part 3: "Planning Your Trip" for contacts.)

Larger watercraft with a deep draft must enter Cumshewa Inlet from Hecate Strait. Shuttle service for kayakers without a vehicle is available in Sandspit, but people with plenty of time and energy have paddled into this area right from the ferry dock at Skidegate Landing.

KAYAKING HAIDA GWAII

A kayak, coupled with your paddle and exploratory spirit, will allow you to experience some of the best places Haida Gwaii has to offer. You can shoulder your kayak aboard the BC Ferry and after arriving at Skidegate Landing, launch your craft and set off thoughout Skidegate Inlet and beyond. Most likely, however, you will arrive with your sleek watercraft perched atop your vehicle. With this obvious flexibility you can drive throughout the islands and launch from virtually any beach or boat ramp serviced by a road.

Some areas are more preferred than others. The wild, west coast has exceptional scenery, ancient villages, and plenty of wilderness. This area, however, is fully exposed to the open Pacific making it desirable only to the most experienced kayakers familiar with isolation, heavy ocean swells, and paddling under challenging conditions. For these reasons, most kayakers choose the lee side of Haida Gwaii with its myriad islands, inlets, bays, and beaches. A spectacular wilderness experience is practically guaranteed among these more sheltered waterways.

You have an abundance of choices. Masset, Skidegate, and Cumshewa Inlets all offer premium kayaking opportunities. You can also dip your paddle in Rennell Sound if you wish to have a modest west coast experience. These areas are covered in considerable detail in chapters 2.1, 2.3, 2.5.

The Gwaii Haanas Park Reserve and Marine Conservation Area holds the most promise for kayakers. Those wishing to access this prime destination have two main choices upon arriving at the starting point of Moresby Camp.

The waters surrounding Louise Island are ideal for kayaking. They are generally protected from strong winds. Freshwater creeks are plentiful as are campsites on sheltered beaches. TRAVIS CARTER

If you plan to be independent and paddle your entire trip without any assistance, then you can launch directly from the beach or boat dock at the Moresby Camp facility. Allow six to eight days to explore Cumshewa Inlet or circumnavigate Louise Island. If your destinations include Juan Perez Sound, Burnaby Narrows, or SGang Gwaay Llnagaay (World Heritage Site of Ninstints), then allow a minimum of fifteen days to visit the many cultural, historical and biological sites throughout the archipelago.

Unfortunately, not everyone can spend two or more weeks paddling and camping. When time restrictions factor into your holiday, consider chartering a faster boat capable of carrying kayaks. They can quickly transport your group and gear to a prearranged destination in Juan Perez Sound or points farther south. Visitors can then enjoy the wildlife, beaches and islands at a more leisurely pace.

A few companies make a paddling trip even easier. One Haida Gwaii outfit offers the convenience of a floating residence. They will transport you and your gear to their facility anchored near the shoreline. Once you have settled in, they will provide you with all the necessary gear, prepare the meals and offer suggestions as to the most popular or most isolated spots to visit. At day's end, you will return "home" to warm surroundings and very comfortable sleeping quarters. Should the weather turn cool or wet, this option can turn an uncomfortable camping trip into a much more memorable holiday.

Other tour operators have an appealing variation of a floating lodge. They use a mother ship as a home base. Each day they motor or sail short distances then anchor in a secluded area or calm bay. Guests aboard ship can then enjoy their evening meal in new surroundings or paddle off into the sunset, returning just as the last evening light fades away. They can also look forward to warm, comfortable sleeping quarters.

Any of these paddling holidays will be even more memorable if you make plans based on your abilities and the kind of wilderness experience you enjoy the most. We suggest reviewing chapters 2.5 and 2.6 on Louise Island circumnavigation and Gwaii Haanas National Park Reserve area. Once you know your preferred destinations, arrival time and length of stay, then follow the steps outlined in Part 3: Planning Your Trip. We also recommend you visit gohaidagwaii.ca or queencharlottevisitorcentre.com. These sites have an abundance of photos, contact numbers, and additional information that will help you with planning.

Most travellers agree that being well prepared will go along way towards making your paddle adventure on Haida Gwaii a top-ten experience.

2.6 GWAII HAANAS NATIONAL PARK RESERVE, NATIONAL MARINE CONSERVATION AREA RESERVE, AND HAIDA HERITAGE SITE

Many thousands of years ago, a small but determined group of travellers somehow crossed what is now Hecate Strait and made their way through a tangle of densely forested islands, past shimmering mountains and cascading streams. They may have been following a run of fish, tracking a wounded whale, or searching for fresh crabapples or berries; or they may have been looking for a home. Whether by chance or by purpose, they reached what is arguably one of the continent's great places of natural beauty. Gwaii Haanas—"a place of beauty"—is a world like no other.

The Haida have always recognized the beauty and rich nature of these islands. So, too, have the timber companies. For over sixty years, they logged magnificent stands of spruce, red cedar, and hemlock for the sole purpose of feeding a hungry lumber market. As more trees fell and clear-cuts increased, many people both on and off the islands began to oppose this seemingly uncontrolled resource extraction. Regrettably, however, it took some time for our governments to realize that a problem of seismic proportions was about to erupt. As a result, ever-increasing tensions between the Haida and the logging companies culminated in a dramatic standoff on Lyell Island. This drew international attention that forced governments, along with the logging companies, to begin serious discussions with the Haida in an effort to find solutions.

Over time, a unique partnership evolved. Representatives of the Council of the Haida Nation and the Government of Canada cooperatively manage Gwaii Haanas. Administering a park reserve with so many interests at stake has been challenging, but it has yielded excellent results.

We are certain the two thousand or so annual visitors would agree.

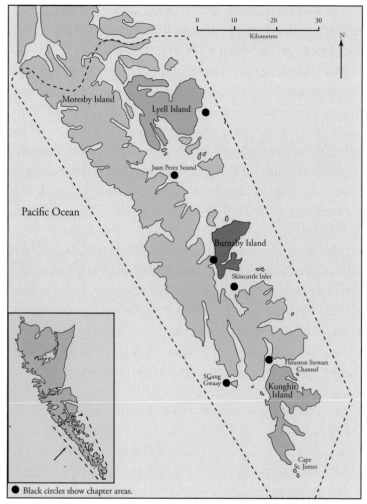

Black circles show chapter areas.

Visiting Gwaii Haanas

Gwaii Haanas's northern boundary crosses Tasu Sound on Moresby Island, the ridge of the Tangil Peninsula, and extends out to sea far enough so that all outer islands south to Cape St. James are included. The park encompasses about 15 percent of the land in the island archipelago.

There are no maintained roads, trails, or public developments in Gwaii Haanas: access is by air or from the water. When planning your trip, keep in mind that there are no public services south of Sandspit. A few people, however, do live legally within the park boundaries. Families at Rose Harbour operate bed-and-breakfast facilities, and seasonal Watchmen live at K'uuna Llnagaay (Skedans), T'aanuu Llnagaay (Tanu), Hlk'yah GaawGa (Windy Bay) and SGang Gwaay Llnagaay (Ninstints). Parks Canada operates two warden stations: one is located at the south end of Huxley Island in Juan Perez Sound; the other is on Ellen Island in Houston Stewart Channel.

Recreationists organizing their own tour must contact the Gwaii Haanas office well in advance of their departure date to book their time. Budget your travel time, as you must attend an orientation session prior to entering the park reserve. Fees also apply to both individuals and tour groups. (See "Part 3: Planning Your Trip.")

If you are kayaking, you should allow two weeks to go from Moresby Camp (see page 216) to SGang Gwaay. That's a lot of paddling. Since the inlets of northern Moresby Island may have less appeal, we recommend that you charter a boat to take you to the village of T'aanuu, within Juan Perez Sound, or to Rose Harbour (page 180).

Motorized pleasure craft can launch at Moresby Camp and within a day can be as far south as Lyell Island. Weather permitting, inflatable and small hard-hulled boats can go almost anywhere, providing you carry enough gas to make the return trip. Inflatables have several advantages—they are generally more seaworthy, can carry substantial amounts of gear, and can still be towed behind yachts. On one of our trips, we chartered a vessel south to Rose Harbour, then returned at a leisurely pace in our own inflatable.

If you are a novice at these types of boating, we recommend signing up with a tour company. Several companies lead trips between May and September. Some of them often feature acclaimed specialists as guides. The Village of Queen Charlotte Visitor Centre, the Gwaii Haanas office, travel agents, outdoor periodicals, or even retail stores specializing in outdoor recreation should be able to provide contacts. The Visitor Centre website also lists on-island tour operators.

Most visitors to Gwaii Haanas tend to head for the main attractions—ancient village sites and scenic areas throughout Juan Perez Sound. We chose to highlight six areas worthy of exploration that include these, plus numerous lesser-known sites. No doubt you will find additional favourites of your own!

Many people pack along a fishing rod with the idea of supplementing their meals with fresh salmon, cod, or other favourite finfish. Be aware that fishing closures for some species are in effect in specific locations. (See "Fishing on Haida Gwaii," page 69, for more information on where you can cast your lure.)

One final note. Notwithstanding the beauty and the cultural and natural diversity of Gwaii Haanas, the park reserve is not a pristine wilderness. Several places along the east coast show signs of previous non-Indigenous habitation or of industry that began within the twentieth century. We found some of these sites compelling, others much less so. Nevertheless, they are part of Gwaii Haanas's rich historical heritage.

For further information, contact:
The Superintendent,
Gwaii Haanas National Park Reserve, National Marine Conservation Area Reserve and Haida Heritage Site

Haida Heritage Centre
60 Second Beach Road, Skidegate, BC V0T 1S0
Phone: 250-559-8818
Fax: 250-559-8366
Toll-free 1-877-559-8818
Email: gwaii.haanas@pc.gc.ca
Website: pc.gc.ca/gwaiihaanas

NAME CHANGES

Agreeing on names for Haida heritage villages was one of many challenges facing the joint management of Gwaii Haanas. Since it will likely take years for maps to reflect these name changes, here is a quick guide to the most frequently visited sites. The unique appearance of these Haida names are the result of an oral language being written using the Roman alphabet. There may be more name changes in the future.

Former Name	Haida Name
Skedans	K'uuna Llnagaay
Tanu	T'aanuu Llnagaay
Windy Bay area	Hlk'yah GaawGa
Village at Windy Bay	Hlk'yah Llnagaay
Hotspring Island	Gandll K'in Gwaay.yaay
Anthony Island	SGang Gwaay
Ninstints	SGang Gwaay Llnagaay

The Haida Heritage Centre officially opened in 2007. It houses the finest display of Haida art and culture on the islands. On-site tours occur during the summer months.

MUSEUMS AND CULTURAL CENTRES

The Haida Heritage Centre officially opened its doors in July 2007. The complex, which consists of several contemporary Haida-style houses, is perhaps the finest introduction to Haida culture anywhere. The entrance, or Greeting House, is a beautiful combination of cedar, glass, and aluminum. An ancient pole from K'uuna Llnagaay (Skedans) greets you in the foyer. From here, you can explore the interconnected Performing House, Eating House, Canoe House, Trading House, and Saving Things House. Near one end of the Greeting House you can stand next to three poles, from the villages of T'aanuu Llnagaay (Tanu) and K'uuna Llnagaay. Outside, six contemporary poles represent large villages from the southern half of Haida Gwaii.

To reach the Haida Heritage Centre, drive east of the ferry landing toward Skidegate. You will soon see the buildings and

The Dixon Entrance Maritime Museum in Masset recognizes pioneers and maritime workers. Youth under sixteen enter for free.

parking lot on your right. The centre is open daily from early June to mid-September. Off-season hours vary, but the complex is usually open Tuesday through Saturday. Entrance fees range from $5 to $12. Children under five are admitted free.

Port Clements's museum focuses on logging, commercial fishing, homesteading, and farming equipment. It's open year-round; daily hours of operation are posted outside the front door. If you arrive outside of scheduled openings, feel free to look at the antiquated logging machinery on the outside grounds. Some of these pieces date back to the 1930s.

The Dixon Entrance Maritime Museum, located at the north end of Masset, boasts an impressive collection of maritime and pioneer artifacts. The building is a museum piece in itself; it was Masset's first hospital. Parents with children will enjoy coming here, as eager young fingers are welcome to touch virtually anything they like! An added bonus is that persons under sixteen are admitted free.

Another attraction is Sandspit Airport. Although it's not a museum, the displays and photographs contained here are certainly worth a close look if time permits.

JUAN PEREZ AND DARWIN SOUNDS

Juan Perez Sound is a wide body of water lying east of Moresby Island and south of Lyell Island. This sound and its protected passage, Darwin Sound, are probably the busiest waters in the South Moresby region. From March through September, numerous commercial and recreational boats visit the area. The vistas that surround Juan Perez Sound are arguably the best in Haida Gwaii.

The shores of the sounds and their mountain backdrops are very rugged. The infinite combinations of landforms and perspectives create some of the most pleasing scenery in Gwaii Haanas. Even when the view becomes monochromatic on rainy days, it's still striking. With the confusion of colour removed, you can better observe the subtle qualities of line and texture.

One such "Misty Isles" day we entered Anna Inlet at the north end of Darwin Sound. Clouds all but obscured the 1,020-metre summits around us. One could easily imagine Valkyries living among the shrouded crags above. The peace of the inlet was calming, the surface of the water dimpled only here and there by diving birds. Ashore, the former mining community of Lockeport lay surrounded by grassy meadows, with a pretty alder forest for a backdrop. Anna Creek tumbled down like wine spilled by the Norse gods; its crisp, cold water tasted divine.

Other than the grassy meadows at Lockeport, suitable camp sites throughout Darwin Sound are scattered and few. Bedrock lines most of the shore, and the forest has fewer clearings. Watch for grassy or sandy shorelines within sheltered bays along the eastern edge of Darwin Sound.

The cove on Shuttle Island can serve as a camp in a pinch. In the opposite bay on Moresby Island, water gushes from a plastic pipe tied to a substantial float. Yachters should top up their water tanks here, since the only other source of reliable piped water is much farther south, in Louscoone Inlet.

George Dawson, an extraordinary Canadian with a formidable reputation in geology, first surveyed this area in 1878. His writings are still standard references for researchers. The names applied to features in this region—Darwin, Lyell, Ramsay, Murchison, Faraday, Sedgwick, Richardson, and Bischof—are tributes to geologists or other scientists whom he admired.

The tiny islands named after K.G. Bischof, a German geochemist, are clustered in an open circle at the north end of Juan Perez Sound. Rugged and attractive, they provide temporary shelter for boats waiting to cross the sound. This is a popular spot for camping, but unfortunately it lacks fresh water. If you're just waiting for the winds to subside, pull your kayak out on the 200-metre-long, Y-shaped islet in the southwest corner and enjoy the fine vistas of Juan Perez Sound.

Immediately north of the Bischofs lies Beresford Inlet. This long narrow inlet is the result of a geological fault running along its entire length. Fresh water is available from creeks at its head if you happen to run short while on the Bischofs. Watch out for strong tidal currents and hidden rocks in the inlet.

The name of an English geologist, de la Beche, is commemorated by both an island and a rugged inlet that cuts into the coast of Moresby Island. Behind them the San Christoval Range rises 1,800 metres to face Juan Perez Sound. These mountains

Some of the finest vistas on Haida Gwaii await those who spend time in this area. Even during rain showers, the heavens over tiny Flower Pot Island display the sound's beauty. TOM PARKIN

are sparsely treed, and their summits are close to shore. Consequently, their semi-open rock slopes make for relatively quick ascents. Even though no trails lead to the peaks, this is one of the better places to reach the high country in Gwaii Haanas.

De la Beche Inlet offers pretty boating opportunities but is unsuitable for camping, as there are no beaches. Skittagetan Lagoon has dangerous rocks, so access is limited to paddlers. Even in the very protected harbour of nearby Sac Bay, a 30-metre yacht dragged its anchor while everyone slept. No one awoke until the hull bumped a rock at the bay's entrance. Strong downdrafts called "williwaws" had shifted the vessel. Fortunately, no damage was done. Faced with such unpredictable winds, yachters should always be prepared to set a second anchor.

For short hikes, boaters frequently go ashore to visit the unnamed lakes above Sac Bay and Haswell Bay. Pull on your gumboots, because there are no defined trails over the boggy ground. Enthusiasts will want to continue up the open rock slopes to the ridge of the San Christovals, where a fantastic view of Juan Perez Sound awaits.

Farther south, hidden behind Marco Island, a beach with a stream provides a good camping spot. If necessary, kayakers and small boaters can wait here for conditions to improve before crossing to Gandll K'in Gwaay.yaay. As you start out, watch for seals hauled out on rocks at the east end of Marco Island.

Gandll K'in Gwaay.yaay, an 8-hectare island, was once one of the most favoured destinations in Gwaii Haanas. For unknown millennia, a number of hot springs fortuitously seeped to the surface above high tide, forming pools amidst the fractured rocks. Whether you were a first time traveller or had made numerous forays throughout Juan Perez Sound, these exquisite hot pools were like a liquid magnet for all those who ventured ashore. Why? There could be no better place to take in the sheer beauty of the San Cristovals, the ever-changing waterways and the peaceful-ness of a late day soak.

Our field companion likened it to living within a Toni Onley painting. Luxuriating up to your neck in hot water as the sun slid over the San Cristovals was the pièce de résistance of experiences in southern Gwaii Haanas.

But alas! The very forces of nature that built the San Cristovals and provided such outstanding natural beauty conspired to take part of the experience away. On the evening of October 17, 2012, massive plates deep beneath Moresby Island and almost directly below the hot springs suddenly shifted. What followed was a magnitude-7.7 earthquake, the second largest ever recorded in Canada. The island network shook and rattled for what seemed like eternity to residents throughout Haida Gwaii. They were not alone. Coastal communities including Prince Rupert, Kitimat, and Bella Coola along with interior cities such as Prince George and Quesnel also felt the ground tremble and shake.

The island communities bore the brunt of the earthquake. Tsunami warnings were issued followed by evacuation orders for coastal residents. An urgent scramble for higher ground followed. Some people remained on high ground all night, fearful of aftershocks or extremely high tides.

For such a tremendous release of subterranean energy and power, there were remarkably few injuries or structural damage. The biggest loss was not noticed until several days later. Park staff, on a routine visit to Gandll K'in Gwaay.yaay, quickly noticed a lack of steam. To their dismay, the pools were empty and the surrounding rocks cold to the touch. Something had turned off the hot-water tap!

That something is believed to be a magnitude-4.0 aftershock, the epicentre of which was less than a kilometre beneath Hotspring Island. For reasons still being investigated, the strong shaking created a realignment of subterranean hydrothermal vents. As a result, clear, hot water no longer fills the pools and cracks above the high-tide marker. Hot water, however, still reaches the island.

In the flurry of activity following the quake, scientists discovered heated water in a few places. Unfortunately, they are all below high tide. To this day, lamenting over the loss of the hot pools continues, even though there is nothing anyone can do. One philosophical islander simply remarked, "The earth gives, and the earth takes away."

Fortunately, the scenery, sights, sounds, and solace of Juan Perez Sound remain among the finest in the western world. And given that the island archipelago receives many minor earthquakes throughout the year, the next one might shake the bedrock just enough to allow hot water to once again fill the island pools. Perhaps the earth will give back as well.

GETTING THERE

This widespread area is accessible to aircraft and boats. Yachters approaching from the north can moor in the small cove on the west side of Hoya Passage, in a tiny cove within the Bischof Islands (fair weather only), on the north side of Murchison Island, and on the north side of Ramsey Island. If you are approaching from the south, Section Cove on the northwest corner of Burnaby Island or Skaat Harbour offer good moorage in most weather conditions.

Helpful Information

Haida Gwaii Watchmen have a house on Gandll K'in Gwaay.yaay (Hotspring Island), but overnighting here or on nearby House and Little House Islands is not permitted. Call ahead on VHF channel 6 before you go to shore on Gandll K'in Gwaay.yaay. Parks Canada has a warden field station (intermittently staffed) at the south end of Huxley Island. In an emergency, it can be reached on VHF channel 16, or by satellite phone at 1-877-852-3100 or 1-780-852-3100. Potable water from a pipe attached to a substantial float is available in a small cove on Moresby Island opposite Shuttle Island.

Pets are prohibited on Gandll K'in Gwaay.yaay (Hotspring Island). Visiting hours are 8:30 a.m. to one hour before sunset. A portion of the northwest shore of Ramsay Island is closed from April 1 through June 30 due to sensitive ancient murrelet nesting colonies.

Many people consider Lyell Island to be the centrepiece of the Gwaii Haanas region. It was here that the Haida made their stand to protest logging, and it was pictures of Lyell Island clear-cuts that first attracted the attention of most Canadians to the issues. The national media was present when the Haida were arrested in 1985 for blocking the loggers' access. Although northern and eastern portions of the island were extensively clear-cut before the protests began, the Hlk'yah GaawGa (Windy Bay area) watershed and Dodge Point were eventually saved from the saw. This part of Lyell Island and the much smaller satellite islands to the east are worthy of a day's exploration.

The entrance to this bay is exposed, and we recommend postponing your passage along the outside of Lyell Island if the weather is poor or threatening. Strong tides also run past both Gogit and Fuller Points. Check your tide tables and weather channels before heading this way. If you do become stormbound here, there is good camping with fresh water from the creek. Looking Around and Blinking House, located near the campground, is a modified traditional Haida-designed structure with wooden sleeping platforms. It was officially opened in 1987. In August 2013, a legacy pole was raised here to commemorate twenty years of cooperative management since the signing of the Gwaii Haanas Agreement by the Haida Nation and the Government of Canada. This was the first monumental pole raising in the Gwaii Haanas area in over 130 years. Hlk'yah Llnagaay is also the site of an ancient village, and remnants of former houses can be seen on the opposite shore. Former residents had access to the stands of magnificent trees immediately behind. It was this rainforest that inspired the fight to save Gwaii Haanas: its beauty was recognized

Examining a Haida test hole in a western red cedar. Trees of this size, if solid inside, could have been used for canoes. The purpose of the test hole was to be sure the trunk was firm and without rot.

Haida Gwaii, Region by Region

These figures on the new Windy Bay pole recognize the protesters who locked arms and blockaded the Lyell Island logging operations. TRAVIS DOANE

long ago. Today, a boardwalk leading to the largest trees winds through this famous forest.

In 1900, biologist William Osgood spent five weeks studying the flora and fauna of these islands. In his writings about the rainforest, he said: "The spruces stand in magnificent groves, the grandeur of which is appreciated only when one gets above the tangle of underbrush and obtains an unobstructed view of the tall, straight, reddish barked trunks, column after column extending far back into the forest, until the dim light is finally obscured and individual trees can no longer be distinguished."

It sounds rather like the Parthenon, and Hlk'yah GaawGa is certainly a temple of nature. There is little undergrowth to obstruct movement, and a deep carpet of moss invites your tread across the forest floor. To step off the trail for a moment alone is humbling, yet inspiring. The trees are so big that one feels insignificant creeping over their spreading roots. The cedars in this valley rise to 70 metres. Nearing one thousand years old, some are among the most ancient living organisms in this country.

Very little direct sunlight penetrates below the forest canopy, and sounds are muffled. Occasionally the song of some small bird faintly reaches your ear. You might recognize the muffled notes of a Townsend's warbler, a golden-crowned kinglet or a chestnut-backed chickadee. Other bird calls carry surprisingly well. The double bell tone of a common raven resonates through the trunks, "dong-dong." From the sky above, a bald eagle cries its creaky stutter. It's easy to understand why the Haida attributed supernatural qualities to eagles and ravens.

The Haida came into these woods to gather plants and to cut western red cedar for medicines, clothes, canoes, and building materials. Many of the huge trees still show signs of use: some have their bark stripped off; others have been "holed" in a test for internal rot. There is no way to pinpoint the location of specific specimens, but a boardwalk trail will guide you through some of the finest examples; you may discover others if you decide to wander off the trail. If you do step away from the trail, be aware that it is very easy to become disoriented in these woods. Stay within sight of your hiking partners.

Where bark has been removed from red cedar, the resulting scar is usually easy to spot. The Haida collected the bark by making horizontal cuts, then pulling out and ripping strips up the trunk. They separated the fibres and wove them into clothing and various coverings. The soft bark was also made into rope, fishnets, baskets, and numerous items of a twined or woven nature. This activity did not kill the tree. (The process of collecting bark is still done throughout Haida Gwaii.)

Cedars at Hlk'yah GaawGa were also used for construction. The men sought large, straight trees for house timbers, canoes, and totem poles. Depending on its intended use, a tree would be tested for core rot. Once selected, trees were felled by chipping and/or burning. We discovered one horizontal log that had been partially cut into boards.

There is so much evidence of tree use here that this watershed could be considered a living museum. Cedar was (and still is) a multi-purpose material for the Haida, and was virtually their exclusive choice in wood. It is soft, light, straight-grained, easy to split, and holds paint well. It also contains a fragrant natural oil that makes it resistant to decay, even in the sodden Northwest Coast climate.

As surely as cedar is the wood of life for the Haida, salmon is their food of life. Windy Bay Creek has the distinction of being the largest and most productive spawning stream in Gwaii Haanas. When autumn rains raise water levels, chum, pink, and coho salmon return to lay eggs in the gravel where they hatched. Pinks are the most abundant: in late September they can number as many as 55,000 fish. Coho complete their life cycle from late October through November.

Five kilometres to the north, Dodge Point was the site of Gwaii Haanas's largest breeding colonies of ancient murrelets. In 1982 this colony was estimated to contain more than ten thousand nests. Today the numbers have been decimated due to rat predation. Because murrelets need the spaced trees and open floors of old-growth forests, they become grounded if obstructed by low-level vegetation. They need lots of open space to manoeuvre around tree trunks. They nest in underground burrows, hidden among the roots of mature spruce and cedar trees. In late March, adults return to the colony and select burrows within sight of the sea. After hatching, young birds leave their burrows at night, following the calls from their parents, who wait for them just offshore. Once on the water, the adults and chicks head out to sea. You may see them near Tuft Islets at the end of May or early in June.

All the islands off the east coast of Lyell are good places to see a variety of marine fauna. The Tar Islands are frequently used by seals for haul-outs. Killer whales know this and often cruise this coast for prey. We once encountered a pod of five orca at Agglomerate Island. While we stood transfixed on a ledge only a few feet above the water, the whales engaged in a seemingly spontaneous display of playful behaviour literally beneath our feet. For a full thirty minutes these magnificent marine mammals interacted with one another and with us. They swam in gentle spirals and rolls around each other, rubbed against kelp stalks and spyhopped (raised their heads straight out of the water) to check our activity on shore, all of this within 6 metres of where we stood. Finally, after their engaging performance was over, it seemed to be our turn, and the whales lay on the surface of the water to listen while we tried to entertain them with our singing. When at last they departed, it seemed only because they were bored with our human antics. We were frustrated by our inability to communicate with these intelligent mammals. Yet there was no doubt in our minds that they had chosen to spend time in our presence. We felt oddly grateful and privileged to witness this rare display.

GETTING THERE

Both Hlk'yah GaawGa (Windy Bay area) and Hlk'yah Llnagaay (Village at Windy Bay) remain unmarked on topographic maps and marine charts. Located between Gogit Point and Fuller Point, the bay, creek, and ancient village are accessible only by boat.

Visitors may camp here for one night, longer only if weather-bound. In emergencies, you may stay in Looking Around and Blinking House but check with the Haida Watchmen first.

BURNABY NARROWS

Burnaby Strait connects the waters of Juan Perez Sound and Skincuttle Inlet. The strait tapers to a section 50 metres wide that charts and maps label Dolomite Narrows. The local name— Burnaby Narrows—is, however, widely accepted. This is a premier location for viewing intertidal life. There are also points of interest north and south of the narrows.

Burnaby Strait is widest at its northern end. On the northwest corner of Burnaby Island, Section Cove has campsites, fresh water, a sandy beach, and a mooring buoy for larger craft. There may also be chained logs anchored near the shore. They are chained together to make floating pens for the Haida fishery for Pacific herring spawn. In spring, large blades of the kelp called *Macrocystis* hang from the logs. As the herring gather in huge schools, they are netted and put in these pens until they spawn on the kelp. The herring lay small white eggs directly on the kelp, sometimes several layers deep. The resulting algal caviar, known as K'aaw, is a delicacy for First Nations people and the Japanese. K'aaw may be eaten raw, quick-fried, dipped in hot water, frozen, or dried. In past years, this industry has generated more than $10 million in overseas sales.

Heading south toward the narrows you'll pass the entrance to Island Bay. Motor or paddle very slowly and keep your chart in hand, for the bay is guarded by seventeen islands and at least as many rocks. All of these provide a picturesque foreground to Yatza Mountain, part of the San Christoval Range. On clear days

Bat stars abound in the sheltered waters of Burnaby Narrows. They feed on dead animals, seaweed, sponges, and sea urchins. Their range of colours makes the sea bottom at the narrows resemble a tapestry.

its summit provides fine views, though no defined trails lead to the top. A cascade at the far end of Island Bay offers a refreshing drink and a place to fill water containers. In 1961 the carcass of a great white shark discovered here was the first ever recorded in the province. At least a dozen more great whites have washed ashore throughout Haida Gwaii since then.

Your trip to Burnaby Narrows needs to be carefully timed. If you plan on heading right through, do so on high slack tides. If you want to spend an hour or two viewing the profuse intertidal life, it's best to arrive just before or after low tide. You'll find it almost impossible to walk here without stepping on something alive. For this reason, Parks Canada requests visitors to drift through the area. As you float over the shallows, the crystal clear water affords excellent views of a marine ecosystem in action.

The abundance of marine life is due to the strong tidal action through the narrows, which brings a constant supply of nutrients

Sea urchins thrive in the waters around Haida Gwaii. Their prickly spines drop off when the echinoderm dies leaving a shell that can be safely tucked away in your packsack. TRAVIS CARTER

HAIDA GWAII

Raccoons frequent Burnaby Narrows at low tide. They often hide among shoreline logs and vegetation. JIM THORNE

to these creatures. Most are filter-feeders, including clams, barnacles, and mussels. They strain the water they take in through special brushes called cirri, which trap minute, free-floating organisms. Equally conspicuous, sea stars blanket the bottom like a tapestry of the heavens. Each has a different colour, and when surrounded by textured algae they make terrific photographic compositions.

You may also notice curious mounds in the mud, or sandy-coloured rings resembling rubber toilet plungers. The large, spherical moon snail creates both. This carnivorous shellfish plows beneath the surface in search of clams, which it envelops with its fleshy foot. Once a clam is trapped, the snail rasps a small hole through the clamshell, allowing access to its innards. The purpose of the rubbery rings puzzles many people: in fact, they

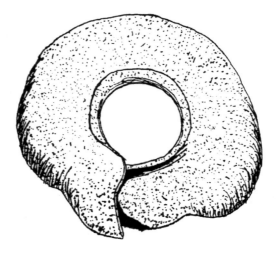

The egg case of a moon snail is a layer of eggs sandwiched between two layers of sand. Hundreds of these doughnut-shaped cases may appear in tidal areas.

are used for reproduction. As the snails extrude their eggs in a gelatinous sheet, sand binds to the sticky mass, forming a thin collar that hardens, then splits. The grey ring of sand and eggs remains on top of the muddy ocean floor. About midsummer, this egg case breaks down, releasing thousands of free-swimming moon snail larvae.

Red rock crabs also live hereabouts. These crustaceans are smaller and have less meat than the commercially favoured Dungeness crab. Their black-tipped pincers possess considerable strength, adding new meaning to the term "armed and dangerous." One of our travelling companions discovered this the hard way when demonstrating the method of capturing crabs by hand. Using an approved technique, he grasped the shell from the rear, only to find that his specimen was unusually agile, deftly pinching his index finger with the strength of a vice. Blood, pincer, and crab flew in different directions as he recoiled in pain. Clenched teeth later gave way to a smug smile, however, as he cracked open the dismembered limbs and savoured the tasty meat of the culprit.

Be prepared to share this environment with some other wildlife. During our early-morning explorations we encountered raccoons, eagles, and ravens foraging for breakfast. Black bears frequently visit the narrows, which is one very good reason camping is not allowed here.

Only the fast-rising tide will limit your time in this exciting area. When the water becomes too deep for viewing, set out to explore nearby bays and coves. To the immediate south, Bag Harbour is the site of a former seasonal Haida village. The remnants of several salmon weirs can be seen in the bed of the stream that enters here, and a rusted boiler and a heap of shells on the shore are vestiges of a clam cannery that operated here between 1908 and 1910.

Although this is one of the richest shellfish beds on our Pacific coast, these clams should not be eaten. Burnaby Narrows and other places around Gwaii Haanas have frequent algae blooms known as red tide, caused by tiny micro-organisms in the water. These organisms contain a toxin that is harmless to clams but potentially deadly for humans. Since regular testing for this poison does not occur, harvesting of clams is permanently prohibited throughout Gwaii Haanas.

Bag Harbour is an excellent small-boat refuge. You can safely wait here for Burnaby Narrows to flood if you're travelling north. You can also anchor while you explore the surrounding forests, beaches, and salmon stream.

Every visitor to this part of Gwaii Haanas should try to include at least one full day in the Burnaby Narrows area. Although intertidal life flourishes throughout the islands, the Narrows are unique. Floating over one of the richest areas of intertidal life has been a highlight of their visit for many travellers to Haida Gwaii.

GETTING THERE

Burnaby Narrows (also called Dolomite Narrows) is accessible only to boats. At most low tides, the narrows dry and passage through them is impossible. Marine markers aid navigation at high tide, but motorized boats should proceed with caution. Large craft can find good anchorage at Section Cove (at the northwest end of Burnaby Island) or at Bag Harbour (southwest of the narrows).

Camping is not permitted here, although you can picnic on the grassy east side. You will find suitable campsites, some with small streams, at the entrance to Island Bay (north of the narrows) or in Bag Harbour and Tangle Cove (south of the narrows).

ON-THE-SPOT PREPARATION AND RECIPES FOR CRAB AND CLAMS ON HAIDA GWAII

PLEASE NOTE Fisheries and Oceans lists possession limits for both crab and clams. We hope you will respect these and take only what you can eat while visiting Haida Gwaii. When we visit, it's nice to know there will be some for us!

Razor Clam Preparation

If possible, transport live clams in a bucket of seawater, in which clams tend to purge themselves of some sand. Cover the bottom of a large pot with 1.5 cm of salted water and bring to a boil. Place clams in pot, leave lid ajar, and steam for one to three minutes until clams open. Remove and allow to cool. With a sharp knife, open the clams and remove all meat. Separate the foot and siphon from other body parts. Wash thoroughly to remove sand. Cut into small, tasty pieces.

Creamy Campfire Chowder

    2 cups of diced clams
    1 medium onion, chopped
    2 slices of bacon (cooked)
    ¼ cup of diced green pepper
    1 cup diced potatoes
    ½ tsp salt and a dash of pepper (preferably cayenne)
    ¼ tsp thyme
    2 cups of milk or tomato juice

In a clean pot, add all the ingredients with pre-steamed clams, stir until creamy and the vegetables are tender, then serve.

Dungeness Crab Preparation

Transport live crabs in a bucket until you are ready to eat. For those unfamiliar with handling crabs, first place the live crab on its back and hit the underside dead centre with a rock or knife handle; the crab will die instantly. Next, grasp the legs and pincers in each hand, twisting first inwards and then out. The limbs will separate quite easily from the shell. Remove any of the remaining gills and rinse in seawater. Submerge crab legs in boiling salted water for about fifteen to twenty minutes, depending on the size.

> **Campfire Crab**
>
> After the crab is cooked, remove from the water, allow time to cool, then separate legs from main body. Break each leg at the joints, then crack open the covering with nutcrackers or a rock. Strong fingers can sometimes break the outer covering. A small fork can help remove meat from narrow sections.
>
> Remove the white meat and enjoy. For added delight, dip morsels in melted butter, garlic butter, or a seafood sauce. Crab can also be added to salad or used as a side dish with your main meal.

SKINCUTTLE INLET

Skincuttle Inlet is a 6-kilometre-wide opening that enters Hecate Strait between Burnaby and Moresby islands. Within the inlet are five scattered groups of smaller islands. Many inlets, bays, and a strait divide the shoreline into attractive anchorages. Surrounding hills rise to 350 metres and form a solid wooded aspect. Low tides expose the sculpted rocks along the shoreline, on the smallest islands and above Harriet Harbour.

Anyone interested in minerals or geology will enjoy several days of exploration in Skincuttle Inlet. Mining here dates back to 1862. You'll find huge open pits, several underground tunnels, and the remains of three mining communities, a former cannery, and a nearby commune.

Jedway was first established in the early 1900s, when its copper deposits attracted prospectors. Although the miners searched throughout the inlet, their home base was along the west side of Harriet Harbour. The townsite included two wharfs, a sawmill, and numerous cabins. Today, the site is completely overgrown.

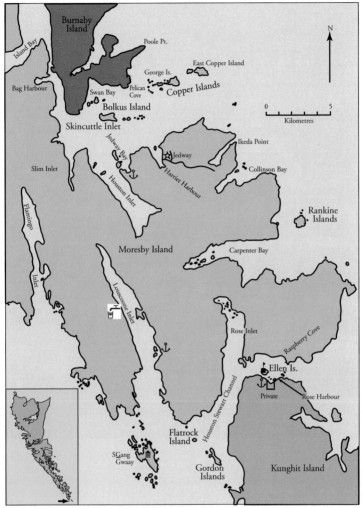

Before this became a park reserve, diggers hunting for antique bottles scavenged the dump. Removing any items now, however, contravenes park reserve policy.

Above Harriet Harbour, waste rock forms a loose slope below an open pit. Pieces of heavy magnetite, a rich ore of iron, still

Kayakers exploring Skincuttle Inlet will find sea caves at Poole Point and a former iron mine at Jedway. TOM PARKIN

litter the ground. Jedway was one of two iron-ore mines in Gwaii Haanas that shipped concentrate to Japanese steel mills (the other was at Tasu on the west coast of Moresby Island). The mine operated between 1961 and 1968, employing 130 full-time staff.

The Haida name for the island shielding this pretty bay is Jiidawaay, meaning "lasso with a rope." As mentioned, magnetite was mined here and significant amounts of it still remain. It may cause compasses to give inaccurate readings, so use caution and your GPS if you are travelling during times of limited visibility. Companies at industrial sites such as this commonly dumped their scrap metal in the sea. If you set your anchor, you could snag some of this debris. As if that weren't enough, this seemingly protected bay is prone to strong southerly downdrafts.

Harriet Island offers some protection for anchored boats should you decide to go ashore. The townsite of Jedway has been cleaned, but some tailing ponds remain. These should be avoided. The roads leading to the mines are still open for walking. The least obstructed route parallels the harbour before leading uphill. It will take slow walkers two hours to reach the ridge between Jedway and Ikeda Cove, a vantage point that offers fine sunset views of Skincuttle Inlet.

From the ridge, the road descends toward Ikeda Cove, stopping short of the water and leading to additional workings on the south slope. During construction of this road the workings of an earlier copper mine were partially obliterated. If you look along the upper side, you may spot a mine portal and the dump piles of this 1906–20 operation, which was managed by the successful Japanese businessman Arichika Ikeda.

After it was sorted by hand, ore was carted to the loading wharf on a 1-metre-gauge tramway for shipping to a smelter on Vancouver Island. In the piles left at the ore bunkers you can find chalcopyrite, a brassy mineral sometimes called copper pyrite. From the road's lowest point, you can follow the rails to the old camp at the water's edge.

We were wary of the water draining from these mines and we do not recommend it for drinking. Instead, fresh water can be

Sunset views from the ridge overlooking Jedway are spectacular.

obtained from the streams that run into Harriet Harbour along the western shoreline.

A Japanese abalone cannery also used to operate in Jedway Bay. In the woods behind the rotting buildings is a touching inscription on a wooden grave marker. The grave of Mrs. Taniyo Isozaki dates from the dark decades when the Japanese were ostracized by the white community. Sadly, we know little about her or the cannery operation.

A fellow by the name of Francis Poole was the first European resident in Skincuttle Inlet. This English engineer prospected for copper here in 1862–63 and later published an account of his explorations. Poole's venture failed, his miners mutinied, and his life was threatened several times. Remarkably, he still wrote appreciatively of the area: "I stood by the beach for fully half an hour, thinking how difficult it would be to find a sweeter spot in all the world, and how at no distant date that very beach would assuredly give way to the wharves and landing places of a flourishing commercial town. Harriet Harbour has only to be known in order to be seized upon in the interests of trade and colonization."

Poole never realized his own vision, however, since he was unsuccessful in his quest for copper. His mines were located in the limestone on Copper Island and at Pelican Cove on Burnaby Island. Old shafts and camp remains are still visible at the sites where he laboured.

Poole Point on Burnaby Island is named after him, but some of the holes here are from erosion, not mining. This point is subject to strong winds, and it is difficult to land on its stony beaches. Those who do make it ashore will be fascinated by the cave. Heavy seas have carved the granite rocks into a horseshoe-shaped cavern that has two openings on the same shore. The major opening gapes 10 by 6 metres. The adjacent hole has a partially collapsed ceiling, creating a separated arch. At low tide you can kayak into the flooded passage, though ocean surges can make this dangerous. Around the arch's base, the sea swirls stones, grinding circular holes in the bedrock. Such grinders are called millstones and their depressions, potholes.

Also on Burnaby Island, Swan Bay is of minor interest. This idyllic setting was once the homestead of some families seeking an alternative lifestyle. They struggled for six or seven years before deciding to move elsewhere. One of their homes resembled a large mushroom, but little evidence remains of their venture. Today, this is the site of the Swan Bay Rediscovery Camp sponsored by the Skidegate Band Council. Young people in attendance learn about traditional Haida culture. Visitors are requested to give the bay a wide berth.

At high tide, seawater fills this unusual cavern. Your kayak will fit inside provided the surface remains calm. Once inside, you can look straight up to the heavens.

HAIDA GWAII

We had an enjoyable time motoring around Skincuttle Inlet, exploring the bays and walking the beaches. We saw plenty of wildlife that balanced nicely with the historical remnants and mineral extraction. Even hiking to the ridge above Jedway was interesting. Everyone in our party had a measurable appreciation of geology and enjoyed examining what remains of the mines. Skincuttle Inlet will certainly add another dimension to your Gwaii Haanas visit.

GETTING THERE

This large inlet is accessible to all aircraft and boats. Yachters will find fair-weather anchorage in Harriet Harbour or a more protected mooring in Jedway Bay.

Campsites abound in this area, but a few places are permanently closed. These include the isthmus between the two eastern Swan Islets, Bolkus Island, Slug Islet, and East Copper Island across the middle of Skincuttle Inlet. Rankine Islands, southeast of Skincuttle Inlet, are also closed. All of these locations have sensitive seabird nesting sites.

HOUSTON STEWART CHANNEL

Many people begin or complete their Gwaii Haanas explorations in Houston Stewart Channel since this area is as far south as most groups go. The channel has suitable pickup and drop-off places, offers refuge from poor weather and is close to a major place of interest—SGang Gwaay, an island and ancient village with a UNESCO World Heritage designation.

Early sailing ships also sought shelter in Houston Stewart Channel, anchoring here on trading visits. At first, trade dealings with the Haida were friendly, but unfortunately hostilities did occur. At least four ships were attacked, and two were burned. There was considerable loss of life on both sides. These tragic events are retold from a Indigenous perspective in Christie Harris's novel *Raven's Cry*.

In 1853, sailors aboard the *Virago* discovered fresh stream water on the north side of the channel. They also found lush red salmonberries, which they called raspberries. Now known as Raspberry Cove, this is a good campsite. Unfortunately, tiny, biting flies called no-see-ums can be a problem, and the cove's popularity with kayakers means you may find this site rather crowded.

Directly across from the cove lies Rose Harbour, a former whaling station that employed as many as one hundred men seasonally between 1910 and 1942. It was not unusual for management to bring their families in for the summer. Records indicate that in those thirty-two years more than two thousand whales were processed and shipped as barrels of oil, mink food, and fertilizer. The foul smell generated a lot of wisecracks about the station's floral name—named for the same George Rose who is commemorated at Nai-Kun (Rose Spit). The whaling company eventually went bankrupt and most of its machinery was dismantled. (W.A. Hagelund wrote an anecdotal history of whaling here and on Graham Island in his book, *Whalers No More*.)

Two digesters, used to render whale blubber and bones, still sit rusting on the beach at Rose Harbour. A plain monument nearby is dedicated to Asian workers who died while employed here. Steam boilers remain hidden behind the trees and modern buildings, and several homes are now built on this site. Families have resided here since 1978, living off the land and sea. If you go

In its day, whaling was an accepted commercial enterprise. This marine behemoth was only one of two thousand whales processed at Rose Harbour. The whale's flesh was rendered into oil, cosmetics, and fertilizer. BC ARCHIVES E-01609

ashore to see the remains of the whaling station, please respect the residents' property and privacy.

A pleasant trip ashore awaits nearby in 5-kilometre-long Rose Inlet. Inflatables and kayaks require careful navigation through rocks and kelp to reach the broad salt marsh at the inlet's terminus. Such a large foraging area is rare in Gwaii Haanas, making this important habitat. Deer and bear graze in the meadow, and it's also popular with migrating waterfowl.

Beyond the western end of Rose Inlet, all that separate you from the Pacific horizon are small island clusters. Despite its name, this ocean is rarely pacific. Strong waves and ocean swells batter both sides of Kunghit Island. Paddling a kayak along these exposed shorelines requires special skills. Both sides of Kunghit Island are usually avoided by smaller craft.

At the very mouth of the channel is Flatrock Island, a mesa-topped monolith alive with nesting glaucous-winged gulls and pelagic cormorants. We also spotted a rare horned puffin flying in wide circles around this rocky roost. Going ashore here is extremely difficult, so the birds are best studied from the water. The nearby Gordon Islands have some pretty nooks, but only kayakers can easily navigate through them. Sometimes glass fishing floats from Japan can be found in this remote coastal location.

The best-known island cluster west of Rose Inlet contains SG̲ang Gwaay (formerly Anthony Island), which is the location of SG̲ang Gwaay Llnagaay, often referred to as Ninstints (described in the next section, SG̲ang Gwaay World Heritage Site). Around SG̲ang Gwaay, the smaller islets are excellent for birdwatching. Nine of the thirteen species of seabirds that breed in BC nest in this one area: an estimated forty thousand pairs. They use every type of available habitat—burrows, rock crevices, open rock, or thin vegetation. A nesting horned puffin was first recorded in BC at this location. Our favourite, however, is the tufted puffin. Their colourful faces and fat bodies, with wings that seem to revolve around their midsections, give them the look of stunt planes at an air show. The islets all around SG̲ang Gwaay are protected areas for these birds, so please remain in your boat while exploring and birdwatching.

This is also a great place to see mammals. Northern sea lions rest on the outermost rocks, exposed to surf and spray, and you can watch for harbour seals among the islets or river otters within Houston Stewart Channel.

There is an exceptional diversity of submarine mammals as well. If you're hoping to see whales on your trip, either end of Houston Stewart Channel is a likely locale. Watch for spouting grey and minke whales near shore, or humpbacks breaching farther out. Killer whales will sometimes cruise right through the channel.

Houston Stewart Channel is one of the most remote locations in BC. Birds and mammals are abundant. Most people return with an exciting story about breaching whales, whirling puffins, or sharing a campfire with a kayaker from almost anywhere in the world.

Nowhere else on Haida Gwaii is quite like it.

GETTING THERE

Houston Stewart Channel separates Moresby Island from smaller Kunghit Island to the south. The channel is accessible to aircraft and boats. There are mooring buoys in Rose Harbour, as well as within Louscoone Inlet.

Rose Harbour has bed-and-breakfast facilities and offers a boat-tour service out to SGangGwaay (Anthony Island).

Parks Canada has a field warden station (intermittently staffed) on the eastern side of Ellen Island. For emergencies, they monitor VHF channel 16 during the day or can be reached with a satellite phone at 1-877-852-3100 or 1-780-852-3100.

No-access sites include Bowles Point on the eastern side of Kunghit Island, all of the rocks and islets surrounding SGangGwaay, and Kerouard Islands at the southern extremities of Kunghit Island. Camping is not permitted on SGang Gwaay.

Water from a pipe can be found about halfway along the west side of Louscoone Inlet.

**FISHING IN GWAII HAANAS NATIONAL PARK
RESERVE, NATIONAL MARINE CONSERVATION
AREA PRESERVE, AND HAIDA HERITAGE SITE**

Limited saltwater fishing is allowed within the park reserve. During orientations or when registering for a visit, inquire about any current fishing closures. There is a permanent closure in all freshwater rivers, lakes, and creeks. In addition, Rockfish Conservation Areas exist in two locations. One of these is in the waters north, south, and east of SGang Gwaay (Anthony Island). The second is generally north, east, and south of Lyell and Tanu Island, and throughout Crescent Inlet. Parks Canada or the Village of Queen Charlotte Visitor Centre can provide you with a map showing the exact boundaries of these two areas.

The harvesting of any bivalve shellfish is not permitted due to the high risk of Paralytic Shellfish Poisoning (PSP).

SGANG GWAAY WORLD HERITAGE SITE

This tiny island seems an unlikely place to find the masterpieces of the Haida's creative genius, but SGang Gwaay has been recognized as having international significance for its artistic heritage. Some of the world's greatest totem poles still stand here in the ground where they were raised.

The Haida name of SGang Gwaay—the Wailing Island—is most appropriate. The name originates from the sound of surging waves forcing air through a hole in a rock—a sound like a woman keening or wailing. European traders called the village Ninstints—a mispronunciation of Nan Sdins, the name of the village chief. It is correctly referred to as SGang Gwaay Llnagaay, the Wailing Island town.

The historic village, once the home of at least three hundred Haida and one of the largest villages in the Gwaii Haanas region, is now uninhabited and decaying. Archaeologists have compared it favourably to the lost jungle cities of Mexico and Cambodia. The United Nations finally recognized this legacy in wood in 1981 by declaring SGang Gwaay a World Heritage Site, ranking it alongside Egypt's pyramids and France's palace at Versailles. SGang Gwaay presents an exceptional testimony to a civilization that very nearly disappeared.

This village was the last homeland of the Gangxid, a sub-division of the Haida Nation whose territory was the southern Gwaii Haanas region. They occupied this site for at least two thousand years, using it as a year-round residence. During the summer, people scattered throughout the territory to hunt, fish, and gather edible plants. They occupied their time in winter with carving, construction and social ceremonies, usually in conjunction with other villages.

SGang Gwaay was a difficult place for guests and enemies to approach. The winds of winter, and sometimes those of summer, are among the strongest in Canada. Yet the village itself is sheltered on the lee side of the island. A smaller island lies in front, restricting passage to a concealed cove behind. Here canoes once lay beached before numerous houses. When low tide dries the bay, you can still see the canoe runs cleared through the beach cobbles.

Visitors are often humbled into silence upon arriving here. Decaying wooden faces on the poles stare out to sea as if to ignore the intrusion, and a straggling row of bestial eyes can be intimidating. You feel like asking permission from the spirits to tread among these towering relics. The presence of the dead is pervasive, so perhaps it's fitting that the majority of the standing poles are mortuaries, honouring the people who led this village. The bodies

Haida Gwaii, Region by Region

The village of SGang Gwaay Llnagaay is a World Heritage Site, recognized for its superior poles well over a hundred years old. Visitors are welcomed by Haida Watchmen who will guide you throughout the old village.

of the dead were entombed in enclosures at the top of the poles. Other poles include tall memorials commemorating an ancestor lost at sea or elsewhere.

These poles do not depict pagans or demons, nor were they worshipped. The animal and human figures on them represent family crests and mythology, and are similar to European coats of arms or Scottish tartans. These symbols make a statement about genealogy and possibly the individual commemorated. Tragically, many of these meanings were forgotten or lost when, during the 1800s, raging smallpox epidemics nearly wiped out the entire population. We were able to identify some of the figures such as bears, whales, and birds.

Oddly, some of the animals symbolized on the poles weren't residents of Haida Gwaii in those days or, in some cases, even to this day. These include the beaver (with cross-hatched tail), the frog (with toothless grin), and the grizzly bear (with protruding

Many of the poles here are mortuary poles. The remains of a chief or other important person would be interred at the top.

SG̲ang Gwaay Llnagaay recreated by artist Gordon Miller. It was the most isolated and protected of all major Haida villages. GORDON MILLER

tongue). These animals strongly suggest the Haida were familiar with mainland creatures. Other figures are recognizable as eagles and killer whales. Some poles are virtually unidentifiable, having fallen and subsequently been covered in moss.

Of the twenty-six poles remaining at SG̲ang Gwaay Llnagaay (many were removed to museums), several have begun to lean and a few have toppled. This decay is part of a cultural progression. Traditionally when poles aged, they were removed and replaced. The old ones would be cut up and given out at a potlatch. Recently, Parks Canada has worked together with the Haida elders to straighten some of the leaning poles.

Decay has seriously affected the remains of the dwellings. Collapsed beams and posts lie behind the poles, the remnants of twenty houses. The largest of these was 14.3 metres by 14.9 metres and had an excavated floor. Only two houses here had such terraced interiors. George MacDonald's booklet, *Ninstints:*

Haida World Heritage Site, provides excellent drawings of their design, while artist Gordon Miller renders the village in exquisite detail as it may have appeared during its peak. This is an excellent onsite guide to identifying the houses and poles.

The Gangxid suffered more than other Haida in their early contacts with Europeans and Americans. Led by a prideful and embittered chief, they attacked four trading vessels in as many years, twice destroying entire ships and crews. In the last conflict, which occurred in 1795, the chief, K'uuya, and fifty warriors were killed with no loss to the traders.

Following K'uuya's death, the Gangxid kept much to themselves for many decades. Their isolation, however, was no protection from the new diseases white men brought. Smallpox first struck late in the eighteenth century, probably transmitted by Russian fur traders. A subsequent epidemic was thought to have been deliberately introduced in 1862 when a "sick" man was sent ashore in Skincuttle Inlet. The Haida social fabric was further torn apart when they obtained liquor and when many of their young people moved to a temporary camp on the outskirts of Victoria on Vancouver Island. By 1884, SGang Gwaay Llnagaay had only thirty surviving residents. They were eventually invited to move to Skidegate. Today only a few descendants can trace their family back to the once-great Gangxid tribe.

The rainforest soon took over. For many years the village site was largely forgotten, visited only by the occasional hunter or fisher. In 1938, a few poles were removed and taken to Prince Rupert. During the 1950s, after negotiations with the Skidegate Band Council, even more were removed under an initiative by the Royal BC Museum. Eventually, some of these poles were returned to the islands and can now be seen at the Haida Heritage Centre at Skidegate. Seven remain at the Museum of Anthropology at the

University of British Columbia. Thankfully, enough poles were left onsite to give visitors a glimpse into one of the Haida traditions from years past. The plan now is to keep the poles in place and slow their deterioration as much as possible. Haida Gwaii Watchmen come each summer to monitor the thousands of visitors passing through here.

This is both a blessing and a curse. While no one will argue with the necessity of tourism to justify the poles' preservation, large numbers of people can have a detrimental impact. Visitors are reminded to tread carefully and keep to the established paths. In addition, the limit of only twelve people ashore at any one time will help keep the whole site as natural and intact as possible.

This legacy, richly deserving of our respect, was admirably summarized by Wilson Duff and Michael Kew in their 1957 *Report of the Provincial Museum*:

> A few fragments of memory, a few bright glimpses in the writings of the past, some old and weathered totem-poles in a storage shed, and the mouldering remnants of once-magnificent carved post and houses on the site of the old village—these are all that survive of the tribe and village chiefs K'uuya and Ninstints. What was destroyed here was not just a few hundred individual human lives. Human beings must die anyway. It was something even more complex and even more human—a vigorous and functioning society, the product of just as long an evolution as our own, well suited to its environment and vital enough to participate in human cultural achievements not duplicated anywhere else. What was destroyed was one more bright tile in the complicated and wonderful mosaic of man's achievement on earth. Mankind is the loser. We are the losers.

GETTING THERE

SGang Gwaay (Anthony Island) is home to the famous Haida village of SGang Gwaay Llnagaay (Ninstints). The island sits 3 km
off the western end of Houston Stewart Channel, on the edge of
the Pacific Ocean. It is accessible only by boat. Please note that
the shore in front of the village is off limits to all boats; the landing site is a small cove on the north end of the island. A trail leads
through to the totem poles and house sites.

Camping is not allowed on the island. Also, all of the rocks
and islets surrounding SGang Gwaay are closed to visitors. Good
campsites exist at nearby Louscoone Point and within Louscoone Inlet, where there is also fresh water. A pipe is hooked up
to a buoy about halfway along the west side. Kayakers may want
to consider staying at these sites. If you camp in Houston Stewart
Channel, it is a challenge to tour SGang Gwaay and paddle both
ways in a day. Seasonal Haida Watchmen live on SGang Gwaay.
You are requested to radio ahead on VHF channel 6 to request
permission to come ashore.

FLY TO SGANG GWAAY

While visiting the islands, seeing an ancient Haida village is
a must. Large, open inflatables will transport adventurers to
Skedans and SGang Gwaay. If a boat trip is too long, consider
chartering a plane. Although a flight will cost more, you and
four others will be rewarded. Your aircraft will zip down to Rose
Harbour in under two hours allowing plenty of time to view the

village's many mortuary poles before heading home in time for dinner. The pilot will likely return on a different flight path giving you a first class view of the island tapestry a few hundred metres beneath your feet. This is also an ideal elevation to observe whales, sea lions, bears, eagles, and any number of watercraft. The flight will undoubtedly rank high on your list of great things you did on Haida Gwaii. For more information, call Inland Air at 1-888-624-2577.

PART 3

PLANNING YOUR TRIP

P REPARING FOR YOUR trip to Haida Gwaii should be an enjoyable and hopefully easy undertaking. This section includes
as much information as possible to help first-time or
returning visitors plan their excursion. If your plans include a
B&B, charter, or tour, we highly recommend making advance
reservations. Phoning, emailing, or investigating the websites
listed here will speed up this process. Haida Gwaii may seem off
the beaten track, but tours, charters, and accommodations can
still fill quickly. Keep in mind also that names, park regulations,
or facilities can change faster than a swimming salmon. Phone
ahead to avoid disappointment.

Some travellers prefer to go it alone, letting the tides and
weather set their day's agenda. Even so, it makes good sense to
have a contingency plan. Whether you're travelling by car, boat,
plane, or bike, this section has heaps of helpful suggestions
to keep you warm, dry, and on the right trail, hopefully with a
salmon or crab cooking over the fire.

3.1 OVERNIGHTING ON HAIDA GWAII

Overnight accommodation on the islands ranges from modern hotels and motels to bed-and-breakfast facilities and

simple campsites. These are located throughout the island communities.

The number of bed-and-breakfasts on Haida Gwaii has grown over the past decade, largely in response to tourist popularity. We have highlighted ten of them, and two fishing lodges, basing our selection on signage, the host's experience, quality of accommodation, special features, and atmosphere—all indicators that the operators are familiar with the islands and know how to cater to their guests.

The B&Bs listed here share several characteristics. All are close to a river or the ocean, offer comfortable rooms, and, in most cases, look out on magnificent views. In addition, their hosts can link you up to aerial tours, fishing charters, kayak rentals, or boat trips. Whatever you plan to do while you're on the islands, they'll help you make the right connections. Bear in mind that all these accommodations have a policy of no smoking indoors and will not normally accept pets. If you travel with a four-legged friend, be sure to mention this before making your reservation.

The fishing lodges featured here cater mostly to off-island fishers. Both have excellent facilities and do their best to make sure your fishing trip is memorable. One doubles as both a B&B and fishing lodge.

For additional information on motels, inns, and lodges, consult the annual *Accommodation Guide* or *Bed and Breakfast Directory* published by the BC Ministry of Tourism. Both guides (available free from any of the more than 140 visitor centres located throughout the province) list accommodations meeting preset standards.

The Village of Queen Charlotte Visitor Centre will also give you the most current listing of accommodations. They can be contacted at:

Copper Beech Guest House

PO Box 819, 3220 Wharf St.
Village of Queen Charlotte, BC V0T 1S0
PHONE 250-559-8316
FAX 250-559-8952
EMAIL info@gcinfo.ca
WEBSITE qcinfo.ca

BED & BREAKFASTS

Northern Graham Island
Copper Beech Guest House
HOST Susan Musgrave
ADDRESS PO Box 97, 1590 Delkatla
Masset, Haida Gwaii, BC V0T 1M0
PHONE 1-855-626-5441

FAX 1-250-626-5441

EMAIL cbh@copperbeechhouse.com

WEBSITE copperbeechhouse.com

UNITS 5

RATES $100–$140

FEATURES Copper Beech Guest House has a long history of entertaining visitors. For over twenty years, innumerable guests ranging from casual overnighters to Canadian prime ministers have nestled comfortably between the sheets in one of the eclectic rooms. While sipping your morning coffee, you can soak in the view of Masset Inlet, the beaches, and the boats moored in the quiet harbour.

Breakfast is "Off-the-Continental." It includes coffee, a selection of Murchie's teas, juice, fresh fruits, and wild berries in season. Homemade granola and yogurt, and a choice of breads, muffins, scones, or pastries will delight your morning palate. The menu also includes eggs, any style, plus crab, chanterelle, and goat cheese omelets in the summer months.

If you are literary minded, Susan would be pleased to assist you with any writing projects you have in mind or in progress. Contact her ahead of time to make arrangements for this additional service.

GUEST COMMENTS "Thank you so much for our visit. I place Copper Beech Guest House at the top of our near perfect vacation."

Eagles Feast House and Haida Gwaii Lodge

HOST April White, Haida Artist

ADDRESS PO Box 381, 2120 Harrison Ave. Masset, BC V0T 1M0

PHONE 250-626-6072 (local) or 1-877-485-7572 (info)

Eagles Feast House

EMAIL bothofus@eaglesfeast.com
WEBSITE eaglesfeast.com
UNITS 12
RATES $85–$175

FEATURES Staying in Masset will be further enhanced by special services such as WiFi, wheelchair accessibility, and accommodation of special dietary needs. Breakfasts can be simple to gourmet and, when possible, prepared using locally grown ingredients. The B&B doubles as a gallery featuring your host's art work.

In both Masset and Old Massett, many of the Graham Island's finest features are minutes or short drives away. Fishing charters, adventure tours, kayaking, the best beaches, Tow Hill, and Naikoon Park are just a few. You can also visit Haida studios, shops, carvers, and view contemporary poles throughout Old Massett.

Alaska View Lodge ALASKA VIEW LODGE

GUEST COMMENTS "We loved everything about our stay. A wonderful experience sharing your heritage and seeing your amazing art."

Alaska View Lodge

HOSTS Rick and Dana Bourne

ADDRESS Box 12291, Tow Hill Rd, Masset, BC V0T 1M0

PHONE 250-626-3333

TOLL FREE 1-800-661-0019

EMAIL alaskaview@langara.com

WEBSITE alaskaviewlodge.com

UNITS 6, plus 2 beach houses

RATES B&B: $125–$180; beach house: $250–$310

FEATURES Hot tub, satellite TV, bed and breakfast or all meals. Alaska View Lodge is sheltered by the lush rainforests of Naikoon Provincial Park, yet your picture window offers views of Dixon

Hiellen Longhouse Village

Entrance and distant Alaskan islands. In addition to top-rated accommodation, it offers world-class fishing in both fresh and salt water, beachcombing along dramatic coastlines, hiking through lush rainforests, tours by kayak and floatplane, and visits to Haida cultural sites and museums.

GUEST COMMENTS "We enjoyed our stay here immensely—the rolling surf, the long walks on the beach, agate searches (addictive) and the peace and quiet so difficult to find in Vancouver."

Hiellen Longhouse Village
HOST Patricia Moore
PO Box 175, Masset, BC VOT 1MO
PHONE 250-626-3337
TOLL FREE 1-888-378-4422
EMAIL hiellenlonghouses@gmail.com
WEBSITE haidalonghouses.ca

UNITS 7 cabins and 10 rooms in the longhouse

RATES $125 for cabins; longhouse rates upon request

FEATURES The Hiellen Longhouse Village features unique accommodation on Haida Gwaii. Situated on the edge of the Hiellen River and surrounded by a spruce and hemlock forest, you might imagine you are living in the past. The seven Haida-style cabins and longhouse are built on the site of a substantial Eagle and Raven Crest village.

Guests can stay in cabins, suitably equipped with fridge, stove, queen bed, and bunk, as well as an eating area for a family of four. Larger groups may prefer to stay in the longhouse featuring private rooms, a central kitchen, and a wood stove. Bedding is available upon request.

This small village is safely sheltered yet maintains a feeling of outdoor camping.

Southern Graham Island – Tlell to Village of Queen Charlotte

Riverside Lodging

HOST Margaret Condrotte

ADDRESS Box 89, Richardson Rd, Tlell, BC V0T 1Y0

PHONE 250-557-4418

TOLL FREE 1-888-853-5522

EMAIL margaret@qcislands.net

WEBSITE qcislands.net/margaret

UNITS 4

RATES $95 single; $110 for double

FEATURES You can't get much closer to the Tlell River without falling in. Perfect for anglers. Margaret welcomes visitors to her riverside accommodations, certain they will enjoy the

Riverside Lodging

peace and quiet of the Tlell area. The central location allows you to cast a line in the river, walk to nearby shops and galleries, or drive to Naikoon Provincial Park in just a few minutes. Adult oriented.

Self-contained rooms are all non-smoking, but each has access to a private balcony. A common kitchen is available for all guests to prepare their meals.

GUEST COMMENTS "Fantastic! Just like home, but better fishing."

Cäcilia's Bed and Breakfast

HOST Cäcilia Honisch

ADDRESS Box 3, Highway 16, Tlell, BC V0T 1Y0

PHONE/FAX 250-557-4664

EMAIL ceebysea@qcislands.net

UNITS 5

RATES $30–$50 per person

Cäcilia's Bed and Breakfast

FEATURES From this rustic log house or cabin nestled behind the dunes, 4 hectares of beachfront property await you. Bring your camera, paintbrush, or binoculars. There is room inside for larger groups if you plan a seminar, workshop, or meeting. They also offer a cedar steam sauna and massage, along with Ayurvedic spa treatments. Start your day with either muesli or waffles topped with your choice of huckleberry jam or real maple syrup. What a treat!

GUEST COMMENTS "Hospitality was superb. The best B&B we've been in since Britain. Wonderful atmosphere."

Chateau Norm
HOST Norman Wagner
ADDRESS 4112 Oceanview Drive
PO Box 92, Village of Queen Charlotte, BC V0T 1S0
PHONE 250-559-8455

Chateau Norm NORM WAGNER

EMAIL norm@chateaunorm.com
WEBSITE chateaunorm.com
UNITS 4
RATES $80–$200

FEATURES Loaded! Wireless internet, satellite TV, hot tub, pool table, bicycles and kayaks, and oceanfront fire pit. When it comes to oceanfront accommodation, it's hard to beat the view of Skidegate Inlet from Norm's front deck or dining room table. Read your book, munch on fresh crab caught right on the beach, or photograph eagles. On many summer afternoons, you will be treated to an eagle jamboree as the magnificent birds feast on fish left at the boat ramp, a mere 200 metres away. A fully stocked kitchen awaits you each morning before you set out on your day's adventure.

GUEST COMMENTS "A restful night. The eagles were a continuous treat. Comfortable, relaxed ... great!"

Spruce Point Lodge

Spruce Point Lodge

HOST Nancy Hett and Mary Kellie
ADDRESS Box 735, Village of Queen Charlotte, BC V0T 1S0
PHONE/FAX 250-559-8234
EMAIL sprpoint@qcislands.net
WEBSITE qcislands.net/sprpoint
UNITS 7
RATES $95–$120

FEATURES Great view of Skidegate Inlet. Onsite pottery shop, boat tours, kayak rentals, and fishing charters. All tours leave right from Spruce Point, whose location at the west end of the Village of Queen Charlotte offers a panoramic view of the inlet. Each room is self-contained, quiet, and comfortable. A full breakfast, including home baking, is delivered to your room each morning. Sip your coffee on the balcony, or relish your morning feast in the quiet of your room.

Dorothy and Mike's Guest House and Cottages MIKE GARRETT

GUEST COMMENTS "The room with the best view, and the best breakfast we've ever had. We will definitely be back."

Dorothy and Mike's Guest House and Cottages

HOSTS Dorothy and Mike Garrett

ADDRESS Box 595, 3125 2nd Ave

Village of Queen Charlotte, BC VOT ISO

PHONE/FAX 250-559-8439

EMAIL doromike@qcislands.net

WEBSITE qcislands.net/doromike

UNITS 7, plus 2 cottages

RATES $79–$125 (Kids under 12 stay free.)

FEATURES Relax on the deck overlooking the ocean, surrounded by flowers and forest. It would be hard not to enjoy this oasis in the middle of the Village of Queen Charlotte. Choose from queen or twin rooms or suites with private entrances and fully equipped

Seaport Bed & Breakfast MORESBY EXPLORERS

kitchens. You can look forward to complimentary coffee and tea served on the balcony overlooking Skidegate Inlet.

GUEST COMMENTS "This was a great respite from windy beaches—a wonderful place, and a great host. We will return."

Moresby Island

Seaport Bed & Breakfast

HOST Moresby Explorers

ADDRESS Box 127, 365 Beach Rd, Sandspit, BC V0T 1T0

PHONE 250-637-2215

TOLL FREE 1-800-806-7633

EMAIL info@moresbyexplorers.com

WEBSITE moresbyexplorers.com/seaport

UNITS 8 rooms

RATES $95–$150; off-season rates available

FEATURES A ten-minute walk to the airport, spectacular sunset view from the front deck, a local reference library and book exchange. Seaport Bed & Breakfast is a centrally located waterfront accommodation in Sandspit. Stay warm and cozy in rooms featuring a queen and twin bed in the main Seaport building, or in a queen bed in our rustic, self-contained studio cabin, making your choice of overnight stay as comfortable as possible. Begin each summer morning with a full homemade breakfast before relaxing on the large covered deck overlooking the bay.

GUEST COMMENTS "This place is practically brand new, with a beautiful view, friendly staff, great food, and a perfect launch spot for tours of Gwaii Haanas!"

FISHING LODGES

Naden Lodge

ADDRESS Box 648, 1496 Delkatla Rd, Masset, BC V0T 1M0
PHONE 250-626-3322
TOLL FREE 1-800-771-8933
EMAIL info@nadenlodge.com
WEBSITE nadenlodge.com
UNITS 6 bedrooms
RATES $4,700-$4,900 (3- to 4-day all-inclusive packages)

FEATURES When ocean fishing is on your agenda, Naden Lodge will have all the amenities you need for a memorable fishing trip at the northern end of Haida Gwaii. Naden Lodge, located along Masset's waterfront, is mere minutes from Masset Airport. Direct return flights from Calgary, or other major western Canadian centres, aboard a private aircraft are a part of the all-inclusive package.

Naden Lodge NADEN LODGE

Once you have settled in to your luxury room, get ready for some of the best salmon and halibut fishing in the world aboard one of the fully guided premium 27-foot Boston Whalers. Once your fishing day ends, a chef-prepared dinner and a relaxing evening await. The lodge features an extra large hot tub, pool table, and many other amenities. All meals, beverages, fish processing, shipping, and tackle are included in the package.

GUEST COMMENTS "You really looked after us while we stayed with you. We were your *guests*, not just some of the people staying at the lodge. I really appreciated that extra friendly touch the big lodges just don't have."

Kumdis River Lodge

HOST Bill Harrison

ADDRESS Box 419, Port Clements, BC V0T 1R0

Kumdis River Lodge KUMDIS RIVER LODGE

PHONE 250-557-4217
TOLL FREE 1-800-668-7544
EMAIL info@langara.com
WEBSITE langara.com
UNITS One cabin for up to 8 guests
RATES $3,095–$3,795 (3-, 4-, and 5-day all-inclusive packages)

FEATURES Bike and kayak rentals, heli-tours to remote island locations. Optional packages upon request.

Kumdis River Lodge offers a true get-away-from-it-all experience. Located on the historic site of Graham Centre, the lodge is tucked away by itself, hidden along the shoreline of Masset Inlet. From this home base you can fish numerous lakes, rivers, and estuaries for cutthroat, Dollies, and some of the best steelhead anywhere. All fishing packages include airfare from Vancouver, full meals, great accommodation, guides, equipment, and, of course, transportation to choice fishing spots.

GUEST COMMENTS "Wonderful environment. So peaceful. Well-stocked kitchen, a taste of huckleberries and then the hot tub!"

CAMPGROUNDS

Numerous private, provincial, and forestry campgrounds are located throughout the two largest islands. Most are listed below. Forest recreation sites are free. Fees are collected seasonally at provincial sites, but year-round at private sites. Although there are no organized campsites within the Gwaii Haanas area, fees are still collected in advance for both day use or extended trips.

If you intend to travel within Gwaii Haanas for longer than a day, you can choose your own site in most places. Any beach that looks suitable can be used as a campsite, except those in sensitive cultural or bird-nesting areas. Camping is not allowed on SGang Gwaay (Anthony Island), Gandll K'in Gwaay.yaay (Hotspring Island), House, Rankine, East Copper, Bolkus, and Slug Islands, or at Cumshewa, K'uuna Llnagaay (Skedans) and T'aanuu Llnagaay (Tanu) village sites. Burnaby Narrows is also closed due to the high possibility of interacting with the local black bear population. Each year the park reserve has seasonal or sporadic closures which visitors are informed of at their orientation. Be sure to ask at the Gwaii Haanas orientation for closures in other, less well-known areas.

Where there are no services, backcountry campsite etiquette naturally applies: pack out your garbage, bury all sewage below high tide, light fires below the high-tide line and leave your site

Camping on a beach is free, but there are no services. Leave your campsite at least as clean as when you arrived.

as clean or cleaner than you found it. Only your footprints should give away your overnight location!

Graham Island

Tlell area north to Masset and Tow Hill

Agate Beach Campground
(Naikoon Park, north end)

LOCATION 25 km east of Masset

SITES 39

OPEN Year round

AMENITIES Tap water, kitchen shelter with wood stove, outdoor toilets, picnic tables, tent pads, RV accessible

FEES Fees apply May through September

SPECIAL FEATURES All sites are beachfront with world-class view. Bakery nearby operates during summer season.

Misty Meadow Campground (Naikoon Park, south end)

LOCATION At Tlell, 42 km north of the Skidegate Landing ferry dock and 21 km south of Port Clements

SITES 40

OPEN Year round

AMENITIES Tap water, kitchen shelter with wood stove, outdoor toilets, picnic tables, tent pads, RV accessible

FEES Fees apply May through September

SPECIAL FEATURES Beach is minutes away via a wheelchair-accessible trail. Artisans, restaurant, and grocery store nearby.

Hidden Island RV and Resort

LOCATION Tow Hill Road, about 0.5 km east of Masset causeway

SITES 22

OPEN Year round

AMENITIES Tap water, flush toilets, picnic tables, tent pads, full RV hookups, coin operated laundry and showers, internet, cable TV, phone, firewood

FEES Daily fees collected at the office. Reservations accepted. For more information: 1-250-626-5286

TOLL FREE 1-866-303-5286

EMAIL info@hidden-island-resort.ca

WEBSITE hidden-island-resort.ca

SPECIAL FEATURES This centrally located campsite is perfect for fishers, photographers, and those wanting more comfortable amenities. Restaurants and grocery stores are nearby in Masset.

Sunset RV and Camping Park

LOCATION 2 km west of Port Clements along Bayview Drive

SITES 10

OPEN May through October

AMENITIES Tap water, gazebo shelter, outdoor toilets, picnic tables, 4 tent pads, 6 RV sites with 30 amp service, sani-station nearby, firewood

FEES An attendant collects fees daily.

PHONE 250-557-4295

WEBSITE portclements.ca

SPECIAL FEATURES Wheelchair accessible, viewing tower and an ocean-view walking path. Restaurants, grocery store, pub, fuel, and tourist info are nearby.

Graham Island
Village of Queen Charlotte
through to Rennell Sound

Hayden Turner
Community Campground

LOCATION 1.8 km west of the elementary/secondary school in the Village of Queen Charlotte

SITES 8

OPEN Year round

AMENITIES Tap water, outdoor toilets, flush toilets, picnic tables, 2 tent pads, 6 RV sites

FEES Self-registration; reservations not accepted.

PHONE 250-559-8122

SPECIAL FEATURES Ocean views a minute away, close to stores, shopping, marina, fuel, and hospital.

Kagan Bay Recreation Site

LOCATION 5.2 km west of the elementary/secondary school in the Village of Queen Charlotte along a gravel road

SITES 6

OPEN Year round

AMENITIES Outdoor toilets, picnic tables

FEES Free

SPECIAL FEATURES Ocean views

RECOMMENDATION Fill drinking water containers in the Village of Queen Charlotte.

Rennell Sound
(Duu Guusd Heritage Site/Conservancy)

LOCATION 35 km west of the Village of Queen Charlotte or approximately 51 km south of Port Clements via the Queen Charlotte Mainline

SITES 7 at Rennell Sound Recreation Site; 2 at Cone Head Recreation Site; open tenting on Bonanza and Gregory Beaches

OPEN Year round

AMENITIES Picnic tables, outdoor toilets, fire pits, and beach firewood

FEES Free

RECOMMENDATION Fill drinking water containers in the Village of Queen Charlotte or Port Clements.

The Bunkhouse
Campground Resort

LOCATION Corner of Third Ave. and Tenth St. in the Village of Queen Charlotte

SITES 16

OPEN Year round

AMENITIES Showers, flush toilets, laundry, pet friendly, WiFi, and wheelchair access

FEES Collected at the office

PHONE 206-259-6013

501 RV Tent Park

LOCATION Beach Road, the main road entering Sandspit

ADDRESS Box 107, 501-503 Beach Road, Sandspit, BC V0T 1T0

SITES 15

OPEN Year round

AMENITIES Tap water, full hookups, sani-station, flush toilets, picnic tables, tent pads, coin operated laundry and showers, fridge, and freezer. A small craft harbour is nearby.

FEES Fees collected at the office; reservations accepted.

PHONE 250-637-5473

EMAIL 1rvpark@telus.net

Gray Bay Recreation Site
(Kunxalas Heritage Site/Conservancy)

LOCATION Drive 19 km south of Sandspit on Copper Bay Road. Turn left onto Spur 20. Continue for 7 km to Gray Bay.

SITES 20

OPEN Year round

AMENITIES Kitchen shelter, outdoor toilets, picnic tables, tent pads; each site has beach access.

FEES Free

RECOMMENDATION Fill drinking water containers before leaving Sandspit or the Village of Queen Charlotte.

Sheldon's Bay Recreation Site
(Kunxalas Heritage Site/Conservancy)

LOCATION Drive 19 km south of Sandspit on Copper Bay Road. Turn left onto Spur 20. Continue for 3.6 km then turn left on another spur. Continue 7.6 km to Sheldon's Bay.

SITES 4

OPEN Year round

AMENITIES Outdoor toilets, picnic tables, tent pads

FEES Free

RECOMMENDATION Fill drinking water containers before leaving Sandspit or the Village of Queen Charlotte.

Mosquito Lake Recreation Site

LOCATION After departing the ferry at Alliford Bay, make an immediate right turn and drive approximately 17 km following Beach Main and Alliford Bay Main to a large intersection. Turn right again. Mosquito Lake is 6.7 km along this road. A longer, alternative is to drive 19 km south from Sandspit on Copper Bay Road. At spur 20, keep right and continue an additional 16 km to a large intersection. Turn left and continue 6.7 km to Mosquito Lake.

SITES 11

OPEN Year round

AMENITIES Kitchen shelter, outdoor toilets, picnic tables. A small boat launch allows for fishing or paddling on the lake.

FEES Free

RECOMMENDATION Fill drinking water containers before leaving Sandspit or the Village of Queen Charlotte.

Moresby Camp Recreation Site

LOCATION After departing the ferry at Alliford Bay, make an immediate right turn and drive approximately 17 km following Beach Main and Alliford Bay Main to a large intersection. Turn right again. Moresby Camp is a farther 10.8 km. A longer, alternative is to drive 19 km south from Sandspit on Copper Bay Road. At spur 20, keep right and continue an additional 16 km to a large intersection. Turn left and continue 10.8 km to Moresby Camp.

SITES 6

OPEN Year round

AMENITIES Kitchen shelter, outdoor toilets, picnic tables. Concrete boat ramp and dock suitable to launch any trailerable watercraft.

FEES Free

RECOMMENDATION Fill drinking water containers before leaving Sandspit or the Village of Queen Charlotte.

3.2 GWAII HAANAS NATIONAL PARK RESERVE—RESERVATIONS AND ORIENTATION

Visitors planning a visit to Gwaii Haanas or K'uuna Llnagaay (Skedans) independently must make advance reservations. You can do this by calling the Gwaii Haanas office directly at 250-559-8818 or toll free at 877-559-8818. Bookings are generally made after April 1. Part of your booking includes a mandatory orientation, which must be completed prior to entering the park reserve.

If you plan on travelling with a licensed tour company, the reservation and orientation should be included as part of your package. We suggest confirming this with the operators early in your planning stages.

In the past, some people have arrived in Haida Gwaii and suddenly decided to travel into Gwaii Haanas. If the visitor quotas for that particular time are low, it is possible to take the orientation session and leave directly for the park reserve. For peace of mind and to avoid disappointment, it would be much better to think ahead. Parks Canada staff highly recommends planning well and preparing in advance.

The free orientation session lasts about ninety minutes. Presenters will show an informative movie and provide current information on travel, safety, natural, and human history. If visitors plan on returning to the park in subsequent years, Parks Canada requires you to repeat the orientation session. This might seem redundant but campsite locations, regulations, closures, and the latest safety information can change monthly. It is best to be well informed before heading into this unserviced wilderness area.

Boaters entering Gwaii Haanas must also make advance reservations. Call the Gwaii Haanas office well in advance of your intended visit. An orientation package can be mailed to you if you are not visiting any island communities prior to entering the park reserve.

Scheduled times for orientations at the Haida Heritage Centre:
Before June 1: Monday to Friday, by appointment; 48 hours' notice
June 1 to end of August: Monday to Friday, 9:00 a.m.
July 1 to mid-August: also Saturdays, 9:00 a.m.
After September 1: Monday to Friday, by appointment; 48 hours' notice

Orientations may be booked outside of scheduled times, but within normal working hours. Gwaii Haanas staff will try to accommodate you, provided they have at least forty-eight hours' notice and available staff. Sessions scheduled outside of normal hours cost $78.50. Orientation sessions may also be held at the Sandspit Airport by special booking with at least forty-eight hours' notice.

When making plane or ferry reservations, plan to arrive twenty-four hours prior to your departure for Gwaii Haanas to be certain you have time to attend an orientation session. Fees apply for all visitors to Gwaii Haanas. They are based on either a daily or seasonal time limit. If you plan on staying longer than six days in the park reserve, you will save money by purchasing a seasonal pass. Fees are also assessed differently for seniors, youth, and groups. To find the exact costs for your expedition, phone the park office or access the reserve website listed below. Should you be travelling with a tour company, double check to see if fees are included in the company's price.

Reservations, orientation sessions, and fees may change with little advance notice. We suggest you visit the park office or call the following numbers to get accurate, up-to-the-minute information.

Gwaii Haanas National Park Reserve and Haida Heritage Site
Haida Heritage Centre
60 Second Beach Road, Skidegate, BC V0T 1S0
Phone: 250-559-8818
Fax: 250-559-8366
Toll Free: 1-877-559-8818
Email: gwaii.haanas@pc.gc.ca
Website: pc.gc.ca/gwaiihaanas

PERMITS FOR HAIDA RESERVES

You must obtain permission from the appropriate band office before entering ancient Haida villages. The village council office in Old Massett governs sites on northern Graham Island; phone 250-626-3337 or fax 250-626-5440. The Gwaii Haanas National Park Reserve, National Marine Conservation Area Reserve and Haida Heritage Site administers most villages in the southern parts of the islands. It can be reached at 250-559-8818. The Haida Gwaii

Watchmen Program monitors villages outside of Gwaii Haanas and can be reached at 250-559-8225 or by email (watchmen @skidegate.ca).

3.3 CHARTERING AND TOURS

Visitors who want to explore isolated areas may need to charter a plane, helicopter, or boat to help take them to their destination. Many charter flights are full or half-day trips down to Skungwaii or along the wild, west coast. If you have your own kayak a one-way charter is worth considering. You can paddle in one direction and arrange to have a larger craft transport you and your party for the other portion. Split among a group, chartering is relatively inexpensive.

FLYING

Chartering an aircraft is a fairly simple task. First, decide where you want to go and how many others will be accompanying you. Next, pick your first and second choices for travel dates. You may have to be flexible as weather can cause delays or even cancellations. Finally, contact the airline company, outline your proposed agenda, and let them do the rest.

Be aware, however, that charter rates are set by the hour or the distance flown. If possible, try to fill the aircraft so as to make individual costs as low as possible. Expect additional charges for any landings en route to your final destination. It might be cheaper if your pilot can pick up a second party for the return flight rather than flying back empty. On flights to SGang Gwaay Llnagaay via Rose Harbour, however, the pilot will likely wait for you to return from your excursion ashore.

De Havilland Beavers are the most common fixed wing aircraft on Haida Gwaii. They can carry five passengers with small day packs or four passengers and extra gear. If you have extra

Fixed-wing aircraft and helicopters service the islands and connect with Prince Rupert and Vancouver.

items to transport, weigh everything in advance to allow the airlines to accommodate your needs.

Helicopters (also chartered on an hourly rate) can't carry such heavy loads, but can get you into places where fixed-wing craft can't land. The company at Sandspit usually has fixed tour itineraries and prices. Helicopters are great for a short flight but keep in mind you will be restricted to the amount of gear you can take with you. Nevertheless, what a great way to fly!

Keep in mind a few additional things when planning your flight. There are restrictions as to where aircraft can land in the Gwaii Haanas reserve area. For instance, aircraft are not permitted to land at cultural sites such as SG̱ang Gwaay Llnagaay but can touch down in nearby Rose Harbour or Louscoone Inlet. Also if weather permits, your pilot may be able to fly a different return route, making your flight doubly exciting as you may view a

Several companies offer regular tours throughout Haida Gwaii. Some operate off of a mother ship or floating lodge. JIM THORNE

completely different landscape unfolding beneath your feet. Have your camera ready to go before liftoff, and you'll be rewarded with some terrific aerial photos.

BOATING

Chartering a boat to go fishing, scuba diving, or touring for the day is a relatively simple and safe venture. Numerous islanders specialize in this service. Some have been guiding for years; others not so long. Increased tourism has resulted in improved service over the years, but you should still shop around and compare what you get with what you pay.

For both fishing charters and adventure tours, inspect your prospective vessel beforehand, noting safety equipment and level of maintenance. Ask how long the owners have been in business and how familiar they are with the waters surrounding Haida Gwaii. It's also worthwhile to find out whether the company is insured and under what conditions a refund would be granted.

Those wishing to tackle a scrappy coho or monster halibut will need a fishing licence. Ask your guide if they issue them or where you can get one easily. Guides provide you with a rod and reel, but we suggest you inquire about extras such as rain gear, food, and refreshments. You should also ask about having your fish processed and sent on to a desired location. If you want to take a side trip—perhaps to an old village site—you will need to make this arrangement ahead of time. Your guide may need to get permits in order to go ashore at ancient Haida sites.

Adventurers wanting to transport their kayaks, zodiacs, and related gear to locations such as the west coast or Gwaii Haanas may require a longer charter. If you or your group need an extended trip, ask whether food costs are included, who prepares the meals, and what kind of menu can be expected. In one of our charters, there was an "extra" passenger aboard, which was not made known to us. This made a difference when it came to sleeping arrangements. We also needed to make an additional stop to stash food and fuel before reaching Rose Harbour. Fortunately, we made this request to our skipper ahead of time. He helped us pick our hideaway and, upon arrival, we quickly paddled ashore with little wasted time.

Another option, especially for kayakers, is to have your boat and gear transported to a starting point. From there, you can make the return trip at a leisurely pace fully exploring the islands, bays, and shorelines. Yet another choice is book with companies that have float houses or mother ships. This allows for the maximum amount of paddling and assures a comfortable bed each night.

Many visitors make reservations with a tour company for a few days, a week, or even longer. Several commercial enterprises, both on and off Haida Gwaii, lead tours throughout the islands every summer. If possible, request the company's literature before booking. In addition to the questions noted above, ask whether expert guides will be along, what the guide-to-participant ratio is, and what your sleeping quarters will be like. Unexpectedly having to share a cabin with a fellow shipmate may result in unwanted stress.

We recommend you first contact the Visitor Centre in the Village of Queen Charlotte. They will have a current list of who is leading both fishing charters and adventure tours. They can be reached by phone at 250-559-8316. You can also visit their website, qcinfo.ca, and follow the links to fishing and diving charters, or land tours and adventures. Travel agents, major newspapers, and outdoor magazines often list Haida Gwaii fishing and adventure tours.

Adventure holidays aboard a chartered vessel can provide a memorable lifetime experience. But remember: you'll be further ahead if you check your options long before you check your bags!

TRANSPORTATION AND TRAVEL

On the Water

BC Ferries' MV *Northern Adventure* and MV *Northern Expedition* (winter only) make scheduled crossings between Prince Rupert and Skidegate Landing. The trip takes six to eight hours, depending on marine conditions and time of day. Night crossings are usually longer. There are staterooms, dayrooms, a cafeteria, and lounges onboard. The ship docks at Skidegate Landing on Graham Island. At the same location, a smaller, open-deck ferry, MV *Kwuna*, shuttles vehicles back and forth between Graham and Moresby Island. A schedule is posted at both landings.

A water taxi crosses Skidegate Inlet after ferry hours. Kayak rentals are available at Spruce Point Lodge. (See "Bed and Breakfasts," page 204.)

BC Ferries
For reservations, call toll free from anywhere in North America: 1-888-223-3779
Email: customerservice@bcferries.com
Website: bcferries.com

In the Air

Three companies provide scheduled service from Vancouver to Haida Gwaii. There is a regular floatplane service from Prince Rupert that serves Masset. The same company offers fixed wing service to inter-island locations. One helicopter company is based at Sandspit Airport.

Vancouver to Haida Gwaii (serving Sandspit Airport)
Air Canada Jazz
1-888-247-2262
Website: flyjazz.com

Vancouver to Haida Gwaii (serving Masset Airport)
Pacific Coastal Airlines
1-800-663-2872
Website: pacificcoastal.com

Prince Rupert to Haida Gwaii (serving Masset airport)
Inland Air Charters Ltd.
PO Box 592, Prince Rupert, BC V8J 3R5

Seal Cove Seaplane base, Prince Rupert
Toll Free: 1-888-624-2577
Local telephone: 250-624-2577; Fax: 250-627-1356
Email: info@inlandair.bc.ca
Website: inlandair.bc.ca

Serving inter-island locations
Inland Air Charters Ltd.
PO Box 592, Prince Rupert, BC V8J 3R5
Seal Cove Seaplane base, Prince Rupert
Toll Free: 1-888-624-2577
Local telephone: 250-624-2577; Fax: 250-627-1356
Email: info@inlandair.bc.ca
Website: inlandair.bc.ca

Helijet Charters
PO Box 333, Sandspit, BC V0T 1T0
Phone: 250-637-5344
Toll-Free: 1-877-569-4354
Email: ascott@helijet.com
Website: helijet.com

On Land

A minivan meets all scheduled flights at Sandspit and transports passengers between the airport and the Village of Queen Charlotte. Cars and trucks can be rented in Sandspit, the Village of Queen Charlotte, and Masset. Taxis are available in the Village of Queen Charlotte and Masset.

Hitchhikers usually succeed in getting a ride on most paved roads. On logging roads, you had better keep a book handy. Reaching some of the locations described in this book means travelling on private, gravel-surface back roads owned by logging companies. These all-weather roads are usually well maintained and open to the public. Information on logging activity and company maps can be obtained from their local offices.

For the latest information on roads, maps, tours, or active logging areas, contact:

Ministry of Forests, Lands and Natural Resource Operations
1229 Oceanview Drive
Queen Charlotte City, BC
Mail: Box 39 Queen Charlotte City, BC VOT 1S0
Phone: 250-559-6200
Toll Free: 1-800-663-7867
Fax: 250-559-8342
Email: Forests.QueenCharlotteDistrictOffice@gov.bc.ca
Website: for.gov.bc.ca/dqc

or

Taan Forest
Tours and logging information (Graham Island)
Phone: 250-559-2337
Email: info@taanforest.com
Website: taanforest.com

After obtaining information about active working areas and any road access restrictions, follow the instructions carefully. Off-highway trucks carry loads larger than those hauled by most semi-trailers. Unexpectedly meeting a loaded logging truck on a tight curve can be a heart-thumping experience. Always drive with your headlights on, follow directional signs, and be aware that road conditions and traffic may change with little warning.

3.4 NAVIGATION AND SAFETY

The sea poses a constant challenge to all boaters, regardless of the size of vessel you're travelling in. Wind is usually considered to be the greatest hazard: it can come up suddenly, blow powerfully, and not die down for days. Waves, swells, tides, and currents may also present challenges, particularly if you are forced to paddle or motor against them. The best rule of marine safety is to obtain the latest weather information, equip yourself with charts, VHF radio, GPS, and onboard survival gear, then be prepared for anything.

A wise first step is to obtain a portable VHF radio, readily available in marine supply or electronics shops. For safety, emergencies, and convenience, anyone travelling into Gwaii Haanas or other remote parts of the islands should be equipped with one. Before starting your trip, become familiar with how to use it to both receive and transmit. In addition to using it to obtain regular weather reports, you can use the radio in an emergency to contact the Coast Guard, or nearby mariners, on channel 16. You will also need one to contact Haida Watchmen before landing at villages or other cultural locations where they are posted.

Some people like to carry an altimeter—a barometer that indicates changes in atmospheric pressure. For reference purposes, the pressure at the centre of a very deep low will be about 950 millibars (mb). The centre of a very strong high will read about 1035 mb.

Before launching our boat, we always check to make sure our marine charts are with us. Unlike topographic maps, marine charts mark navigational aids, current flows, and marine hazards. They measure depths in fathoms, which will assist in finding suitable anchorages. Depths are recorded during tidal lows, enabling predictable passage through shallow areas. These charts are indispensable—don't leave the shore without them!

Tide tables are just as important as charts. Published annually by the Department of Fisheries and Oceans, they list the height and time of high and low tides each day. There are several monitoring stations on Haida Gwaii, all of which can be found online at tides.gc.ca. In enclosed waterways such as Masset Inlet, tides are later than along the open coast. Be sure take into account Pacific Daylight Saving Time, in effect from March through October. If you wish to buy tide tables or charts before arriving on the islands, virtually any marina or fishing store will be able to serve your needs.

We further recommend you obtain a copy of *Exploring the North Coast of British Columbia,* by Don Douglass. For boaters unfamiliar with the islands, this book provides detailed maritime information for the most visited areas of southern Haida Gwaii. *Boat Camping Haida Gwaii,* by Neil Frazer, goes one step further by covering many marine locations around Graham and Moresby Island. His main focus is pointing out camping spots for kayakers and small boaters, but he also includes helpful navigation and safety information.

Even if visitors in small boats plan to stay within the protected channels of Moresby Island, they should always bring along extra supplies in the event they find themselves wet, weather-bound, or exhausted. Extra food and clothing alone can be a lifesaver; either for you or some unfortunate fellow explorers.

Before heading into remote areas, it is advisable to file a sail plan with a reliable family member or friend. If you miss your return date, it is nice to know that someone will be watching for you and can contact the Coast Guard on your behalf. The Coast Guard can be reached by calling 1-800-567-5111. Be certain to contact your family or friends immediately upon your return, or you may cause much grief, not to mention unnecessary search-and-rescue costs.

Tide tables and charts are available in most sporting goods and marine supply stores, on the Internet or can be ordered from:

Canadian Hydrographic Service,
Chart Distribution & Sales
Box 6000, Sidney, BC V8L 4B2
Phone: 250-356-6358
Fax: 250-363-6841
Email: chartsales@pac.dfo-mpo.gc.ca

The marine chart reference numbers for the marine areas mentioned in this book are as follows:

Masset Area
Dixon Entrance 3802
Masset Sound and Inlet 3805
Plans–Dixon Entrance 3895
Port Luis to Langara Island 3868
Masset Harbour and Naden Harbour 3892

Skidegate Area
Skidegate Inlet and Channel 3806
Skidegate Channel to Tain Rock (Rennell Sound) 3869

Gwaii Haanas National Park

Reserve and Haida Heritage Site

Cape St. James/Cumshewa Inlet/Tasu Sound* 3853

Houston Stewart Channel 3855

Juan Perez Sound 3808

Carpenter Bay–Burnaby Island 3809

Houston Stewart Channel/Cape St. James 3825

Lawn Hill–Selwyn Inlet 3894

Atli Inlet–Selwyn Inlet 3807

This chart is helpful but inadequate for navigation purposes as the scale is too small.

3.5 CLIMATE AND CLOTHING

The climate of Haida Gwaii is extremely variable. The Queen Charlotte Mountains attain elevations of 1,050 metres—high enough to disrupt tumultuous storm clouds driven in by offshore winds. Coastal areas near the mountains can be particularly windy and wet, while just a few kilometres inland the wind tapers off, the air temperature rises and rainfall is significantly less. This rain-shadow effect is most noticeable on Graham Island, disappearing altogether where the land narrows toward southern Moresby Island. Less than 1 percent of Canada experiences this unusual blend of oceanic storms, cloudy skies, cool summers, and relatively mild, wet winters.

Overall, weather on the islands has two patterns. From mid-May until September, prevailing winds blow from the northwest. In late September, a new system begins to form in the Gulf of Alaska, and the wind blows from the southeast for the rest of winter. Storms are worst from October to January. Cape St. James, the windiest place in Canada, bears the brunt of this force (average wind speed over the past twenty-six years has been 37.7 kilometres per hour).

Rainfall measurements here do not set national records but they are impressive. The average annual precipitation of 4,218 millimetres at Tasu on the west coast makes it the wettest spot on Haida Gwaii. The east-coast communities overall receive less than a quarter of the rain that the west coast experiences. May, June, and July are the driest months. Tlell and Sandspit are recorded as the driest (and the warmest) places on the islands.

Although we encountered some weird weather on some of our summer trips to Haida Gwaii, it was nothing we couldn't handle. In anticipation of at least one rainy day, a rain jacket with a hood was always included. We also packed toques, gloves, and pullover fleeces, which occasionally came in handy. Rubber boots, intended for beach and bog walks, were appreciated if it rained when we were camping. Numerous residents told us, "If you don't like the weather, then wait five minutes and it will change." This proved correct on most of our trips.

COMMUNITIES AND FACILITIES

There are eight communities on the islands today: Old Massett, Masset, Port Clements, Tlell, Skidegate, Skidegate Landing, the Village of Queen Charlotte on Graham Island, and Sandspit on Moresby Island. If you're not travelling with an organized tour, most of the things you might need are available in one or more of these communities. Prices are naturally higher than they might be back home. In fairness, however, a day on Haida Gwaii will probably cost you a lot less than a day at West Edmonton Mall.

Local businesses welcome the influx of tourists, but their variety and quantity of supplies are limited by shipping costs and retail space. If you can't find what you're looking for, don't be afraid to ask. Some stores and attractions lack signage, because the people who live here know where things are.

Facilities in Each Community

Old Massett

- Gift and artist shops
- Village office
- Automotive fuel
- Internet café
- Convenience store

Masset

- Scheduled seaplane service daily
- Vehicle rentals and taxi service
- Marine and automotive fuels, parts, and services
- Government pier and floats
- Boat ramp at sea-plane base
- Motel, cabin, and B&B accommodation
- RV park with showers and hookups
- Sani-dump and car wash at Visitor Centre
- Restaurants, pub, and grocery stores
- Laundromat, pharmacy, liquor store, and credit union
- Hospital and public health nurse
- Royal Canadian Mounted Police
- Nine-hole golf course
- Fishing guides, licences, and tackle
- Airport
- Library
- Maritime Museum
- Royal Canadian Legion

- Delkatla Interpretive Centre
- Sightseeing and cultural tours
- Indoor swimming pool

Port Clements

- Automotive fuels and parts
- Government pier and float, boat ramp
- Motel with laundromat
- Sani-station
- Grocery store with liquor sales
- Licensed restaurant and pub
- B&B
- Gift shops
- Post office
- Library
- Pioneer and logging museum
- Campground and interpretive trail, wildlife viewing

Tlell

- Provincial park campground and headquarters
- Lodge, B&B
- Takeout restaurant
- Laundromat
- Post office, fishing licences
- Gift and craft shops, farm and country store

Skidegate Area

- Scheduled ferry service
- Water and road taxi service
- Boat ramp and boat charters
- Automotive fuels
- B&B
- Grocery store, ATM, marine and fishing supplies
- Haida Heritage Centre
- Sightseeing and cultural tours

- Gift and artist shops
- Village of Queen Charlotte
- Vehicle rentals
- Taxi service
- Automotive fuels, parts, and service
- Government wharf and floats
- Hotel, motel, and B&B
- Campgrounds
- Restaurants and grocery stores
- Laundromat, pharmacy, liquor store, ATM, and credit union
- Hospital and public health nurse
- Royal Canadian Mounted Police
- Boat charters and rentals
- Gift shops
- Travel agent
- Library
- Provincial and federal government offices
- Seaplane charters

Sandspit

- Airport with scheduled daily flights and charters
- Helicopter and seaplane charters
- Vehicle rental, fuel, and parts
- Small-craft harbour
- Government pier and boat ramp
- Hotel, motel, lodge, and B&B accommodation
- RV park
- Restaurants and lounge
- Grocery stores, one with liquor sales
- Outdoor supplies and licences
- Hunting and fishing guides
- Nine-hole golf course
- Library
- Health clinic

Emergency Services

In case of emergency, here are the phone numbers for the police, the hospitals on the islands, and the Coast Guard station in Prince Rupert.

RCMP

Masset area and Port Clements: 250-626-3991

Village of Queen Charlotte and Sandspit: 250-559-4421

HOSPITALS

Masset: 250-626-4700; emergency: 250-626-4711

Village of Queen Charlotte: 250-559-4300;

emergency: 250-559-4506

Sandspit Clinic: 250-637-5403

PRINCE RUPERT COAST GUARD

Air and marine emergencies: 1-800-567-5111

3.6 THE SIX-DAY GUIDE

Faced with so many intriguing options, tourists with a limited amount of time can be a bit overwhelmed trying to figure out how to make the most of their visit. One of the most frequent questions we hear from people planning their first trip to Haida Gwaii is, "Where should we go?" This day planner provides an overall perspective of the shops, sights, beaches, restaurants, and accommodation. On your second visit, you will no doubt head straight for a favoured location. This planner assumes you will have six full days, are travelling in a motorized vehicle, and are either camping or staying in a B&B.

Disembark from the ferry and drive to either Misty Meadows Campground or a B&B near Tlell.

First morning: Hike to *Pesuta* shipwreck or take the beach walk from Misty Meadows Campground. Afternoon: Visit nearby gift and artisan shops.

Second morning: Tour Old Massett and Masset. Be sure to visit Haida gift shops and view poles in Old Massett. Afternoon: Drive to Agate Beach Campground and Tow Hill. Hike to the top of Tow Hill.

Third morning: Drive to Skidegate Landing, take the ferry to Alliford Bay and Sandspit. Walk the short trail to Onward Point. Later, allow some time to view the displays in the Sandspit Airport. If you have additional time and a suitable vehicle, drive on to Gray Bay and perhaps Moresby Camp. Check the ferry schedule at Alliford Bay and arrive at least thirty minutes prior to departure.

Fourth morning: Drive to the Village of Queen Charlotte. Walk along the waterfront pathway, stop in at the visitors' centre, peruse the shops, and rest your feet in a café or restaurant. In the afternoon, drive to nearby Skidegate Village. Allow two to three hours at the Haida Heritage Centre. If you still feel energetic, hike the Spirit Lake Trail, which begins at the northern edge of Skidegate Village.

Fifth morning: Head north to Port Clements and view the old blank canoe and old-growth forest trail. Also drop by the pioneer museum or visit Sunset RV and Camping Park and look for birds from the viewing tower or walk the campground trail. In the afternoon, tour Delkatla Wildlife Sanctuary in Masset. Before settling on the beach for a picnic dinner, drop by the Maritime Museum at the north end of Masset.

Sixth morning: If your ferry departs in the evening, consider scheduling a visit to Rennell Sound. This will be your only glimpse of the west coast. Allow at least five hours for the round trip, especially if you do some beach explorations. BC Ferries prefers vehicles and passengers to arrive at the ferry terminal at least sixty minutes prior to departure.

If you visit Haida Gwaii during the months of May, June, and July, there will be an opportunity to volunteer at a semi-remote marine research station. It provides a special opportunity to monitor birds and mammals living around the islands.
LASKEEK BAY CONSERVATION SOCIETY

PART 4

A NATURAL HISTORY
OF HAIDA GWAII

T HE UNUSUAL NATURAL history of Haida Gwaii, not to mention its promise of superlative outdoor recreation, has made these islands one of Canada's most desirable adventure-travel destinations. Provincial, national, and international designation of reserves to protect landscapes and heritage sites as well as various species and their habitats has ensured the preservation of this region's many special attributes.

The islands' distance from the mainland has restricted the natural influx of animals and plants. As a result, the islands have significantly fewer species than the mainland. There are, however, many endemic subspecies of birds, mammals, fish, and invertebrates. At one time these islands even supported a subspecies of caribou that, tragically, is now extinct. Several species of insects are found only here, and more unique species may be discovered as research continues.

When it comes to plants, there are a dozen species unique to Haida Gwaii. Not surprisingly in this moist climate, many are mosses. Another two dozen plants provide examples of disjunctive populations—that is, species separated from their relatives by great distances. For example, some local specimens are associated with species normally found in Japan, other parts of Asia, and

Scotland. Possibly they found refuge on an unglaciated part of the islands during the ice age.

Such ecological oddities have led to promotion of the islands as the "Galapagos of Canada." This is a reference to the Galapagos Islands, off the coast of Ecuador, which are famous for the evolutionary distinctions of their wildlife, originally studied by Charles Darwin. Biological parallels between Haida Gwaii and the Galapagos are evident, as they are on any isolated islands. For the most part, however, we feel the phrase works better in promotion than in application, because it creates a distorted expectation of the wildlife to be encountered. That said, knowledgeable birders, botanists, nature photographers, and other enthusiasts will be delighted with what they can find here. You can enhance your pleasure by doing some reading before your arrival. *Islands at the Edge: Preserving the Queen Charlotte Islands Wilderness*, by the Island Protection Society, is an excellent introduction to the outstanding natural history of these islands. Unfortunately, the publisher no longer lists this book. If you can't locate it with a used bookseller, a very good alternative is to visit haidagwaiibirds.com. This website is maintained by long-time residents Peter Hamel and Margo Hearne. You will find nicely written accounts of birding and other natural history topics organized month by month. (See also "Their Place to Be.")

4.1 BIRDS

Haida Gwaii has some of the richest islands for bird study in Canada. Millions of birds visit or nest around the archipelago every year, although the number of species to be found here is actually less than on the adjacent mainland. (Remote islands predictably have fewer species.) Today, over 300 species had been recorded on Haida Gwaii, compared to more than 480 throughout BC. Similarly, of about 300 species that breed in BC, only 77 breed here.

Pigeon guillemots are almost all black with bright red legs. Look for them around docks, old pilings, and while crossing inlets.

However, the unusual and rare birds of these islands are guaranteed to delight casual birdwatchers, and compulsive bird listers will have an opportunity to record Asian strays.

Birdwatching on Haida Gwaii doesn't always require binoculars. As you walk along the beaches you'll pass beneath bald eagles perched on overhanging branches, while song sparrows, dark-eyed juncos and even hermit thrushes will boldly continue feeding among the driftwood as you approach. On the water, common loons and white-winged scoters are easily identified before they dive.

If, on the other hand, you want to see sandhill cranes dancing, witness the flight of a peregrine falcon, or search for Siberian

Brant are technically sea geese. During migration, they rest and feed on eelgrass at low tide. Look for them at Sandspit or areas of extensive mud flats.

shorebirds, you'll probably need a field guide, a good pair of binoculars, or a spotting scope.

Bird enthusiasts come here specifically to see rare, colonial, or unusual birds. Of the recorded species, more than 70 percent are non-perching birds. Many of these are associated with aquatic habitats: loons, albatross, shearwaters, shorebirds, and alcids fall into this category. During migration, hundreds of thousands of birds from these families visit Haida Gwaii.

Of the four species of loon, both the common and the red-throated breed on lakes on Haida Gwaii. The smaller, lighter, red-throated loon can take off from short stretches of water, which enables it to inhabit small lakes and ponds. Although they raise their young here, they fly to the ocean for food. An estimated four hundred pairs of red-throated loons nest throughout the islands—one of the highest breeding densities in the world for this species.

Birders seem to have an even keener desire to see a third species, the yellow-billed loon. Although they breed exclusively in

Rhinoceros auklets belong to a family of highly specialized seabirds. They feed on fish, use their wings to propel themselves underwater, and come ashore at night to nest or feed their young in a burrow.

the high Arctic, individuals remain scattered along BC's coast throughout the year, especially on these islands. Numerous sightings occur during spring and summer, with fewer during autumn and winter. Look for them year-round in Skidegate Inlet, off Rose Spit, in sheltered bays, or even on the open water of Old Massett.

Some birds travel to Haida Gwaii from more distant places. After breeding throughout the southern and eastern Pacific, shearwaters and albatross head to northern latitudes, where they may be sighted from spring through fall. Of the six species of shearwater, the sooty shearwaters are the most numerous. At least a million of these birds spend the summer in Hecate Strait. Due to upwelling currents, Rose Spit is also a favourite feeding place for sooty and several other species of shearwater.

While searching for shearwaters, you might spot a much larger, dark-bodied bird with a 2-metre wingspan. Sightings of black-footed albatross (and the even rarer Laysan albatross) are well documented on Haida Gwaii. A few have been spotted in Hecate

Glaucous-winged gulls nest on islands throughout Haida Gwaii. Look for them from the deck of the MV *Kwuna* while nearing Alliford Bay. They often congregate on the small rocky islets close to shore.

Strait, but most occur off the west coast, particularly in spring and summer.

Of the forty-four species of shorebirds recorded, only eight are known as breeders. Two of these have made significant extensions to their normal breeding range. Semipalmated plovers nest each spring along North and East Beaches. This is a long way south of their main Arctic breeding grounds, and one of only a few known BC breeding sites. Least sandpipers also normally nest on the tundra, but researchers have counted as many as ninety pairs nesting at Delkatla Wildlife Sanctuary at Masset—probably a very high breeding density for this shorebird. Sanderlings do not breed here, but many stay on through the winter. Annual Christmas bird counts have recorded the highest winter number of this species anywhere in Canada. Look for them sprinting along the water's edge on sandy beaches, or on mud flats.

More than half of BC's total seabird population, an estimated two million pairs, usually nest on small wooded or sparsely vegetated islands. Seabirds flourish on these islands partly because their colonies remain isolated from the mainland. The islands are protected from most predators, have direct access to the ocean and, equally important, offer a variety of nesting sites.

Isolation has also been an important factor in the evolution of three unique subspecies. The northern saw-whet owl, hairy woodpecker, and Steller's jay all live in forested areas. They can be distinguished from their mainland relatives by their darker colours or by markings their relatives don't possess. Island Steller's jays are darker and lack the noticeable white eyebrow typical of mainland birds; saw-whet owls and hairy woodpeckers have darker pigmentation than off-island individuals.

As most birdwatchers know, the thrill of finding a "life bird"—a bird never previously sighted by that birdwatcher—is perhaps surpassed only by discovering a "new" species—a bird never before recorded in that area. Since Haida Gwaii lies along the migratory path of many birds, vagrant birds (unusual wanderers) occasionally appear. A great-tailed grackle identified at Cape St. James must have flown here from the Gulf Coast. The red-faced cormorant, Aleutian tern, and black-tailed gull possibly arrived from Alaska or Siberia. A magnificent frigatebird, sighted off Langara Island in 1981, may have come from the Galapagos Islands on the equator.

Finding migrant and resident birds on the islands is a pleasant task. If you come by ferry, be sure to watch for oceanic birds as soon as you reach open water. The ferry docks in Skidegate Inlet, which is one of the better island birding spots. Kagan Bay, Sandspit and numerous islets host some nesting birds, as well as many migrating ducks and shorebirds. A Baikal teal, red-legged kittiwake, black-and-white warbler, and red-throated pipits were rarities sighted at Sandspit.

Almost all seabird colonies are located in the Gwaii Haanas region or along the west coast north to Langara Island. You'll require a boat or aircraft to reach them. Many have landing restrictions and should be viewed only from the water.

North of Skidegate Inlet, scan the Yakoun River estuary near Port Clements. Sandhill cranes are regulars here throughout the summer, while wintering birds include trumpeter swans, ducks, geese, and eagles. Delkatla Wildlife Sanctuary at Masset shouldn't be missed as its combination of water, shore and forest habitats has attracted more than 113 species. This list includes unusual vagrants such as cattle egrets, marbled godwits, ruffs, and wood sandpipers. Nearby, Masset Sound, McIntyre Bay, and waters to the west have an equal number of interesting birds. Black-tailed gulls, Aleutian terns, and king eider have been found in these areas.

For us, Rose Spit remains a favoured birding hot spot. Its sandy nose hooking into Hecate Strait attracts sea and land birds alike. Shearwaters, fulmars, auklets, and diving ducks can number into the thousands. One summer afternoon more than a hundred sooty shearwaters crossed our spotting-scope view in less than a minute. On a brisk autumn day, after waiting three hours for a pea-soup fog to lift, we checked off thirty-seven species in short order. Among them was a red knot, a wandering tattler, a black-legged kittiwake, a sandhill crane, and two peregrine falcons. Only a Caspian tern, seen the day before, would have made the outing more complete.

SEABIRD ISLANDS

Haida Gwaii is particularly well known for twelve species of nesting seabirds: two species of storm-petrel, a cormorant, a gull, and eight species of alcids, or diving seabirds. They nest on smaller islands using a variety of wooded and open habitats ranging from barren rocks a few metres above high tide to cliffs, grassy knolls, and heavily wooded islands. Although most are difficult to spot

Silhouettes of peregrine falcons. Males are smaller than females and have a wingspan of 34 to 36 centimetres.

due to their nocturnal habits and underground nests, estimated numbers range from one million to two million pairs.

These birds use more than a hundred islands. Major breeding stations with more than 25,000 breeding pairs exist on Langara, Hippa, Lyell, Rankine, SGang Gwaay, and Kerouard islands. Seabirds have selected these sites for good reason: in most cases the colonies are isolated from predators and free of human disturbance. Birds select sites as close as possible to their feeding areas—the pelagic waters of the eastern North Pacific. A variety of habitats exist on most islands, making it possible for several species to nest without seriously affecting one another.

Leach's and fork-tailed storm-petrels are the smallest of all the seabirds on Haida Gwaii. Sometimes called "sea swallows," they are barely larger than those more familiar insect eaters, and they have a similar light, fluttery flight. They nest in burrows and lay a single white egg. Both sexes share incubation, which lasts about fifty days. Every few nights, in complete darkness, the colonies come alive with activity. After foraging at sea, one parent returns to relieve its mate deep within the burrow. They apparently locate each other by call. The returning adult takes over while the other flies off.

Compared to the secretive storm-petrels, pelagic cormorants and glaucous-winged gulls are large and conspicuous breeding birds. Both species prefer rocky islets with little or no vegetation. The gulls occupy the flatter ground, while cormorants prefer ledges and cliff faces. Flocks of gulls circling over an islet or cliffs plastered with white excrement mark the colonies from a long way off and give the impression that the birds are abundant. A surprisingly low number actually breed on Haida Gwaii, however: less than five hundred pairs of cormorants and two thousand pairs of gulls.

Cormorants have the distinction of being the seabird with the greatest reproductive potential. They can lay as many as six eggs, and will lay a second clutch to replace any that are damaged or stolen. Crows and gulls frequently grab cormorant eggs if the adults are inattentive or have been scared off the nest. It's interesting to note that cormorants and gulls, despite being egg enemies, sometimes share the same nesting islet.

Many seabirds have solved the problem of exposed nests, laying their eggs in rock crevices or at the end of long burrows. The largest and most colourful burrow-nesting seabirds are tufted puffins and rhinoceros auklets. Both are dark bodied, but can be distinguished by their bills. The puffin has a bright yellow-and-orange triangle similar to a parrot, hence its nickname "sea parrot." The rhinoceros auklet's thinner bill bears a small horn near the base during breeding season. Both species feed near shore, returning to their burrows on grassy slopes or the forest floor once the sun has set. Their colonies on Haida Gwaii exist only in southern areas at this time. (Although only one nest of the less common horned puffin has ever been found here, probably there are more.)

Ancient murrelets and Cassin's auklets give no indication as to their actual abundance on Haida Gwaii. They number into the hundreds of thousands (nearly 75 percent of the entire world population of the species), yet are among the most secretive birds along our coast. They feed well offshore during the day, returning in total darkness to their burrows beneath the mossy forest floor. Bill snapping and twittering calls are heard as the adults crash-land beneath the trees. These vocalizations may help them orient themselves and locate their young.

Cassin's auklets feed a single black chick on regurgitated crustaceans. Forty days after hatching, the chicks fly away from the colony. Ancient murrelet young are precocial (they can feed themselves soon after birth). Within two days of hatching, the murrelet chicks leave their burrow by night. Guided by their parents' calls, they scramble through the forest to the shoreline. Once on the water, they swim with their parents directly out to sea.

Marbled murrelets have so far eluded every attempt to locate their nests on Haida Gwaii. (Nests have been found on mossy branches of conifers in old-growth forests in other BC coastal locations.) Small groups of these chocolate-coloured murrelets gather offshore, where they dive for fish. At dusk they fly inland to highly secretive destinations. Evidence strongly suggests they nest in the branches of tall trees on the islands. In 1953, amid the debris of a large hemlock felled near Masset, an adult marbled murrelet was discovered dazed but alive. Eggshell fragments were found nearby, but there was no sign of a nest. This robin-sized bird continues to keep its nesting sites a secret on Haida Gwaii.

Any discussion of seabird colonies on Haida Gwaii would be incomplete without mention of peregrine falcons and bald eagles, the seabirds' main predators. Somewhere between sixty and eighty pairs of peregrine falcons nest here. If non-breeding birds are added in, the falcon population probably exceeds two hundred individuals—the greatest density in Canada. Their high numbers are supported by an abundance of food, especially seabirds. They hunt ancient murrelets, Cassin's auklets, and both species of storm-petrels. Shorebirds and smaller waterbirds are preyed upon at other times of the year.

Peregrines are highly specialized predators. They pursue prey directly, catching or knocking it out of the air. During the nesting period, this activity begins at dusk, directly from the eyrie. As darkness closes in, nocturnal seabirds appear from either the sea or their burrows. Peregrine falcons wait aloft, and as the seabirds' shadowy silhouettes appear, the hunter makes a swift, headlong stoop. Speed, surprise, and height give deadly advantage to the predator. Falcons often make successive kills whether hungry or not, judging from the littered remains of seabirds found below their favourite plucking perches.

Naturally, most eyries are located close to a seabird colony. Peregrines prefer to nest on a ledge near the top of a steep cliff, using overhanging roots or plants for shelter. Sometimes they'll take over an old eagle or hawk nest. Adults share parental duties, feeding three or four young even after they've become skilled fliers. Such added care may be crucial to maintaining their population, since young falcons appear to have difficulty catching food on their own. This may be the reason why few young falcons survive the winter.

Bald eagles also prey on seabirds, although they lack the specialized hunting techniques demonstrated by peregrine falcons. The eagles normally feed on fish or carrion, but on Haida Gwaii at least half their diet consists of seabirds. Bald eagles have been observed walking through an old forest, apparently searching for stunned or disoriented murrelets. Studies have also shown that they have developed a taste for gulls, shearwaters, and fulmars. In winter, eagles regularly prey on diving ducks such as scaups and scoters.

Despite the abundance of avian predators, the sheer size of the population of seabirds ensures that more than enough survive to maintain their numbers. A far greater threat comes from other quarters: humans, fire, oil spills, logging, racoons, and rats seriously affect seabird populations. Since 1996, a successful rat eradication program has successfully cleared many seabird-nesting islands of this destructive pest. The results have been positive—several species have experienced a resurgence.

To further protect nesting seabirds, an island in Lepas Bay, the Anthony Islets, and Copper, Jeffrey, Rankine and Kerouard islands have all been designated ecological reserves, or have a special designation. You will need a permit to go ashore on these islands at any time.

Following a few simple rules will minimize human impact on other colonies. One person walking through a colony of cormorants or gulls is enough to cause a major disruption. Gulls, in particular, will attack and kill chicks that cross invisible territorial boundaries. Cormorants will flush from nests when disturbed, leaving their eggs to be devoured by gulls and crows, or their young to bake in the sun. Islands that have nesting gulls and cormorants should be viewed only from the water.

Nocturnal seabird colonies appear abandoned during the day—you can be in the middle of one without knowing it. During the breeding season, nightfall brings thousands of adults crashing through the trees and undergrowth. This seemingly chaotic arrival is followed by a mad dash for the burrow.

The threat to existence comes in many guises. Domestic cats and dogs can create havoc, catching and killing adults before they locate their mates. Beach fires disorient flying birds, and if they are left burning, may advance into the forest. A large oil spill, or logging near a seabird colony, can wipe out entire populations.

For trips to any wilderness island, leave all pets on the boat (or at home), walk around the island only in daylight and do not light fires anywhere. Every island visitor has a responsibility to make sure that millions of seabirds continue to be an integral part of Haida Gwaii.

4.2 MARINE MAMMALS AND REPTILES

The cool waters that surround Haida Gwaii are part of the most favoured habitat in the Pacific for marine mammals. The Alaska current sweeps along the west coast, blending tidal currents, river runoff and areas of upwelling into a nutrient-rich solution. Plankton, fish, and marine invertebrates thrive in this environment. In all, twenty-two species of marine mammals and two reptiles have also been attracted to these islands.

Marine mammals are usually large, spending most of their life in the ocean. In the waters surrounding Haida Gwaii you may spot whales, dolphins, porpoises, seals, sea lions, and sea otters. Of the twenty-two recorded species, most either breed or spend a significant portion of their time in nearshore waters. Of the cetaceans (whales, porpoises, and dolphins), the grey whale is the most predictable. These large and unassuming mammals pass through inshore waters biannually, travelling between their Arctic summering areas and Baja breeding lagoons. This twenty-thousand-kilometre journey is the longest undertaken by any mammal. Alone or in small groups, the whales travel day and night, seldom stopping to eat. Energy is supplied by fat reserves accumulated before the journey begins.

Until recently, the actual spring migration route of grey whales along the central BC coast was unknown. With the help

Sea lions gather in large numbers on low, rocky ledges found at Skedans or SGang Gwaay Islets. The second-largest breeding rookery in BC is farther south at Cape St. James.

of satellite tagging and observation posts, it is now believed the majority of these whales enter Hecate Strait from the south during April and May. They continue northward, rounding Rose Spit then crossing Dixon Entrance. The southbound route in late autumn past Haida Gwaii is poorly known but many believe the whales travel offshore en route to their wintering areas around southern California and Mexico.

As a result of nineteenth-century whaling, an estimated fourteen thousand grey whales were reduced to a few thousand by 1900. (See page 180 for Rose Harbour Whaling Station.) Protection came just in time, and the population rebounded to a peak number of 21,000 in 1998. Humpback whales followed a similar pattern. Whaling decimated their numbers, but after protective measures were enacted in 1966, they made a strong recovery. As their numbers increased, they began to reoccupy coastal waters. Today, the highest densities of humpbacks in BC usually occur near Haida Gwaii, particularly along the east side of the Moresby Island in the national park preserve.

Humpback whales elevate their tail flukes just before diving. The underside has a unique pattern and is used to identify different whales.

Humpback whales are often the 'whale to watch' due to their dramatic displays. They engage in flipper slaps, tail slaps, and just before diving they lift their fluke vertically before disappearing into the depths. They also regularly breach. In spectacular fashion, they will leap completely out of the water only to fall sideways with seawater cascading in all directions. Observers may also witness them bubble net feeding and if equipped with underwater microphones, hear their elaborate and lengthy songs.

Because they lack teeth, grey and humpback whales obtain food by filter feeding. A baleen in their mouth screens bottom-dwelling crustaceans, krill, or schooling fishes. Humpbacks have a unique method of cooperative feeding. This involves a group of whales, usually five to ten, that corral a school of fish such as herring. They create a bubble net causing the small fish to concentrate just long enough for the whales to lunge upwards, mouths open, engulfing the prey as they reach the surface. It is a most sensational experience to witness.

At close range, a bushy blow and small dorsal fin suggests a humpback whale. Watching for their large flippers or tail slaps and dramatic breaches.

Both of these whales can be seen from shore or out on the waters of Haida Gwaii. Humpbacks have a small dorsal fin, smooth back, and raise their tail flukes when sounding. Grey whales lack a distinct dorsal fin. Rather, they exhibit a small hump followed by six to twelve bumps or "knuckles" just in front of the tail. Skidegate Inlet, Rose Spit, Dixon Entrance, and throughout the Gwaii Haanas preserve are excellent observation areas.

A second group of cetaceans possesses teeth capable of seizing fish, squid, birds, seals, and sea lions. Prey is swallowed whole or in chunks; these animals can rip, but not chew, flesh. Nine species occur here, most of which can be expected near shore.

The smallest are blunt-nosed harbour porpoises. These shy mammals prefer sheltered shorelines and waterways, such as Skidegate and Cumshewa Inlets. True to their disposition, they usually travel alone or in groups of two or three. Most people glimpse only a small fin disappearing beneath the surface, as these mammals vanish when approached or disturbed.

Sighting an orca whale makes a Haida Gwaii visit complete. Some pods of orcas, known as transients, prey on mammals such as seals and porpoises.

Dall's porpoises are the exact opposite. These sleek, thick-bodied creatures are full of spirited curiosity and are reputed to be the fastest marine mammal. Their bold black-and-white forms zip through the water, sometimes creating sudden rooster tails of spray. To the delight of boaters, Dall's porpoises love to chase a fast craft and will sometimes ride bow waves. They'll zig, zag, and zip across in front of a boat's prow but will quickly vanish if you slow down for a better look.

Pacific white-sided dolphins sometimes venture into near-shore waters. Unlike Dall's porpoises, white-sided dolphins may be in groups of fifty to a hundred or more. They are playful and sociable, but will probably stay well away from kayaks or larger craft.

The excitement created by porpoises and dolphins is second only to the appearance of *Orcinus orca*, the killer whale. Sighting their tall dorsal fins slicing the water's surface is simultaneously frightening and intriguing. The personality and habits of these graceful marine hunters contradict their reputation as indiscriminate monsters. A twenty-year study, initiated by the late

A harbour porpoise is usually seen at a distance while Dall's porpoises (bottom) will sometimes approach small craft and ride the bow waves.

Dr. Michael Bigg, made enormous strides in furthering our understanding of these mammals. For years it was believed killer whales ate anything that moved—a belief that suggested humans were also fair game. However, logs from thousands of hours of observing these whales show that there is not one valid account of aggressive behaviour toward humans in BC. There is only one single record of a provoked attack, and that was against a boat.

Dr. Bigg and his colleagues also identified three distinct groups of killer whales around Haida Gwaii. One group, referred to as *residents,* usually herds in pods of ten to twenty-five animals and eats only fish. The second group, *transients,* usually moves in pods of two to five whales and eats only marine mammals. Recently a third group, provisionally designated as *offshores,* has been recognized. Much less is known about this last group, although most of the sightings have occurred off Haida Gwaii and Vancouver Island.

If you travel long enough with a pod of transients, you may witness an attack on a harbour seal (their most common prey), or a northern sea lion. These pinnipeds, or fin-footed mammals, are

In small groups, sea lions cruise along outer shorelines or sheltered waterways. Watch for them within Skidegate or Cumshewa Inlets.

common residents throughout the islands. They have hairy coats and love to "haul out" on beaches or rocky islets. They're tolerant, sometimes allowing close approach, but it's advisable to stay at least 100 metres away, even if the sea lions appear accustomed to human presence.

Sea lions habitually congregate on isolated islets, where you can sometimes witness their spectacular behaviour. Occasionally exceeding 1 tonne in weight, these brown beasts may seem ponderous on land, but they are truly graceful when plunging headlong into foaming surf or when swimming. We have seen kayakers paddle over their massive forms, but it is more prudent to keep a comfortable distance, as they could easily upset a small craft. At any time, but particularly during the winter months, they haul out at Rose Spit, Skedans Rocks, and Reef Island.

Sea lions also congregate throughout the year at southerly Cape St. James. In the summer, more than 1,100 sea lions return to this remote tip to breed, making it the second-largest rookery on

A killer whale hopping near the Tar Islets.

the BC coast. Males begin arriving on these wave-washed rocks in May, immediately establishing and defending a territory. Females and other immature animals arrive a few weeks later.

Pregnant females give birth to a single pup soon after arriving. Within the next two weeks, while they nurse their newborn, they mate with one of the territorial males. The females then settle into a routine of feeding well away from the colony before returning to nurse their pups. By late August this social fabric breaks apart, as most males scatter along BC's coast in smaller groups. Females and pups may overwinter near the rookery or perhaps spread out along the coast. Regardless of how far they travel, they usually let the males manage on their own.

Sea lions tend to anger commercial fishers, who blame them for depleting salmon stocks and destroying fishing gear (which they sometimes do). Studies prove, however, that sea lions are opportunistic feeders, dining on whatever fish are most plentiful. They do not particularly favour salmon.

Harbour seals are likewise blamed for gorging on salmon: their habit of raiding spawning streams has given them a bad reputation. Despite this, they, too, are opportunists, catching whatever takes the least amount of energy. This fits their lifestyle well. They spend a lot of time hauled out and resting with others of their kind.

They can, however, be spontaneous and energetic. On one occasion we were startled by a loud splash and turned to see a fleeting shape disappearing into a kelp bed. Suddenly, a round head appeared and curious eyes examined us. After deciding we were harmless, the young seal playfully chomped on a large kelp frond, then dove after an imaginary companion.

Harbour seals seem to spend equal amounts of time on land and in the water; they rest, mate, give birth, and moult on shore and at sea. You will see harbour seals on or around many sheltered rocks or islets throughout the islands. Look for them specifically off Rose Spit, and within Masset, Skidegate, and Cumshewa Inlets. Throughout South Moresby, watch for their mottled forms along the east coast of Lyell Island, at Marco Island and in other protected areas.

Sea otters were once as plentiful as harbour seals. The smallest of all marine mammals, they were highly valued for their fur. British, American, and Russian traders were ruthless in their quest for these dark pelts, which fetched a fabulous price in China. So intense was their desire for wealth that greedy sailors literally traded the shirts off their backs. The Haida were willing accomplices, and they vigorously traded the skins for the wonderful goods the purchasers offered. Only remnant otter populations in Alaska and California survived the slaughter.

Despite their near annihilation, these remaining sea otter populations increased dramatically after 1911 when protective laws were put in place. In the early 1970s, sea otters from Alaska were released on the west coast of Vancouver Island. From this reintroduction, their numbers and range expanded northward to BC's central coast. A small colony with mothers and pups has been established on the Goose Islands, directly east of Cape St. James. Individuals—probably males—have been reported from Rose Spit to Langara Island and along the west coast south to the national park preserve. One hopes they will soon find permanent residency throughout Haida Gwaii.

In addition to the array of marine mammals, two species of turtles have been observed around Haida Gwaii. Green turtles can be expected in tropical waters but on Haida Gwaii, they are rare vagrants. Leatherbacks are the largest species of turtle in the world. They, too, prefer tropical areas but range widely even into temperate waters such as along the BC coast. Turtle sightings have come from Skidegate Inlet, East Beach, Rose Spit, and Langara Island.

Thankfully, attitudes toward all marine animals have changed. Whereas humans once killed them on sight, studying wildlife is now a major recreational activity. As more people experience the thrill of seeing these animals in their natural habitat, our sense of kinship with them, albeit poorly developed, seems to grow. Their intelligence, curiosity, care of offspring, and playfulness are qualities we share. It is our hope that personal experiences will blend with respect and lead to greater understanding of these remarkable creatures.

4.3 LAND MAMMALS AND AMPHIBIANS

During the last ice age, immense sheets of ice covered these islands. However thick this ice may have been, many scientists believe there were parts of the archipelago that remained ice-free. Some speculate that these pockets, or refugia, may have been large enough to allow some mammals to survive. Other species arrived on the islands after the ice melted, but only eleven species were present on Haida Gwaii when the first Europeans arrived. Unfortunately, the intruders' infested ships brought rats and mice, which were previously unknown along the BC coast. The accidental importation of these four-legged foreigners marked the beginning of a rash of species introductions, so that today there are almost an equal number of native and foreign species on the islands.

Hecate Strait and refugia have proved to be effective barriers to mammal dispersal. When animals remain isolated for a long period of time, they begin to differ from their relatives in larger breeding populations. These differences include size and colour variations, and habitat selection. Most native mammals on Haida Gwaii exhibit such characteristics. For example, the black bear here is the largest of its kind in North America. The marten is one of the largest on the continent and is a lighter colour, with an orange tinge to its undercoat. The ermine and river otter are also subspecies unique to these islands.

There are exceptions, however, that encourage debate of refugia. One subspecies of dusky shrew, for example, seems to resemble its mainland cousins. Could it have arrived on the islands in a Haida canoe, or clinging to some floating debris? Such examples are intriguing and fuel speculation among genetic researchers.

Bats differ from all other Haida Gwaii mammals in their ability to fly. They may fly as far as the mainland, but more research is needed to be certain. Four species inhabit these islands. One of only two known colonies of Keen's long-eared myotis in BC was found on Gandll K'in in Gwaay.yaay (Hotspring Island). Curiously, these bats, along with some little brown myotis, roost in rocky cracks and crevices below high tide.

Black bears on Haida Gwaii are among the largest on the continent. Look for them on estuary meadows or turning over beach rocks at low tide.

Originally the caribou was the only ungulate mammal on Haida Gwaii. Unfortunately, little is known about the local species: the last one to be seen was shot in 1908. It apparently fitted the pattern of mammals on isolated islands, being smaller than mainland caribou. The females may have differed from their mainland relatives by not growing antlers. These caribou appear to have maintained a tenuous existence in the bogs on Graham Island. Possibly competition from introduced deer, as well as from hunting, contributed to their demise. Accounts of searching for the last of these animals are documented in Charles Sheldon's book *The Wilderness of the North Pacific Coast Islands*. Although Sheldon did not find any caribou, he certainly would have seen plenty of northern river otters. This long-tailed, short-legged weasel, about the size of a basset hound, frequents virtually every fish-bearing lake, stream, and shoreline across Haida Gwaii. Males may travel by themselves, but otters also congregate in what may be family groups of two to seven individuals. River

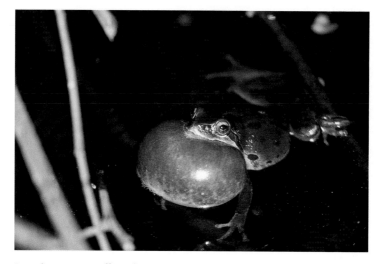

In spring, many small ponds resonate with the mating calls of treefrogs. On still nights their chorus can be heard at a distance of several kilometres.

otters are adept on land and seldom swim far from ocean shorelines. These characteristics make it easier to distinguish them from the rare sea otter. Sea otters rarely come ashore and are very awkward on land.

Amphibians are another story. The western toad is the only amphibian native to the islands. The Pacific treefrog and Northern red-legged frog have recently been introduced. Treefrogs and toads are widely distributed and can be found in fields, meadows, and forests. Since toads probably did not swim across Hecate Strait, they may have survived in a glacial refugia or crossed the water as stowaways.

The islands' biological balance has been altered drastically by introduced animals. The black rat may well have arrived on sailing ships, since captains had no way of ridding their vessels of these vermin. This was not the case with other introductions. By 1901 several attempts to populate the islands with deer had failed, before two subsequent introductions proved successful.

Raccoons were introduced to the islands in the 1940s. Since they prefer to hunt at night, you may only see their tracks along riverbanks and mud flats at low tide.

Red deer from New Zealand were also released. The introduction of squirrels, beaver, elk, raccoons, and mule (Sitka) deer also took place.

Some of the consequences are severe. An absence of predators and abundant food caused a population explosion among the Sitka deer. Competition among them has resulted in a change of diet to *cedar à la bush.* Much to the chagrin of foresters, these small deer eat cedar seedlings faster than they can be planted. Researchers have partially protected plantings by placing transparent cones over the seedlings, but this adds substantial cost to tree farming.

Two other non-native mammals have also become nuisances. Raccoons have a reputation for devouring the eggs of ground-nesting birds. Since these aggressive animals are able swimmers, isolated nesting islets are well within their reach. Seabird colonies have no defence against such marauders and could be decimated by this animal's omnivorous appetite.

The beaver's habit of building dams poses another kind of threat. The lowlands on Graham Island are dotted by countless lakes and ponds. Many of these were completely isolated and contained their own distinct subspecies of stickleback. These minnow-sized fish are of great scientific interest due to their genetic differences. The beaver dams raised the water levels, however, linking the freshwater oases and allowing the sticklebacks to interbreed. This may seem trivial, but to biologists these fish offer important evolutionary clues. Sticklebacks have developed special characteristics that ensure their survival in each lake's particular environment. Beavers are destroying a rare opportunity for the study of adaptation.

It is impossible to predict the behaviour of an animal when it is introduced into a new environment. There is even great danger in the escape of pets and livestock. Domestic goats once roamed at will on Ramsay Island and could have destroyed the vegetation if their populations had expanded. Visitors must keep their pets leashed, particularly in wild areas. Given the knowledge of what has happened, and the uncertainty of what could happen, it would be an act of selfishness and indifference to introduce any more species to Haida Gwaii.

PART 5

THEIR PLACE TO BE

PEOPLE COME TO Haida Gwaii from all over the world, never imagining that the islands' spell may descend upon them and they may never want to leave. We heard first-hand how strong a pull this place can exert, even on the casual visitor, and we present seven profiles of folks who stayed and who help contribute to the special character of Haida Gwaii.

Peter Hamel, *Anglican minister and ornithologist*
Margo Hearne, *naturalist*
Joy LaFortune, *entrepreneur*
Garner Moody, *Haida carver*
Amanda Reid-Stevens, *community activist*
Andrew Merilees, *tourism guide and mayor of Masset*
Wendy Riley, *extraordinary baker and island enthusiast*

PETER HAMEL

In 1982 Peter Hamel was living in Toronto, working hard at the Anglican Church's head office. His job kept him extremely busy, applying church policies to corporate finances, as well as to environmental and Indigenous land issues. This spectrum of responsibilities eventually brought him to Terrace, BC,

for a regional conference. Before the meetings ended he had been invited (divine intervention, perhaps?) to spend a few days on Haida Gwaii. This spontaneous side trip marked a new beginning in his church life. Soon he was ministering to the islands' parish and indulging his love of natural history—particularly birds.

"The first day I was here I went across the road, over the bank and looked across the inlet at all the seabirds," he recalls. "A yellow-billed loon, in breeding plumage, flew by along with Cassin's auklets and marbled murrelets. It was really quite exciting."

For a keen eastern birdwatcher, this was too much to ignore. He made some phone calls, met with his supervisors, then contacted the bishop. Three months later he began a one-year sabbatical as priest at the Masset church.

"I got involved in a number of things right away. A few of us started the first Christmas bird count. Nobody could believe what we saw here. There was a cattle egret in the sanctuary, a Townsend's solitaire on the beach, and I found a thick-billed murre! I fell in love with the place."

One year was not nearly long enough. He returned again in 1994, this time for a longer term. "One of the main things I wanted to do was to really explore, in depth, the spirituality of the islands and nature. I wrote a column for the national church for five years on environmental spirituality. It would be great to rewrite these and connect them with some other theological writings."

The pastorate, however, involves more than just personal endeavours. Many members of his congregation are involved in the community, in political life or education, or they work as fishers, caregivers, or medical professionals. "I see the church as giving support and meaning to what these folks are doing. That is, supporting them in a spiritual way."

He also foresees the church playing a role in the new society that is developing here. The downsizing of the armed forces base meant a loss of civilian jobs but invigorated community spirit. The artistic community seems to have revived, and residents have more control over decisions in their community. On the flip side, economic change in the fisheries and forest industries has hit people hard, like a mean-spirited punch. Many people are hurting, out of work, and with limited prospects.

The church makes its building available for community arts events and has established a successful thrift shop along with a quaint drop-in cafe. The shop is staffed by volunteers, people who want to contribute positively to their community's need. In no small way, the church also promotes the spiritual connections of humanity's place in creation.

Peter eloquently ties all these observations together when asked what Haida Gwaii means to him. "The islands are the vortex of creation. To me, they are the centre of the unfolding universe. It is a place where heaven and earth meet, and where they dialogue. To me, in a real way, you can sense the heartbeat of creation here, and the pivotal point is Rose Spit, where the land and the sea and the sky meet."

MARGO HEARNE

Visitors to Haida Gwaii tend to hear about the Delkatla Wildlife Sanctuary shortly after their arrival. This relatively compact tidal marsh nestles next to the community of Masset and offers leisurely walking trails, viewing towers, and well over a hundred species

of birds. Margo Hearne has been a major influence in this sanctuary's preservation and development.

Twenty-five years ago, Margo left her native Ireland and immigrated to Canada. Short stops in Toronto and Banff National Park were just stepping stones en route to her ultimate goal: Canada's west coast wilderness. Arriving in Haida Gwaii, she knew she had found the right place to be.

"I came out here for the winter with the intention of staying—for the winter," she says. "I liked it a lot. Something about it touched me. It reminded me of Ireland. I remember one time I was sitting where I had a view out over the sanctuary. It was a still evening with a sunset, a rose glow over the water and a little mist rising. I thought, 'This is *really* beautiful.' So I stayed."

She worked in the local hotel through the winter, and the following spring opened the first bookstore in Masset. Two years later she joined her husband on his fishboat. Her fishing career lasted more than fifteen years, until new regulations drove her from the water. "The fish are still out there. There are so many new rules, however, that you can't even get out to the fishing grounds anymore."

Although fishing was her livelihood, her passion became the Delkatla marshes. In 1978, town council appealed for help to manage the marsh, which was a gift to the community from the Masset Rod and Gun Club.

The wetlands were in a far from pristine state, the result of indiscriminate dumping and digging, combined with wandering livestock. The most challenging problem was the causeway. Built in 1963, the earth dam provided a wonderful access to the military base, but it altered the tidal flows. The salt marsh was slowly dying.

Over the next decade, Margo was twice elected to Masset council and was chair of the Wildlife Sanctuary Committee. The area was cleaned up, viewing towers were built, trails constructed and trees trimmed to make it a bit more accessible. In order to fully restore the salt marsh, however, the causeway had to change. So a Canada-wide fundraising campaign was undertaken—they needed $1 million!

Margo persevered, undaunted by the immense tasks of raising the money and manoeuvring through multiple levels of government and private bureaucracies. Finally, in 1995, part of the causeway was removed and replaced with a 30-metre bridge. The rising tide flooded the marshes for the first time in three decades. The restoration of Delkatla took a huge leap forward.

If Margo has her way, there will be more changes to come. "There's nowhere in Masset at the moment for people to find out about what's in the natural world around us. They come here to find out about the outdoors, but there's not a lot of information available." She hopes the new interpretive centre will highlight Delkatla and give visitors an overview of the island's natural history.

Even though she has made Masset her home and become so involved in community affairs, Margo admits it's not always easy living here. Nevertheless, "one of the things we love about Masset is its relative quietude," she says. "I don't think the word is isolation. There is a certain peace and a certain security in knowing that you're quite a bit off the beaten track.

"One of the major attractions for me, as a birdwatcher, is that you get some really wonderful and unusual birds coming through here," she remarks. "And there's that wildness that you're close to all the time. The ocean and the trees and the wind blowing through here. It's really very special."

JOY LAFORTUNE

In 1980 the first scheduled ferry arrived on Haida Gwaii. With it came tourists and car traffic never before experienced on these most isolated islands in Canada. Recognizing a great opportunity, Joy LaFortune turned part of her beachside home into an information centre and gift shop. Over the last quarter-century, Joy has been the first person many visitors meet en route to their favoured island destination. Living most of her life on the islands has given her a unique perspective and love for the islands.

Both her parents' families arrived in the very early 1900s. Although born in the Village of Queen Charlotte, at age five she and her immediate family moved to Port Clements. They firmly grasped the pioneering spirit, carved out a life for themselves, and began to make things happen. Her father was both a fisherman and trapper, while her mother became the agent for the government telephone and telegraph. She also started the first credit union for the islands. "Our living room was a telephone office and a credit union all through my childhood," Joy recalls.

Children faced the additional problem of obtaining schooling, as there were seldom enough kids to fill a classroom. She took more than five years of school by correspondence, then boarded in Masset to complete Grades 10 and 11. "There was no road between Port Clements and Masset, so you had to go by gas boat. It took me as long to get to school in Masset as it takes the kids now to fly to Vancouver."

The phrase "pioneering spirit" may have a romantic ring, but it usually means hard work. In addition to finishing Grade 12 by correspondence, Joy worked as a school janitor for an income of $40 a month. Then, like both her grandfathers before her, she took on the job of postmaster for Port Clements.

With school, the teenage years and early work experience behind her, Joy followed the lure of greener pastures in Vancouver and the Caribbean. Her life abroad, however, did not last long. After living in such exotic locales and travelling the length and breadth of North America, why return to Haida Gwaii? "The weather," she quickly replies. "I live on the beach and it's always beautiful. The beaches: I really, really envy Masset's beaches. And the people: they are a different kind of people. I don't know whether special people come to islands or islands turn them into special people—we have an awful lot of very talented people here."

Joy would like to see more growth and more people. A bigger population base would improve the education system, reduce stress on the hospital, and build on the tax base. "People do not know how wonderful it is here. This is the real problem. If anybody had a clue how gorgeous it is from the first of April till the end of October, we would have a lot more people here."

After being in business since 1976, Joy has seen just about everything. Her first customers were the local fishers and loggers. The ferry service brought a whole new clientele, and the creation of Gwaii Haanas National Park promised to give tourism a huge boost. Unfortunately, leaner years and economic slowdowns have not helped the islands.

A lot of people who jumped on the tourism bandwagon did not last. Joy, however, has adapted with the times, moving her store into "downtown" Charlotte while keeping an ocean view from her shop window. In 2007, Joy decided to retire. She handed over her business to Jackie's Island Jewelers and settled into a somewhat quieter lifestyle. She still enjoys her beachfront home and being close to her grandchildren. What could be better than that?

GARNER MOODY

The Raven and the First Men, Lootaas, and *Spirit of Haida Gwaii* are only three among the many striking creations by the late Bill Reid, a gifted and internationally renowned Haida artist. These later achievements, although awesome in size, complexity, and detail, may ultimately be eclipsed by another outstanding accomplishment—inspiring a new generation of Haida artists. Garner Moody is one such artist.

Garner was fortunate. His Uncle Rufus, renowned for argillite carving, helped him get started. "The old school wasn't being used any more, so Rufus set up a night class. This was just in argillite," Garner explains. "Everybody that kept on [after the night class finished] moved to his house. He let eight to ten kids go into his bathroom and wash up after playing with slate [argillite]. We were just black. The washroom was a mess, as was the kitchen after serving candies, cookies and hot chocolate."

For Expo 86 in Vancouver, BC, Bill Reid was commissioned to carve a large cedar canoe, one measuring more than 16 metres. A canoe of this size had not been carved for more than seventy years, and most of the skills and knowledge had been lost. So Bill hired four promising carvers, including Garner, to help take on this immense project.

"I guess we worked pretty good because Bill picked four guys from Skidegate to go down to Vancouver and work for him down there. He had his workshop on Granville Island and was just starting the Spirit Canoe. We learned how to melt down silver, make silver wire and solder. It was really good. He taught us as he worked on his projects."

Garner spent three months working on the canoe, starting with the raw log. By the time he left to go herring fishing, the canoe's sides were being honed down to less than two inches thick and it had been hollowed out and steamed. The sanding and painting were yet to come.

Bill had a unique style for teaching his students, Garner recalls. "I was working on the human—a bear with a man between his legs with a hat on. So Bill said do the nose. I looked at all the books and everything. All the old-style noses are big, fat, flared noses. So that's what I put on. When Bill saw it, he got his axe and went all over it, chopping it away. I cleaned it up, but when he returned he again said, 'No,' then chopped some more away. Four times he did this. The next thing I know I'm gluing the nose on. It was real discouraging. In the end he was happy with it, but he wondered why we were so darn slow. He was ready to fire us."

After apprenticing in Bill's studio for a year, Garner had had enough of Vancouver, even though the city served him well. "We got to know most of the Vancouver stores: we got to know the buyers, and they got to know us. I don't care for Vancouver now. I'm happy here—it's home. It's good for the kids to grow up here. They have a lot more freedom here than in the city."

Garner has now made Skidegate his home. Elected to the village council, he admits it takes a lot of work. "You have to be in the chambers from 9:30 to 4:30, every day. It's a big commitment. I never realized what it took to run a village."

The future of Skidegate looks immensely promising, particularly with the completion of the Haida Heritage Centre. This houses a Bill Reid teaching centre, tool-making room, performance space, and archives—all linked to the Haida Gwaii Museum. It is an education centre. Ultimately, it is expected to display sixteen poles outside, six of which were raised in 2001. The best carvers in the world will soon be on Skidegate's doorstep.

Their Place to Be

Garner's sense of belonging means all he needs and wants is right here. "You grew up with everybody around here. You know everybody. So why leave?"

AMANDA REID-STEVENS

Anyone who visited Haida Gwaii ten years ago would be pleasantly surprised by the islands today. The downsizing of the armed forces base has actually revitalized the entire Masset community. The museum at Port Clements has tripled in size, Tlell has some new gift shops, Naikoon Provincial Park has improved facilities, and the inside of Sandspit Airport has been given an impressive historical facelift. The most dramatic changes, however, have occurred at Skidegate. Amanda Reid-Stevens is a village resident who has made a significant contribution to the transformation.

Amanda was born in Toronto, but spent most of her teenage years in Skidegate. She remembers having a great time on the islands. "We swam, played baseball, walked the beaches, and partied when my parents weren't watching me too closely. It was a good teenagerhood for me." Unfortunately, the school system of the day did not extend past Grade 10. Correspondence courses or moving away were the only options to complete grade school.

For her senior grades, Amanda spent a year attending a school in Maple Ridge, BC, and her last year in Vancouver. Since returning to Haida Gwaii, she has been an enthusiastic village resident, and for seven years was the general manager of a proactive corporation.

"One of the most significant factors for Native people recently has been Bill C31. This federal law allowed many First Nations people to regain their status. Skidegate was one community that welcomed back, and is still welcoming back, as many people as it can. Over the last decade, the population has nearly tripled. In response to this influx, the band council established the development corporation Gwaalagaa Naay, meaning 'Ambitious House.' Its mandate is to generate economic development and employment opportunities. The corporation, along with the council, is responsible for a lot of the development in Skidegate today."

Skidegate has some excellent facilities. You can purchase gifts, supplies, and staples at the new mini-mall, and perhaps take part in a recreational activity at one of the gymnasiums. The village has the islands' only cosmic bowling alley. Younger children enjoy a state-of-the-art school, one that would make most school districts envious.

For Amanda, the future for the village, and for the islands as a whole, looks exciting. "I see the leaders of Skidegate willing to work with other leaders on the island, through the Gwaii Trust Board, through island communities and through other island boards where representatives (both Indigenous and non-Indigenous) work together to make progress."

The showpiece for the new millennium is the Haida Heritage Centre. "It incorporates an expanded museum, a Bill Reid teaching centre, a theatre, as well as resource, language, interpretive, and administrative facilities. It is great for the village, for the kids, and for future generations that come along. It will hold a lot of our history and keep it safe."

Amanda has a special interest in the centre, particularly since one component, the Bill Reid teaching centre, honours her late father. She was involved in planning for the centre along with a cross-section of people from all over Haida Gwaii. The entire complex is linked with larger educational institutions, including the University of Northern BC, Emily Carr College of Art and Design,

Northwest Community College, and the local school district. People from all over the world can come here to study or be a part of this unique centre.

Regardless of the national or international attention that Haida Gwaii or Skidegate receive, Amanda is more than content with her life on the islands. "They are my home and always will be my home. I feel at peace here, I feel safe and I feel part of a very vibrant Haida and island culture. It's an exciting place to live right now and I wouldn't want to live anywhere else."

ANDREW MERILEES

As Andrew neared the end of his elementary school years, his father invited him along on a field trip. This was no ordinary day trip to a park close by their hometown of Nanaimo. Rather, his father was leading a tour sponsored by the Vancouver Natural History Society. Their destination was the unique group of islands off of British Columbia's north coast known then as the Queen Charlotte Islands. This two-week sojourn was an almost magical adventure that had a lasting effect on his life and career choices.

The special field trip stayed in Andrew's memory as he went on to finish high school, complete two years of college in Nanaimo, and move to Prince George. There, he attended the University of Northern BC and completed his geography degree.

As often happens, a career opportunity took him farther away from Haida Gwaii, but another connection brought him back. He first started working for BC Parks on Vancouver Island then in the northern area of the province. While working as a park contractor, he met Kimiko von Boetticher, who had been living on Haida

Gwaii for over a year. In fairly short order, Kimiko convinced Andrew to make a return trip to the islands he had first visited almost two decades earlier. Andrew quickly noted, "It didn't take a lot of convincing to get me to move!"

When moving to Haida Gwaii, Andrew had several choices as to where he could live. Although Sandspit, the Village of Queen Charlotte, Tlell, and Masset all offer services, each locale had some advantages over the others. Andrew and Kimiko chose Masset, a small community of just over a thousand and the largest municipality on the islands, as their home. Everyone in the community is within walking distance of the inlet, since Masset is nestled near the entrance to Masset Sound on the north shore of Haida Gwaii.

It is exposed, however, to moody Dixon Entrance, where winter storms pass through, sometimes with hurricane-force winds. When asked, "Why Masset?" Andrew replied quickly.

"The community of Masset and particularly Old Massett really welcomed us into their fold. They made us feel we were part of the community. We've had a really good experience here, and we've wanted to give back to it."

Andrew continued to work for BC Parks but also made a shift into the tourism industry. He established his own company and soon became president of Haida Gwaii Tourism Association and a director of the Queen Charlotte Islands Chamber of Commerce. Both of these are important because the islands are in a transition phase: their resource industries are in decline, so there is a hope that tourism and other businesses will help offset the void.

In all communities, planning and decisions usually have a political component. Politics has also been an important part of Andrew's family. His grandfather, James Houghton, was speaker of the Parliament of Queensland in Australia, and his uncle, Harold Merilees, was an MLA in the BC legislature. So it was not too surprising for Andrew to continue this family tradition.

"On Haida Gwaii there is a great need for people to be leaders and lots of roles for people to fill. If you prove you are competent with something you soon get more and more responsibility. Friends soon began to encourage me to run for council. I followed their advice and served two terms on council. In the last election, I ended up in the mayor's chair."

Being involved in a community means much more than just doing your job, volunteering, and running for public office. It also means that you develop a sense of place and a passion for your community and the surrounding environment. None of this has been lost on Andrew.

After living on Haida Gwaii for sixteen years, he has a unique perspective on what the islands mean to him.

"Haida Gwaii has everything you need and nothing that you don't. To me, it's a special place that has many opportunities for people. The islands provide a lot of opportunities for personal and professional self-discovery, which may not be possible in a more urban environment. Masset is also a community with a close relationship to the natural world and the resources that we have here. There is a sense of connectedness to the natural environment which is always close at hand."

Andrew's sense of understanding Haida Gwaii is clearly evident in his voice. There is much more, however, than just words. He has developed a strong sense of community and eagerly gives back to the community that embraced him when he chose Masset as his home.

Andrew's enthusiasm is contagious. If you are planning a trip to Haida Gwaii and would like to tap into his knowledge and insight, he will gladly help you with an experience like no other. His company, Haida Gwaii Discovery Tours, offers all-inclusive island excursions every year. He will also connect you with a variety of other island excursions and events. Feel free to contact him at PO Box 798, Masset, BC V0T 1M0, or visit his website: haidagwaiidiscovery.com.

WENDY RILEY

Wendy is a small town girl who lived in Lantzville before moving to nearby Cassidy to raise her family. Both of these small communities bookend the much larger city of Nanaimo, BC, located on the eastern edge of Vancouver Island. About twenty years ago, however, her countryside home began to change. Wendy recalls, "I've always been a rural type of person and Nanaimo just seemed to be growing way too fast for me. I began thinking about a change." Her daughter, who was living in Terrace called and said, "Mom, you've got to go to Haida Gwaii! That's where you should be."

Acting on this suggestion, she drove to Prince Rupert and boarded the ferry across Hecate Strait. "My first glimpse of the islands was almost a magical moment. There was just something about this place and it was time to move."

Within six months, she left her work at a dental clinic and moved north to Masset. She worked at various jobs for a few years but then was presented with a most interesting idea. A friend who owned a small coffee shop located along the road to Tow Hill queried Wendy about running the business. Since Wendy's college job gave her free time during the summer, she jumped at the chance.

"I drove down the road with a 5-gallon jug of water and a coffee pot and opened the place in the middle of nowhere without electricity, running water, or other amenities. It was totally off grid." Despite these obstacles, she had a feeling it would succeed. Everyone who comes to the islands wants to see Tow Hill and North

Their Place to Be

Beach. To do so would mean driving right by her shop. The location was everything.

Pretty soon, she didn't have any time to do anything else except run the shop which had morphed into a bakery with open air seating and a large parking lot. Fifteen years later the bakery continues to attract island visitors due to scrumptious cinnamon rolls and word-of-mouth advertising.

"Yes, I've never had to do any advertising. Its all been from people who heard about this place from friends in Australia or read about it on the ferry coming over."

Surprisingly, there is no real menu. "We just cook things for lunch that are available to us. That way it keeps it fresh and fun for us. We do what we want to do." This could mean pizza, soup and homemade bread, lunch specials, and, of course, baked desserts.

Visitors from all over the world meet in this little corner of Haida Gwaii. On outside bar stools or nestled on a corner couch, coffee aficionados sip their Spit Fire java while swapping adventure stories and relishing the local flavor. The Moon Over Naikoon Bakery serves its fare to hungry campers starting at 10:00 a.m. and regretfully sends patrons homeward around six in the evening. There are no days off. Wendy and her staff of local helpers keep the doors open every day. Despite the success and publicity, Wendy keeps it all in perspective and attributes much of what she has done to her island home.

"It's difficult to explain unless you've been here and get a sense of the place. The thing that makes it work is that you get your finger in the ground and you realize how lucky you are to be able to live in a place like this where there's food on the beach, food in the forest, and wonderful communities all around you that care about each other. Every once in a while you get present with who you are and what you are. Haida Gwaii makes it really easy to do that."

APPENDICES

A.1 CHECKLIST OF THE BIRDS OF HAIDA GWAII

BR–Breeding, SP–Spring, SU–Summer, AU–Autumn, WI–Winter

•–denotes breeding or occurence in season

BIRDS	BR	SP	SU	AU	WI
Red-throated loon	•	•	•	•	•
Pacific loon		•	•	•	•
Common loon	•	•	•	•	•
Yellow-billed loon		•	•	•	•
Pied-billed grebe	•	•	•	•	•
Horned grebe		•		•	•
Red-necked grebe		•	•	•	•
Eared grebe		•		•	
Western grebe		•	•	•	•
Laysan albatross		•	•	•	•
Black-footed albatross		•	•	•	•
Short-tailed albatross		•	•	•	•
Northern fulmar		•	•	•	•
Murphy's petrel			•		
Pink-footed shearwater		•	•	•	
Flesh-footed shearwater		•	•	•	
Buller's shearwater			•	•	

BIRDS	BR	SP	SU	AU	WI
Sooty shearwater		•	•	•	•
Short-tailed shearwater		•	•	•	•
Manx shearwater			•	•	
Black-vented shearwater			•	•	
Fork-tailed storm-petrel	•	•	•	•	•
Leach's storm-petrel	•	•	•	•	•
Brandt's cormorant		•	•	•	•
Double-crested cormorant		•	•	•	•
Red-faced cormorant		•			
Pelagic cormorant	•	•	•	•	•
Magnificent frigatebird			•		
American bittern				•	•
Great blue heron	•	•	•	•	•
Great egret		•	•	•	
Cattle egret		•		•	
Greater white-fronted goose		•	•	•	•

283

BIRDS	BR	SP	SU	AU	WI
Emperor goose		•		•	•
Snow goose		•	•	•	•
Ross's goose		•			
Brant		•	•	•	•
Canada goose	•	•	•	•	•
Trumpeter swan		•		•	•
Tundra swan		•	•	•	•
Wood duck				•	•
Gadwall		•	•	•	
Eurasian wigeon		•		•	•
American wigeon		•	•	•	•
Mallard	•	•	•	•	•
Blue-winged teal	•	•	•		
Cinnamon teal		•			
Northern shoveler		•	•	•	•
Northern pintail	•	•	•	•	•
Baikal teal		•			
Green-winged teal	•	•	•	•	•
Canvasback		•	•	•	•
Redhead		•	•	•	•
Ring-necked duck		•		•	•
Tufted duck				•	
Greater scaup		•	•	•	•
Lesser scaup		•		•	•
Steller's eider	•	•		•	
Spectacled eider		•			
King eider		•	•	•	•
Common eider		•	•		
Harlequin duck	•	•	•	•	•
Surf scoter		•	•	•	•
White-winged scoter		•	•	•	•
Black scoter		•	•	•	•
Long-tailed duck		•	•	•	•
Bufflehead		•	•	•	•
Common goldeneye		•	•	•	•
Barrow's goldeneye	•	•	•	•	•

BIRDS	BR	SP	SU	AU	WI
Hooded merganser	•	•	•	•	•
Common merganser	•	•	•	•	•
Red-breasted merganser	•	•	•	•	•
Ruddy duck				•	•
Osprey		•	•	•	
Bald eagle	•	•	•	•	•
Northern harrier		•		•	•
Sharp-shinned hawk	•	•	•	•	•
Northern goshawk	•	•	•	•	•
Red-tailed hawk	•	•	•	•	•
Rough-legged hawk			•		
American kestrel	•	•	•		
Merlin		•	•	•	•
Gyrfalcon			•		
Peregrine falcon	•	•	•	•	•
Virginia rail		•	•	•	•
Sora		•	•	•	
American coot		•	•	•	•
Sandhill crane	•	•	•	•	
Black-bellied plover		•	•	•	•
American golden-plover		•	•	•	
Pacific golden-plover		•	•	•	
Lesser sand-plover		•			
Snowy plover			•		
Semipalmated plover	•	•	•	•	•
Killdeer	•	•	•	•	•
Eurasian dotterel		•			
Black oystercatcher	•	•	•	•	•
Spotted sandpiper	•	•	•	•	
Solitary sandpiper		•	•		
Wandering tattler		•	•	•	
Greater yellowlegs		•	•	•	•
Lesser yellowlegs		•	•	•	•
Wood sandpiper			•		

BIRDS	BR	SP	SU	AU	WI
Upland sandpiper		•	•		
Long-billed curlew		•	•		
Whimbrel		•	•		
Hudsonian godwit		•	•		
Bar-tailed godwit		•	•		
Marbled godwit		•	•	•	•
Ruddy turnstone		•	•	•	•
Black turnstone		•	•	•	•
Surfbird		•	•	•	•
Red knot		•	•	•	
Sanderling		•	•	•	•
Semipalmated sandpiper		•	•		
Western sandpiper		•	•	•	
Red-necked stint			•		
Long-toed stint			•		
Least sandpiper	•	•	•	•	•
White-rumped sandpiper			•		
Baird's sandpiper			•	•	
Pectoral sandpiper		•	•	•	
Sharp-tailed sandpiper				•	•
Rock sandpiper		•	•	•	•
Dunlin		•	•	•	•
Curlew sandpiper			•		
Stilt sandpiper		•	•	•	
Buff-breasted sandpiper		•	•		
Ruff				•	•
Short-billed dowitcher	•	•	•		
Long-billed dowitcher		•	•	•	•
Wilson's snipe	•	•	•	•	•
Jack snipe					•
Wilson's phalarope		•	•		
Red-necked phalarope		•	•	•	
Red phalarope		•	•	•	
Rock ptarmigan		•			

BIRDS	BR	SP	SU	AU	WI
Sooty grouse	•	•	•	•	•
Sabine's gull		•	•	•	•
Black-legged kittiwake		•	•	•	•
Red-legged kittiwake					•
Bonaparte's gull		•	•	•	
Franklin's gull		•	•		
Heermann's gull		•			
Black-tailed gull				•	
Mew gull	•	•	•	•	•
Ring-billed gull		•	•	•	
Western gull		•	•	•	•
California gull		•	•	•	•
Herring gull		•	•	•	•
Thayer's gull		•	•	•	•
Slaty-backed gull			•		
Glaucous-winged gull	•	•	•	•	•
Glaucous gull		•	•	•	•
Aleutian tern		•	•		
Arctic tern		•			
Caspian tern		•	•		
South polar skua		•	•	•	
Pomarine jaeger		•	•	•	
Parasitic jaeger		•	•	•	
Long-tailed jaeger		•	•		
Common murre	•	•	•	•	•
Thick-billed murre		•		•	•
Pigeon guillemot	•	•	•	•	•
Marbled murrelet	•	•	•	•	•
Long-billed murrelet			•		
Kittlitz's murrelet					•
Xantus's murrelet			•		
Ancient murrelet	•	•	•	•	•
Cassin's auklet	•	•	•	•	•
Whiskered auklet		•			
Parakeet auklet		•	•	•	
Rhinoceros auklet	•	•	•	•	•

BIRDS	BR	SP	SU	AU	WI
Horned puffin	•	•	•	•	•
Tufted puffin	•	•	•	•	
Band-tailed pigeon	•	•	•	•	
Mourning dove				•	•
Eurasian collared dove	•	•	•	•	•
Great horned owl		•		•	
Snowy owl				•	•
Long-eared owl				•	
Short-eared owl		•		•	•
Northern saw-whet owl	•	•	•	•	•
Common nighthawk		•	•		
Black swift			•		
Vaux's swift		•			
Anna's hummingbird	•	•	•	•	•
Rufous hummingbird	•	•	•	•	•
Belted kingfisher	•	•	•	•	•
Lewis' woodpecker				•	
Red-naped sapsucker		•			
Red-breasted sapsucker	•	•	•	•	•
Downy woodpecker		•	•	•	•
Hairy woodpecker	•	•	•	•	•
Northern flicker	•	•	•	•	•
Hammond's flycatcher		•			
Pacific-slope flycatcher	•	•	•	•	
Say's phoebe		•	•	•	
Eastern kingbird		•	•		
Northern shrike		•		•	•
Hutton's vireo		•			
Steller's jay	•	•	•	•	•
Clark's nutcracker				•	•
Black-billed magpie		•			
American crow				•	
Northwestern crow	•	•	•	•	•
Common raven	•	•	•	•	•
Sky lark				•	

BIRDS	BR	SP	SU	AU	WI
Horned lark		•	•	•	•
Tree swallow	•	•	•	•	•
Violet-green swallow		•	•		
Northern rough-winged swallow		•	•		
Bank swallow				•	
Cliff swallow		•	•		
Barn swallow	•	•	•	•	
Chestnut-backed chickadee	•	•	•	•	•
Red-breasted nuthatch	•	•	•	•	•
Brown creeper	•	•	•	•	•
Pacific wren	•	•	•	•	•
American dipper	•	•	•	•	•
Golden-crowned kinglet	•	•	•	•	•
Ruby-crowned kinglet		•	•	•	•
Northern wheatear				•	
Mountain bluebird		•		•	•
Townsend's solitaire		•	•	•	•
Swainson's thrush	•	•	•		
Hermit thrush		•	•	•	
American robin	•	•	•	•	•
Varied thrush	•	•	•	•	•
Gray catbird		•			
Northern mockingbird		•	•	•	
Brown thrasher		•			
European starling	•	•	•	•	•
Yellow wagtail			•		
Red-throated pipit			•	•	
American pipit	•	•	•	•	•
Bohemian waxwing		•	•	•	•
Cedar waxwing	•	•	•	•	•
Prothonotary warbler			•		
Orange-crowned warbler	•	•	•	•	
Yellow warbler		•	•	•	

286

BIRDS	BR	SP	SU	AU	WI
Yellow-rumped warbler		•	•	•	•
Townsend's warbler	•	•	•	•	
Prairie warbler		•			•
Palm warbler		•	•		•
Blackpoll warbler		•	•		
Black and white warbler				•	
Black-throated warbler				•	
Northern waterthrush			•		
Common yellowthroat				•	
Wilson's warbler	•	•	•		
Western tanager		•			
Spotted towhee		•			•
American tree sparrow				•	•
Chipping sparrow			•		
Savannah sparrow		•	•	•	•
Fox sparrow	•	•	•	•	•
Song sparrow	•	•	•	•	•
Lincoln's sparrow	•	•	•	•	•
Swamp sparrow				•	•
White-throated sparrow		•		•	•
Harris's sparrow			•		
White-crowned sparrow		•		•	•
Golden-crowned sparrow		•	•	•	•
Dark-eyed junco	•	•	•	•	•
Lapland longspur		•	•	•	•
Smith's longspur		•		•	

BIRDS	BR	SP	SU	AU	WI
Rustic bunting			•	•	
Little bunting					•
Snow bunting		•		•	•
Black-headed grosbeak		•	•		
Red-winged blackbird	•	•	•	•	•
Western meadowlark			•		
Yellow-headed blackbird		•	•		
Rusty blackbird				•	•
Brewer's blackbird		•	•	•	•
Great-tailed grackle		•			
Brown-headed cowbird		•	•	•	
Brambling		•	•	•	•
Gray-crowned rosy-finch		•		•	
Pine grosbeak	•	•	•	•	•
Purple finch				•	•
Cassin's finch			•		
House finch			•		
Red crossbill	•	•	•	•	•
White-winged crossbill		•		•	•
Common redpoll				•	•
Hoary redpoll			•		
Pine siskin	•	•	•	•	•
American goldfinch		•	•		•
Evening grosbeak		•		•	•
House sparrow	•	•	•	•	

Based on records from Peter Hamel and Margo Hearne and *The Birds of BC*, volumes 1-4, by Wayne Campbell et al.

A.2 CHECKLIST OF THE LAND MAMMALS AND AMPHIBIANS OF HAIDA GWAII

MAMMALS	NATIVE	INTRODUCED	EXTIRPATED
Dusky shrew	•		
Silver-haired bat	•		
California myotis	•		
Keen's long-eared myotis	•		
Little brown myotis	•		
Muskrat		1925	
Beaver		1936, 1949	
Keen's mouse	•		
Norway rat		early 1980s	
Black rat		date unknown	
Red squirrel		1950	
Northern river otter	•		
Marten	•		
Ermine (weasel)	•		
Raccoon		1940s	
Black bear	•		
Red deer (from New Zealand)		1918	•
Elk (Rocky Mountain)		1929–30	
Mule deer (Sitka deer)		1901, 1925	
Dawson's caribou	•		•

Based on Royal British Columbia Museum handbooks
by David W. Nagorsen and David Shackleton

AMPHIBIANS	NATIVE	INTRODUCED	EXTIRPATED
Western toad	•		
Pacific treefrog		1960s	
Red-legged treefrog		2006	

Based on *Amphibians and Reptiles of British Columbia*,
by Brent Matsuda, David Green, and Patrick Gregory

A.3 CHECKLIST OF THE MARINE MAMMALS AND REPTILES OF HAIDA GWAII

MAMMALS	NEARSHORE	OFFSHORE
Sea otter	·	
Northern fur seal	·	
Northern sea lion	·	
California sea lion	·	
Northern elephant seal	·	
Harbour seal	·	
Right whale		·
Minke whale	·	
Sei whale		·
Blue whale		·
Fin whale		·
Humpback whale	·	
Short-finned pilot whale	·	
Risso's dolphin		·
Pacific white-sided dolphin	·	
Killer whale	·	
Grey whale	·	
Harbour porpoise	·	
Dall's porpoise	·	
Sperm whale		·
North Pacific bottle-nosed whale		·
Bering Sea beaked whale		·
Goose-beaked whale		·
REPTILES	NEARSHORE	OFFSHORE
Leatherback (marine turtle)		·

Based on *Marine Mammals of British Columbia*, by John K.B. Ford

A.4 HUNTING ON HAIDA GWAII

Possibly the first recreational hunter on Haida Gwaii was Charles Sheldon, who searched for Dawson caribou here in November 1906. He endured three weeks of ghastly weather in the unsuccessful pursuit of that now-extinct animal. Despite his failed quest, he writes with a keen interest in natural history, and his observations in *The Wilderness of the North Pacific Coast Islands* provide an interesting perspective on hunting over a century ago. (See "Further Reading," page 297.)

Modern hunters like hunting deer because there is a nine-month season and high limits. Mule (Sitka) deer were originally introduced to provide islanders with a fresh meat source. With no natural predators on the islands, however, they soon became overabundant. Though relatively small, these deer are tender and flavourful. Hunting has reduced deer numbers near populated areas, but they are still plentiful on back roads. Their tolerance of people makes them particularly popular with bow hunters, although larger bucks are more cautious about showing themselves. Locals claim that deer hunting is most productive during the rut in November. When it snows, the animals will forage for kelp washed up on the beaches. At any time of year they can be found grazing in grassy meadows, along roadsides, and in estuaries.

There is also limited hunting for a small elk herd that was introduced on Graham Island. Unlike their deer cousins, these animals have not expanded their numbers and rarely stray from their territory on the upper Tlell River watershed.

Black bears are always of interest to hunters, especially to those hoping for the chance to have their trophy entered in the record book. This is because the particular subspecies on Haida Gwaii is the largest in North America.

Sitka deer on Haida Gwaii are small in stature but large in numbers. Hunters enjoy the long season and high bag limits.

In recent years, however, attitudes and regulations have shifted toward observing and photographing rather than bagging the bears. The bear hunt on Haida Gwaii is now carefully controlled and the number of bears harvested is limited to four animals per season. A compulsory inspection is also mandatory for all bears shot on Haida Gwaii.

Waterfowl hunting is permitted on Haida Gwaii as well, though not on a scale to warrant planning a trip exclusively for this purpose. Protected bays with large estuary flats are favoured habitat for Canada geese and ducks. These birds stage here when storms keep them off migration flights.

Hunting in Naikoon Provincial Park may occur but only from September 15 to March 31. Hunting is prohibited in Gwaii Haanas National Park Reserve and Haida Heritage Site or in any Ecological Reserves.

For more information, the following website or contacts should provide current details regarding licences, fees, quotas, inspectors, and other relevant information.

Most in-province sporting goods stores distribute free paper copies of BC Hunting and Trapping regulations.

To find BC Hunting and Trapping regulations online, visit: env.gov.bc.ca/fw/wildlife/hunting/regulations/

Ministry of Environment's Conservation Officer Service
126 2nd Ave, Village of Queen Charlotte, BC V0T 1S0
Phone: 250-559-8431
or
Smithers regional office: 250-847-7260; fax: 250-847-7728

ACKNOWLEDGEMENTS

THIS GUIDE, first released in 1989, is now in its fifth edition. The continued success is due in no small part to many individuals who volunteered their expertise with advice and fact checking. I relied on island authors, researchers, commercial fishers, biologists, politicians, archaeologists, BC Forest Service personnel, loggers, geologists, DFO personnel, cyclists, proofreaders, camp cooks, and computer experts. In particular, Jim and Elizabeth Thorne were excellent field companions. They were extremely helpful with island exploring, proofreading, photography, and computer expertise. While accepting final responsibility for any errors or omissions, I'd like to thank the following people, who helped over the last twenty-seven years:

Steve Aitkins
Kate Alexander
Lin Armstrong
Dan Bate
Kathryn Bernick
Gerry Bindert
Jody Bissett
Don Blood

Michael Brown
Karen Carter
Travis Carter
Wayne Campbell
Sheila Charneski
Dr. John Clague
Simone Clark
Earl Coatta

Dr. Jim Darling
Anne Day
Michele Deakin
Andrew Dejardin
Travis Doane
Norman Dressler
Doug Eastcott
Brian Eccles

Graeme Ellis
Ceitlynn Epners
Anna Gajda
Janet
    Gifford-Brown
Ted Griff
Dr. Jim Haggarty
Peter Hamel
Margo Hearne
Carolyn Hesseltine
Bill Holme
Brenda Horwood
Rick Howie
Lynda Jackson
Darcey Janes
Carl Johansen
Gary Kaiser
Drue Kendrick

Jeff King
Joy LaFortune
Guy Kimola
Moira Lemon
Captain David
    Littlejohn
Ed Lochbaum
Flavien Mabit
Ken Maitland
Rosemary
    Maitland
Steven McConnell
Andrew Merilees
Sean Muise
David Nagorsen
Kevin Neary
Dr. Wayne Nelson
Gord Nettleton

Tom Parkin
Max Patzalt
John Pinder-Moss
Dr. Jim Pojar
Dr. Hans Roemer
Tom Rutherford
Lindsay Seegmiller
Lucy Stefanyk
Doug Steventon
Maggie Stronge
Stephen Suddes
Richard Thomson
Jim Thorne
Liz Thorne
Walter Thorne
Barb Wilson
John Woods
Mary Ann Zarichuk

FURTHER READING

Brown, A. Sutherland. *Geology of the Queen Charlotte Islands, BC.*
Victoria: Department of Mines and Petroleum Resources,
bulletin #54, 1968.

Campbell, R. Wayne, et al. *The Birds of British Columbia—Loons through
Woodpeckers,* Volumes 1 & 2. Victoria: Royal BC Museum, 1989.

——. *The Birds of British Columbia—Flycatchers through Vireos,* Volume 3.
Victoria: Royal BC Museum, 1997.

——. *The Birds of British Columbia—Wood Warblers through Old World Sparrows,* Volume 4. Victoria: Royal BC Museum, 2001.

Carey, Neil G. *Puffin Cove.* Vancouver: Hancock House, 1982.

Carr, Emily. *Klee Wyck.* Toronto: Clarke, Irwin & Co., 1971.

Carter, Jimmy. *An Outdoor Journal.* Toronto: Bantam Books, 1988.

Collison, F., M. McNamara, and J. Nelson, eds. *Yakoun, River of Life.* Council of the Haida Nation, 1990.

Collison, William H. *In the Wake of the War Canoe.* Victoria: Sono Nis
Press, 1981.

Dalzell, Kathleen E. *The Queen Charlotte Islands,* Volume 1 (1774–1966).
Queen Charlotte City: Bill Ellis, Publisher, 1968.

——. *The Queen Charlotte Islands,* Volume 2 (Of Places and Names). Queen
Charlotte City: Bill Ellis, Publisher, 1973.

——. *The Beloved Island,* Madeira Park: Harbour Publishing, 1998.

Dawson, George M. *Report on the Queen Charlotte Islands, including*

Appendix A: On the Haida Indians. Montreal: Geological Survey of Canada, 1880.

Douglas, Sheila. *Trees and Shrubs of the Queen Charlotte Islands: An Illustrated Guide.* Queen Charlotte City: Islands Ecological Research, 1991.

Douglass, Don, and Reanne Hemmingway-Douglass. *Exploring the North Coast of British Columbia: Blunden Harbour to Dixon Entrance including the Queen Charlotte Islands.* Fine Edge Productions, 1997.

Duff, Wilson, and Michael Kew. *Anthony Island: A Home of the Haidas.* Report of the Provincial Museum. Victoria: Provincial Museum, 1957.

Ford, John, G. Ellis, and K. Balcomb. *Killer Whales.* Vancouver: UBC Press, 1994.

Ford, John and G. Ellis. *Transients: Mammal-Hunting Killer Whales.* Vancouver: UBC Press, 1999.

Ford, John. *Marine Mammals of British Columbia.* Royal BC Museum Handbook Vol. 6, 2014.

Frazer, Neil. *Boat Camping Haida Gwaii.* Madeira Park: Harbour Publishing, 2001.

Hagelund, William A. *Whalers No More.* Madeira Park: Harbour Publishing, 1987.

Harris, Christie. *Raven's Cry.* Toronto: McClelland and Stewart, 1966.

Islands Protection Society. *Islands at the Edge: Preserving the Queen Charlotte Islands Wilderness.* Vancouver: Douglas and McIntyre, 1984.

Hatler, David, David Nagorsen, and Alison Beal. *Carnivores of British Columbia Vol. 5.* Victoria: Royal BC Museum Handbook, 2008.

Long, Bob. *Fishing the Queen Charlotte Islands.* Sandspit: Raser Enterprises Ltd., 1988.

MacDonald, George F. *Ninstints: Haida World Heritage Site.* Vancouver: UBC Press, 1983.

——. *Chiefs of the Sea and Sky.* Vancouver: UBC Press, 1989.

——. *Haida Art.* Vancouver: Douglas and McIntyre, 1996.

Matsuda, Brent, David Green, and Patrick Gregory. *Amphibians and Reptiles of British Columbia.* Victoria, BC: Royal British Columbia Museum, 2006.

Nagorsen, David W., and R. Mark Brigham. *Bats of British Columbia.* Royal British Columbia Museum Handbook. Vancouver: UBC Press, 1993.

Nagorsen, David W. *Opossums, Shrews and Moles of British Columbia.* Royal British Columbia Museum Handbook. Vancouver: UBC Press, 1996.

——. *Rodents and Lagomorphs of British Columbia.* Royal British Columbia Museum Handbook. Vancouver: UBC Press, 2005.

Osgood, Wilfred H. *Natural History of the Queen Charlotte Islands, BC.* Washington: Government Printing Office, 1901.

Poole, Francis. *Queen Charlotte Islands: A Narrative of Discovery and Adventure in the North Pacific.* London: Hurst and Blackett, 1872; reprinted Vancouver: J.J. Douglas, 1972.

Scudder, Geoffrey, and Nicholas Gessler, eds. *The Outer Shores.* Queen Charlotte Islands Museum, 1989.

Shackleton, David. *Hoofed Mammals of British Columbia.* Royal British Columbia Museum Handbook. Vancouver: UBC Press, 1999.

Sheldon, Charles. *The Wilderness of the North Pacific Coast Islands.* New York: Charles Scribner's Sons, 1912.

Smyly, John, and Carolyn Smyly. *Those Born at Koona.* Vancouver: Hancock House, 1973.

South Moresby Resource Planning Team. *South Moresby Land Use Alternatives.* Victoria: Queen's Printer, 1983.

Stewart, Hilary. *Cedar.* Vancouver: Douglas and McIntyre, 1984.

——. *Looking at Totem Poles.* Vancouver: Douglas and McIntyre, 1993.

INDEX

The letter "c" after a number indicates a photo caption.

A

adventure tours, 197, 222, 224
  See also tour companies
Agate Beach Campground, 211
Air Canada Jazz, 225
Alaska View Lodge, 198
amphibians, 264, 264c, 288
arts/artisans, 80, 137–38,
  150c, 184, 197, 212, 237
  resurgence of, 13, 269, 274
  See also Carr, Emily; Moody,
  Garner; Reid, Bill
ATVs, for exploring, 88c,
  100–101, 103
auklets, 68, 127, 243c, 246,
  248–50, 268

B

BC (British Columbia)
  Ferries, 18, 27, 40, 142,
  224–25, 238
beachcombing, 38, 67, 81,
  100–101, 122,
  141, 199
bears
  black, 21, 92, 169, 210,
  262, 263c
  grizzly, 21, 186
bed-and-breakfasts (B&Bs),
  183, 193–94
bicycling, 27, 40–41, 100–101,
  109, 123–24, 203
Bigg, Dr. Michael, 257

birds
  list of species, 283–87
  migration of, 30, 38, 74, 77,
  78c, 79, 106, 242c,
  252, 291
  See also eagles; falcons;
  loons; murrelets;
  ravens; sandhill cranes;
  seabirds; shearwaters;
  shorebirds
birdwatching, 26, 30, 38,
  182, 241, 245, 271
boating, 36, 82, 147, 154,
  228–29
  See also charters
bogs, 93–95, 97
Bunkhouse Campground
  Resort, The, 214
Burnaby Island, 157,
  164, 177

C

Cäcilia's Bed and Breakfast,
  201, 202c
camping, 47, 83, 139
  beach, 45c, 140, 211c
  sites for, 125, 158, 210
canneries, 20, 102–3, 138–39,
  169, 176
canoes, 23c, 30, 52–57, 82
  building of, 11, 54
caribou, 239, 263, 288, 290
Carr, Emily, 136

cedar trees, 6, 37, 48, 54, 145
  for canoes, 11, 13, 52, 274
  carvings of, 80, 137
  house building, 9, 49c
  test holes in, 159c, 161–62
charters
  aircraft, 69, 191, 220–
  21, 226
  boat, 143, 147, 222–23
  fishing, 72, 194, 197, 204,
  222, 224
charts, marine. *See* marine
  charts
Chateau Norm, 202, 203c
Christmas bird count, 268
climate, 16, 52, 231, 239
  See also weather
  conditions
Collison, Rev. William Henry,
  15, 24, 52
Cone Head Recreation
  Site, 42
Copper Beech Guest House,
  195–96
crabs, 73, 83, 86c, 102,
  168, 171
  See also fishing

D

De Havilland Beavers, 220
Delkatla Wildlife Sanctuary,
  Masset, 244, 246,
  269, 271

Dixon, Captain George, 4, 14, 63

Dixon Entrance Maritime Museum, 151

dolphins, 256, 289

Dorothy and Mike's Guest House and Cottages, 205

dunes, sand, 80, 92, 105–6, 113, 115–16, 117c, 118

Duu Guusd Heritage Site/ Conservancy, Rennell Sound, 214

E

eagles, 121, 161, 169
  bald, 45, 76, 161, 241, 249–50

Eagles Feast House, 196, 197c

earthquake, 155–56

ecological reserves, 51, 80, 93, 251, 291

Ellen Island, 147, 183

F

falcons, peregrine, 65c, 67, 76, 79, 106, 241, 246, 247c, 249–50

fishing, 35–36, 38
  commercial, 7, 25, 64, 134
  crab, 83, 86c, 89c
  freshwater, 70, 198
  halibut, 45, 67c, 70–72, 82–83, 208, 223
  licences for, 120, 223
  salmon, 25–26, 29, 34–35, 38, 47, 67c, 69–72, 81, 208
  saltwater, 70–71, 73, 102, 184, 199
  sport, 64, 81, 119c, 120, 134
  See also charters; fishing lodges

fishing lodges, 65, 67c, 71c, 72, 194, 207–10
  floating, 64–65, 72, 134, 144, 222c

501 RV Tent Park, 215

floating lodges, 64, 72, 134, 144, 222c

forest industry. See logging operations

fossils, 29, 30c, 31

G

Gandll K'in Gwaay.yaay (Hotspring Island), 149, 155–57, 210

golfing, 90–91

Graham Island, 2, 54, 195, 197, 211, 231
  sand dunes on, 115–16

Gwaii Haanas Agreement, 158

Gwaii Haanas National Park Reserve and Haida Heritage Site, 2, 6–7, 17, 140, 142, 148, 291
  reservations, fees, orientation, enter permits, 217–19

Gwaii Trust Board, 277

H

Haida culture, traditional, 9, 65, 177
  history of, 5, 13, 16–17, 112, 239–40

Haida fishery, for Pacific herring, 164

Haida Gwaii Lodge, 196

Haida Gwaii Museum, 275

Haida Gwaii Tourism Association, 279

Haida Gwaii Watchmen. See Haida Watchmen

Haida Heritage Centre, 12c, 13, 16c, 150, 189, 275, 277

Haida Heritage Site. See Gwaii Haanas National Park Reserve

Haida heritage villages, 10c, 27, 149, 185, 191
  permits to enter, 219

Haida myth, of human creation, 105

Haida Nation, 5, 158, 185
  Council, 145

Haida poles. See totem poles

Haida Watchmen, 147, 157, 164, 186c, 190–91, 220, 228

halibut, 25, 65
  See also fishing

Hamel, Peter, 78, 240, 267, 269

Hayden Turner Community Campground, 213

Hearne, Margo, 78, 240, 267, 269–71

Helijet Charters, 226

herring, Pacific, 38, 134, 164, 254, 275
  See also fishing

Hidden Island RV and Resort, 212

Hiellen Longhouse Village, 199–200

hiking, 54, 91, 108–9, 114, 154, 161, 179, 199
  routes, 33c, 36–37, 67, 82, 110, 121–22, 124, 237
  shelters for, 92, 113

hitchhiking, 226

Hlk'yah GaawGa (Windy Bay), 147, 149, 158, 160, 162–63

homesteading, 16, 27, 29, 57, 59, 80, 177

Hudson's Bay Company (HBC), trading posts, 14

hunting, 52, 82, 108, 185, 290–91

I

Inland Air Charters Ltd., 225–26

interpretative centres, 78–79, 115, 271

interpretative plaques, 51, 115

intertidal life, 27, 31, 43–45, 164–65, 169

Island Protection Society, 240

islanders
    lifestyle of, 7–8, 177
    profiles of, 267–82

K

Kagan Bay Recreation Site, 213
kayaking, 30, 103, 127, 174c,
    180, 182, 199
    and camping, 137, 191, 229
    rentals, 194, 204, 209, 225
    routes for, 140, 142,
      143c, 147
    transporting kayaks, 27,
      141, 223
Kumdis River Lodge, 208–9
Kunghit Island, 181–83
Kunxalas Heritage Site/
    Conservancy, 215
K'uuna Llnagaay (Skedans),
    127, 129c–130c, 136–37,
    140, 147, 210, 217

L

LaFortune, Joy, 267, 272–73
Langara Island, 64, 65c,
    66–69, 71, 245, 261
Laskeek Bay Conservation
    Society, 127
logging operations, 1, 6, 16,
    47–48, 129–32, 145, 269
    private roads, 227–28
    protest on Lyell Island,
      158, 160c
Loo Plex, 56, 57c
loons, 242, 268, 283
Lootaas, 55–56, 274
Louise Island, 17, 71, 126–27,
    136, 138, 140–41, 143
Louise Island
    Circumnavigation, 144
lumber operations. *See*
    logging operations
Lyell Island, 145, 147, 152, 158,
    160c, 260

M

mammals, land, 261–62, 263c,
    264, 266

list of species, 288
See also bears; caribou;
    otters; raccoons
mammals, marine, 27, 163,
    182, 252, 256–57,
    260–61
    list of species, 288
    See also dolphins; otters;
      porpoises; sea lions;
      seals; whales
Marco Island, 155, 260
marine charts, 29, 45, 124, 135,
    163, 229–30
marine research station,
    volunteering, 127, 238c
Masset
    accommodation, 195–99,
      207, 212
    airport, 225
Maude Island, 30c, 31–32,
    35–36
Merilees, Andrew, 267,
    278–80
mines, iron-ore / copper,
    174–75
missionaries, 15–16, 162
Misty Meadow Campground,
    212
Moody, Garner, 12c, 267,
    274–75
Moresby Camp Recreation
    Site, 216
Moresby Island, 2, 6, 37, 125c,
    231, 253
Mosquito Lake Recreation
    Site, 216
murrelets, 68, 162, 249, 268

N

Naden Lodge, 207, 208c
Naikoon Provincial Park,
    2, 3c, 17, 80, 105, 198,
    201, 276
National Marine
    Conservation Area
    Reserve, 142, 145,
    148, 219
Native land claims, 2

O

Old Massett, 7, 197, 219, 232,
    237, 279
otters
    pelt trade, 1, 14, 64, 260
    river, 124, 139, 182,
      262–64
    sea, 252, 264

P

Pacific Coast Fisheries, 138
Pacific Coastal Airlines, 225
Pesuta, shipwreck, 110c, 111,
    120, 237
plant life, 37, 44, 51, 80,
    94–96, 106, 109c
    in the sand dunes,
      117, 118c
poles. *See* totem poles
porpoises, 255–56
Port Clements, 7, 17, 54, 56, 82,
    151, 237, 246
    travelling to, 41, 47, 51, 61
potlatch celebrations, 9,
    13, 188

Q

Queen Charlotte Islands
    Chamber of Commerce,
    279

R

raccoons, 167c, 169, 265,
    265c, 266
rainfall, measurements
    of, 232
rainforest, 121, 158, 160,
    189, 199
ravens, 161, 169
    as symbol, 105
red tide, 169
Reid, Bill, 55–56, 80, 274–
    75, 277
Reid-Stevens, Amanda, 267,
    276–78
Rennell Sound Recreation
    Site, 41, 44, 45c,
    47, 142

reptiles, 252, 289
  See also turtles
Riley, Wendy, 267, 281–82
Riverside Lodging, 200, 201c
Rose Harbour Whaling
  Station, 253
Rose Spit
  birding and animal spot,
    243, 246, 253, 255,
    260–61
  dune formation at,
    115, 117c
  and human creation myth,
    80, 105, 269

S

salmon, 65, 148, 169
  as food for marine
    mammals, 259–60
  as "food of life," 162
  runs of, 81, 119, 121
  See also fishing
sand dunes. *See* dunes, sand
sandhill cranes, 76, 77c, 92,
    106, 124, 241, 246
Sandspit, 7, 40, 72c, 141, 147,
    232, 237
  accommodation, 206–7,
    215, 221
  birding, 242c, 245
Sandspit Airport, 38–39, 69,
    152, 218, 225, 237, 276
Sandspit Rod and Gun Club, 73
sea lions, 137, 182, 252, 253c,
    257–59
seabirds, 26–27, 34c, 182,
    244–45, 268
  nesting, 246–48
  protection of, 251–52, 266
  See also birds;
    birdwatching
seals, harbour, 257, 260
Seaport Bed & Breakfast,
    206–7
SGang Gwaay Llnagaay World
    Heritage Site, 9, 11, 15c,
    143, 147, 182, 184, 186c,
    188–89, 191, 220–21

shearwaters, 26, 106, 242–43,
    246, 251
  See also birds;
    birdwatching
shorebirds, 38, 74, 78, 106, 124,
    242, 244–45, 250
  See also birds;
    birdwatching
Skidegate (Hlgaagilda
    'Llnagaay), 3c, 12c, 36,
    55, 57c, 133, 141, 230,
    275, 277
  heritage centre in, 9, 56,
    150
Skidegate Band Council, 136,
    177, 189
smallpox epidemic, 189
Spirit Canoe, 274
Spruce Point Lodge, 204
St. Mary's Spring, 5c, 8
steelhead, 70, 71c, 81, 119, 209
  See also fishing
Sunset RV and Camping
    Park, 212
Swan Bay Rediscovery
    Camp, 177

T

T'aanuu Llnagaay (Tanu),
    132–33, 147, 150, 210
tide pools, 46c, 141
  See also intertidal life
tide tables, 58, 111, 114, 126c,
    158, 229–30
Tlell, 7, 17, 40, 82, 114–15, 117c,
    200–201, 212, 232
Tlell Anvil Trail, 120–22
totem poles, 12c, 15c, 129c,
    131c, 136c, 158, 184–85,
    189–91, 197
  as displaying Haida tradi-
    tions, 150, 190
  made from cedar, 9, 162
  as mortuary poles, 186,
    187c, 192
  symbols on, 137, 188
  three-pole mortuary,
    Edenshaw, 66

tour companies, 148, 223
tourism, 273
  and chartering services,
    222
  for economic growth, 7, 61
  and totem poles, 190
  See also adventure tours;
    charters
trip-planning guide, 236–38
turtles, 261, 289

V

Village of Queen Charlotte, 7,
    29, 32c, 39, 41, 72, 120,
    232, 236–37
  accommodation, 195, 202,
    204–5, 213–14
Village of Queen Charlotte
    Visitor Centre,
    194, 224

W

weather conditions, 71,
    231–32
  preparation for, 90, 111,
    144, 158, 228
  See also climate; winter
    conditions
whales
  grey, 252–55
  humpback, 253–54, 255c
  killer (orca), 107, 163, 183,
    256–57, 259c
  watching, 37–38, 39c
whaling, 180, 181c, 253
Willows Golf and Country
    Club, 90–91
Windy Bay pole
  as commemorating Lyell
    Island logging protest,
    160c
winter conditions, 24, 41, 45,
    52, 179, 193
  See also weather
    conditions

Index

ABOUT THE AUTHOR

DENNIS HORWOOD has always had a passion for the outdoors and the biological side of science. From an early age, he watched and fed birds at his Victoria home. His interest in marine biology led him to earn a BSc. at the University of Victoria.

Following several years of working for Parks Canada and BC Parks, he entered the public school system in Kitimat where he taught science and outdoor education. While living in Kitimat, he wrote a regular natural history column for the local newspaper and authored *Birds of the Kitimat Valley*. His photos have appeared in numerous books and magazines, including *Alaska* and *Nature Canada*.

Living in the northwest corner of BC presented excellent opportunities for exploring. Haida Gwaii topped his list of one of the best places to visit. In the last ten years, he and his wife, Brenda, have sailed throughout Douglas Channel and Inside Passage. He has also been involved with the province's ecological reserves, contributed to a coastal eelgrass initiative, and recently published over forty years of avian records for the Kitimat Arm and Kitimat River estuary.